Qt 5 and OpenCV 4 Computer Vision Projects

Get up to speed with cross-platform computer vision app development by building seven practical projects

Zhuo Qingliang

BIRMINGHAM - MUMBAI

Qt 5 and OpenCV 4 Computer Vision Projects

Commissioning Editor: Richa Tripathi
Acquisition Editor: Sandeep Mishra
Content Development Editor: Digvijay Bagul
Senior Editor: Afshaan Khan
Technical Editor: Abin Sebastian
Copy Editor: Safis Editing
Project Coordinator: Carol Lewis
Proofreader: Safis Editing
Indexer: Rekha Nair
Production Designers: Aparna Bhagat, Alishon Mendonsa

First published: June 2019

Production reference: 1190619

Published by Packt Publishing Ltd.
Livery Place
35 Livery Street
Birmingham
B3 2PB, UK.

ISBN 978-1-78953-258-6

www.packtpub.com

To the one who keeps me motivated.

To my wife and my son for their love, support, and inspiration.

And to the open source communities and the people who are working hard to build a better world for all of us.

– Zhuo Qingliang

Packt.com

Subscribe to our online digital library for full access to over 7,000 books and videos, as well as industry leading tools to help you plan your personal development and advance your career. For more information, please visit our website.

Why subscribe?

- Spend less time learning and more time coding with practical eBooks and Videos from over 4,000 industry professionals

- Improve your learning with Skill Plans built especially for you

- Get a free eBook or video every month

- Fully searchable for easy access to vital information

- Copy and paste, print, and bookmark content

Did you know that Packt offers eBook versions of every book published, with PDF and ePub files available? You can upgrade to the eBook version at www.packt.com and as a print book customer, you are entitled to a discount on the eBook copy. Get in touch with us at customercare@packtpub.com for more details.

At www.packt.com, you can also read a collection of free technical articles, sign up for a range of free newsletters, and receive exclusive discounts and offers on Packt books and eBooks.

Contributors

About the author

Zhuo Qingliang (also known as KDr2 online) is presently working at Beijing Paoding Technology Co. Ltd., a start-up Fintech company in China that is dedicated to improving the financial industry by using artificial intelligence technologies. He has over 10 years' experience in Linux, C, C++, Python, Perl, and Java development. He is interested in programming, doing consulting work, participating in and contributing to the open source community (of course, includes the Julia community).

I would like to thank my wife, Feng Xiaoyi, who gave me much encouragement and help while I was writing this book. I would also like to thank my boy, Zhuo Shi; he and his toys played an essential role in the videos of this book.

About the reviewer

Christian Stehno studied computer science, receiving his diploma from Oldenburg University, Germany. Since 2000 he worked in computer science, first as a researcher on theoretical computer science at Oldenburg University, later switching to embedded system design at OFFIS institute. In 2010, he started his own company, CoSynth, which develops embedded sensor and camera systems for industrial automation. In addition, he is a long-time member of the Irrlicht 3D engine developer team.

Packt is searching for authors like you

If you're interested in becoming an author for Packt, please visit `authors.packtpub.com` and apply today. We have worked with thousands of developers and tech professionals, just like you, to help them share their insight with the global tech community. You can make a general application, apply for a specific hot topic that we are recruiting an author for, or submit your own idea.

Table of Contents

Preface

We are entering the age of intelligence. Today, more and more digital devices and applications deliver features facilitated by artificial intelligence technology. Computer vision technology is an important part of artificial intelligence technology, while the OpenCV library is one of the most comprehensive and mature libraries for computer vision technology. OpenCV goes beyond traditional computer vision technology; it incorporates many other technologies, such as DNN, CUDA, OpenGL, and OpenCL, and is evolving into a more powerful library. But, at the same time, its GUI facility, which is not the main feature of the library, isn't evolving very much. Meanwhile, among the many GUI development libraries and frameworks, there is one that is the best at crossing platforms, has the best ease of use, and has the greatest widget diversity—the Qt library. The goal of this book is to combine OpenCV and Qt to develop fully-fledged applications providing many interesting features.

This book is a practical guide to the OpenCV library and GUI application development with Qt. We'll develop a complete application in each chapter. In each of those applications, a number of computer vision algorithms, Qt widgets, and other facilities will be covered, and a well-designed user interface with functional features will be created.

This book is the result of months of hard work, and it would not have been possible without the invaluable help of the Packt team and the technical reviewer.

Who this book is for

This book is designed for all those developers who want to know how to use the OpenCV library to process images and videos, for those who want to learn GUI development with Qt, for those who want to know how to use deep learning in the computer vision domain, and for those who are interested in developing fully-fledged computer vision applications.

What this book covers

Chapter 1, *Building an Image Viewer*, covers building our first application with Qt. We will build an image viewer, with which we can browse images in a folder. We'll also be able to zoom in or out of the image while viewing it.

Chapter 2, *Editing Images Like a Pro*, combines the Qt library and the OpenCV library to build a new application, an image editor. In this chapter, we will start by blurring an image to learn how to edit an image. Then, we will learn how to use many other editing effects, such as eroding, sharpening, cartoon effects, and geometric transformation. Each of these features will be incorporated as a Qt plugin, so the plugin mechanism of the Qt library will also be covered.

Chapter 3, *Home Security Applications*, covers building an application for home security. With a webcam, this application can detect motion and send notifications to a mobile phone upon motion being detected. We will learn how to deal with cameras and videos, how to analyze motion and detect movement with OpenCV, and how to send notifications via IFTTT in this chapter.

Chapter 4, *Fun with Faces*, explores how to detect faces and facial landmarks with OpenCV. We will build an application to detect faces and facial landmarks in the video in real time in this chapter, and, with the facial landmarks detected, we will apply some funny masks to the faces.

Chapter 5, *Optical Character Recognition*, introduces the Tesseract library to you. With the help of this library, we will extract text from images such as photos of book pages and scanned documents. In order to extract text from photos of common scenes, we will use a deep learning model named EAST to detect the text areas in photos, and then pass those areas to the Tesseract library. In order to extract text on the screen conveniently, we will also learn how to grab the screen as an image with the Qt library.

Chapter 6, *Object Detection in Real Time*, shows how to use cascade classifiers to detect objects. Besides using pretrained classifiers, we will also learn how to train classifiers by ourselves. Then, we will introduce how to detect objects by using deep learning models, and a model named YOLOv3 will be used to demonstrate the usage of this approach.

Chapter 7, *Real-Time Car Detection and Distance Measurement*, covers creating an application to detect cars and measure distances. In the application, we will learn how to measure distances between objects from a bird's eye view and how to measure distances between objects and the camera at eye level view.

Chapter 8, *Using OpenGL for High-Speed Filtering of Images*, the final chapter of the book, introduces an approach to heterogeneous computing. In this chapter, we first have a brief introduction to the OpenGL specification, and then use it to filter images on the GPU. This is not a typical way to use OpenGL, and it is not typical to do heterogeneous computing either, so we can refer to OpenCL or CUDA if we want to do heterogeneous computing in a mature way.

Appendix A, *Assessments*, contains answers to all the assessment questions.

To get the most out of this book

In order to achieve the overall outcome of this book, the following are the prerequisites:

- You need to have some basic knowledge of C++ and C programming languages.
- You need to have Qt v5.0 or above installed.
- You need to have a webcam attached to your computer.
- Many libraries, such as OpenCV and Tesseract, are also required. The instructions to install them are included in the chapter in which each library is first used.
- A knowledge of deep learning and heterogeneous computing will be an advantage in helping to understand some chapters.

Download the example code files

You can download the example code files for this book from your account at www.packt.com. If you purchased this book elsewhere, you can visit www.packt.com/support and register to have the files emailed directly to you.

You can download the code files by following these steps:

1. Log in or register at www.packt.com.
2. Select the **SUPPORT** tab.
3. Click on **Code Downloads & Errata**.
4. Enter the name of the book in the **Search** box and follow the onscreen instructions.

Once the file is downloaded, please make sure that you unzip or extract the folder using the latest version of:

- WinRAR/7-Zip for Windows
- Zipeg/iZip/UnRarX for Mac
- 7-Zip/PeaZip for Linux

The code bundle for the book is also hosted on GitHub at `https://github.com/PacktPublishing/Qt-5-and-OpenCV-4-Computer-Vision-Projects`. In case there's an update to the code, it will be updated on the existing GitHub repository.

We also have other code bundles from our rich catalog of books and videos available at `https://github.com/PacktPublishing/`. Check them out!

Download the color images

We also provide a PDF file that has color images of the screenshots/diagrams used in this book. You can download it here: `http://www.packtpub.com/sites/default/files/downloads/9781789532586_ColorImages.pdf`.

Code in Action

Visit the following link to check out videos of the code being run: `http://bit.ly/2FfYSDS`.

Conventions used

There are a number of text conventions used throughout this book.

`CodeInText`: Indicates code words in text, class or type names. Here is an example: "The Qt project file, `ImageViewer.pro`, should be renamed `ImageEditor.pro`. You can do this in your file manager or in a Terminal."

A block of code is set as follows:

```
QMenu *editMenu;
QToolBar *editToolBar;
QAction *blurAction;
```

When we wish to draw your attention to a particular part of a code block, a comment will be appended to end of the lines:

```
// for editting
void blurImage();
```

Any command-line input or output is written as follows:

```
$ mkdir Chapter-02
$ cp -r Chapter-01/ImageViewer/ Chapter-02/ImageEditor
$ ls Chapter-02
ImageEditor
$ cd Chapter-02/ImageEditor
$ make clean
$ rm -f ImageViewer
```

The $ symbol is the shell prompt, and the text after it is a command. The lines that don't start with a $ are the output of the preceding command.

Warnings or important notes appear like this.

Tips and tricks appear like this.

Get in touch

Feedback from our readers is always welcome.

General feedback: If you have questions about any aspect of this book, mention the book title in the subject of your message and email us at customercare@packtpub.com.

Errata: Although we have taken every care to ensure the accuracy of our content, mistakes do happen. If you have found a mistake in this book, we would be grateful if you would report this to us. Please visit www.packt.com/submit-errata, selecting your book, clicking on the Errata Submission Form link, and entering the details.

Piracy: If you come across any illegal copies of our works in any form on the internet, we would be grateful if you would provide us with the location address or website name. Please contact us at copyright@packt.com with a link to the material.

If you are interested in becoming an author: If there is a topic that you have expertise in, and you are interested in either writing or contributing to a book, please visit authors.packtpub.com.

Reviews

Please leave a review. Once you have read and used this book, why not leave a review on the site that you purchased it from? Potential readers can then see and use your unbiased opinion to make purchase decisions, we at Packt can understand what you think about our products, and our authors can see your feedback on their book. Thank you!

For more information about Packt, please visit `packt.com`.

Building an Image Viewer

1

Computer vision is the technology that enables computers to achieve a high-level understanding of digital images and videos, rather than only treating them as bytes or pixels. It is widely used for scene reconstruction, event detection, video tracking, object recognition, 3D pose estimation, motion estimation, and image restoration.

OpenCV (open source computer vision) is a library that implements almost all computer vision methods and algorithms. Qt is a cross-platform application framework and widget toolkit for creating applications with graphical user interfaces that can run on all major desktop platforms, most embedded platforms, and even mobile platforms.

These two powerful libraries are used together by many developers to create professional software with a solid GUI in industries that benefit from computer vision technology. In this book, we will demonstrate how to build these types of functional application with Qt 5 and OpenCV 4, which has friendly graphical user interfaces and several functions associated with computer vision technology.

In this first chapter, we will start by building a simple GUI application for image viewing with Qt 5.

The following topics will be covered in this chapter as follows:

- Designing the user interface
- Reading and displaying images with Qt
- Zooming in and out of images
- Saving a copy of images in any supported format
- Responding to hotkeys in a Qt application

Technical requirements

Ensure that you at least have Qt version 5 installed and have some basic knowledge of C++ and Qt programming. A compatible C++ compiler is also required, that is, GCC 5 or later on Linux, Clang 7.0 or later on macOS, and MSVC 2015 or later on Microsoft Windows.

Since some pertinent basic knowledge is required as a prerequisite, the Qt installation and compiler environment setup are not included in this book. There are many books, online documents, or tutorials available (for example, *GUI Programming with C++ and Qt5*, by *Lee Zhi Eng*, as well as the official Qt library documentation) to help teach these basic configuration processes step by step; users can refer to these by themselves if necessary.

With all of these prerequisites in place, let's start the development of our first application—the simple image viewer.

All the code for this chapter can be found in our code repository at `https://github.com/ PacktPublishing/Qt-5-and-OpenCV-4-Computer-Vision-Projects/tree/master/Chapter-01`.

Check out the following video to see the code in action: `http://bit.ly/2KoYWFx`

Designing the user interface

The first part of building an application is to define what the application will do. In this chapter, we will develop an image viewer app. The features it should have are as follows:

- Open an image from our hard disk
- Zoom in/out
- View the previous or next image within the same folder
- Save a copy of the current image as another file (with a different path or filename) in another format

There are many image viewer applications that we can follow, such as gThumb on Linux and Preview app on macOS. However, our application will be simpler than those in that we have undertaken some preplanning. This involved the use of Pencil to draw the wireframe of the application prototype.

Pencil is a functional prototyping tool. With it, you can create mockups easily. It is open-source and platform-independent software. The latest version of Pencil is now an Electron-based application. It runs well on Windows, Linux, and macOS. You can download it freely from `https://pencil.evolus.vn/`.

The following is a wireframe showing our application prototype:

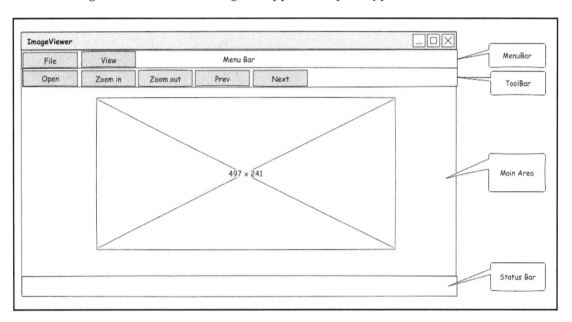

As you can see in the preceding diagram, we have four areas in the main window: the **MenuBar**, the **ToolBar**, the **Main Area**, and the **Status Bar**.

The menu bar has two menu options on it—the **File** and **View** menus. Each menu will have its own set of actions. The **File** menu consists of the following three actions as follows:

- **Open**: This option opens an image from the hard disk.
- **Save as**: This option saves a copy of the current image as another file (with a different path or filename) in any supported format.
- **Exit**: This option exits the application.

The **View** menu consists of four actions as follows:

- **Zoom in**: This option zooms in to the image.
- **Zoom out**: This option zooms out of the image.
- **Prev**: This option opens the previous image in the current folder.
- **Next**: This option opens the next image in the current folder.

The toolbar consists of several buttons that can also be found in the menu options. We place them on the toolbar to give the users shortcuts to trigger these actions. So, it is necessary to include all frequently used actions, including the following:

- Open
- Zoom in
- Zoom out
- Previous image
- Next image

The main area is used to show the image that is opened by the application.

The status bar is used to show some information pertaining to the image that we are viewing, such as its path, dimensions, and its size in bytes.

You can find the source file for this design in our code repository on GitHub: `https://github.com/PacktPublishing/Qt-5-and-OpenCV-4-Computer-Vision-Projects`. The file merely resides in the root directory of the repository, named `WireFrames.epgz`. Don't forget that it should be opened using the Pencil application.

Starting the project from scratch

In this section, we will build the image viewer application from scratch. No assumptions are made as to what **integrated development environment** (**IDE**) or editor you are using. We will just focus on the code itself and how to build the application using `qmake` in a Terminal.

First, let's create a new directory for our project, named `ImageViewer`. I use Linux and execute this in a Terminal, as follows:

```
$ pwd
/home/kdr2/Work/Books/Qt5-And-OpenCV4-Computer-Vision-Projects/Chapter-01
$ mkdir ImageViewer
$
```

Then, we create a C++ source file named `main.cpp` in that directory with the following content:

```
#include <QApplication>
#include <QMainWindow>

int main(int argc, char *argv[])
{
    QApplication app(argc, argv);
    QMainWindow window;
    window.setWindowTitle("ImageViewer");
    window.show();
    return app.exec();
}
```

This file will be the gateway to our application. In this file, we first include dedicated header files for a GUI-based Qt application provided by the Qt library. Then, we define the main function, as most C++ applications do. In the main function, we define an instance of the `QApplication` class, which represents our image viewer application while it is running, and an instance of `QMainWindow`, which will be the main UI window, and which we designed in the preceding section. After creating the `QMainWindow` instance, we call some methods of it: `setWindowTitle` to set the title of the window and `show` to let the window emerge. Finally, we call the `exec` method of the application instance to enter the main event loop of the Qt application. This will make the application wait until `exit()` is called, and then return the value that was set to `exit()`.

Once the `main.cpp` file is saved in our project directory, we enter the directory in the Terminal and run `qmake -project` to generate the Qt project file, as follows:

```
$ cd ImageViewer/
$ ls
main.cpp
$ qmake -project
$ ls
ImageViewer.pro main.cpp
$
```

As you can see, a file named `ImageViewer.pro` is generated. This file contains many directives and configurations of the Qt project and `qmake` will use this `ImageViewer.pro` file to generate a makefile later. Let's examine that project file. Its content is listed in the following snippet after we omit all the comment lines that start with #, as follows:

```
TEMPLATE = app
TARGET = ImageViewer
```

```
INCLUDEPATH += .

DEFINES += QT_DEPRECATED_WARNINGS

SOURCES += main.cpp
```

Let's go through this line by line.

The first line, `TEMPLATE = app`, specifies `app` as the template to use when generating the project. Many other values are allowed here, for example, `lib` and `subdirs`. We are building an application that can be run directly, so the value `app` is the proper one for us. Using other values are beyond the scope of this chapter; you can refer to the qmake manual at `http://doc.qt.io/qt-5/qmake-manual.html` yourself to explore them.

The second line, `TARGET = ImageViewer`, specifies the name of the executable for the application. So, we will get an executable file named `ImageViewer` once the project is built.

The remaining lines define several options for the compiler, such as the include path, macro definitions, and input source files. You can easily ascertain which line does what based on the variable names in these lines.

Now, let's build the project, run `qmake -makefile` to generate the makefile, and then run `make` to build the project, that is, compile the source to our target executable:

```
$ qmake -makefile
$ ls
ImageViewer.pro main.cpp Makefile
$ make
g++ -c -pipe -O2 -Wall -W -D_REENTRANT -fPIC -DQT_DEPRECATED_WARNINGS -
DQT_NO_DEBUG -DQT_GUI_LIB -DQT_CORE_LIB -I. -I. -isystem
/usr/include/x86_64-linux-gnu/qt5 -isystem /usr/include/x86_64-linux-
gnu/qt5/QtGui -isystem /usr/include/x86_64-linux-gnu/qt5/QtCore -I. -
isystem /usr/include/libdrm -I/usr/lib/x86_64-linux-gnu/qt5/mkspecs/linux-
g++
    -o main.o main.cpp
main.cpp:1:10: fatal error: QApplication: No such file or directory
 #include <QApplication>
          ^~~~~~~~~~~~~~
compilation terminated.
make: *** [Makefile:395: main.o] Error 1
$
```

Oops! We get a big error. This is because, with effect from Qt version 5, all the native GUI features have been moved from the core module to a separate module, the widgets module. We should tell qmake that our application depends on that module by adding the line greaterThan(QT_MAJOR_VERSION, 4): QT += widgets to the project file. Following this modification, the content of ImageViewer.pro appears as follows:

```
TEMPLATE = app
TARGET = ImageViewer
greaterThan(QT_MAJOR_VERSION, 4): QT += widgets

INCLUDEPATH += .

DEFINES += QT_DEPRECATED_WARNINGS

SOURCES += main.cpp
```

Now, let's build the application again by issuing the qmake –makefile and make commands in the Terminal as follows:

```
$ qmake –makefile
$ make
g++ -c -pipe -O2 -Wall -W -D_REENTRANT -fPIC -DQT_DEPRECATED_WARNINGS -
DQT_NO_DEBUG -DQT_WIDGETS_LIB -DQT_GUI_LIB -DQT_CORE_LIB -I. -I. -isystem
/usr/include/x86_64-linux-gnu/qt5 -isystem /usr/include/x86_64-linux-
gnu/qt5/QtWidgets -isystem /usr/include/x86_64-linux-gnu/qt5/QtGui -isystem
/usr/include/x86_64-linux-gnu/qt5/QtCore -I. -isystem /usr/include/libdrm -
I/usr/lib/x86_64-linux-gnu/qt5/mkspecs/linux-g++ -o main.o main.cpp
g++ -Wl,-O1 -o ImageViewer main.o -lQt5Widgets -lQt5Gui -lQt5Core -lGL
-lpthread
$ ls
ImageViewer ImageViewer.pro main.cpp main.o Makefile
$
```

Hooray! We finally get the executable file, ImageViewer, in the project directory. Now, let's execute it and see what the window looks like:

As we can see, it's just a blank window. We will implement the full user interface as per our designed wireframe in the next section, *Setting up the full user interface*.

 Although we didn't mention any IDE or editor and built the application in a Terminal with qmake, you can use any IDE with which you are familiar, for instance, Qt Creator. Especially on Windows, the terminal (cmd or MinGW) does not perform as well as Terminals on Linux and macOS, so please feel free to use an IDE.

Setting up the full user interface

Let's proceed with the development. In the preceding section, we built a blank window and now we are going to add the menu bar, toolbar, image display component, and the status bar to the window.

First, instead of using the QMainWindow class, we will define a class ourselves, named MainWindow, which extends the QMainWindow class. Let's see its declaration in mainwindow.h:

```
class MainWindow : public QMainWindow
{
    Q_OBJECT

public:
    explicit MainWindow(QWidget *parent = nullptr);
    ~MainWindow();

private:
    void initUI();

private:
    QMenu *fileMenu;
    QMenu *viewMenu;

    QToolBar *fileToolBar;
    QToolBar *viewToolBar;

    QGraphicsScene *imageScene;
    QGraphicsView *imageView;

    QStatusBar *mainStatusBar;
    QLabel *mainStatusLabel;
};
```

Everything is straightforward. Q_OBJECT is a crucial macro provided by the Qt library. If we want to declare a class that has customized signals and slots of its own, or that uses any other facility from the Qt meta-object system, we must incorporate this crucial macro in our class declaration, or, more precisely, in the private section of our class, like we just did. The initUI method initializes all widgets that are declared in the private section. The imageScene and imageView widgets will be placed in the main area of the window to display images. Other widgets are self-explanatory from their type and name, so I will not say too much about them in order to keep the chapter concise.

 To keep the chapter concise, I have not included each source file in the text in its entirety when I introduce it. For example, most of the time, the #include ... directions at the beginning of the files are omitted. You can refer to the source file in the code repository on GitHub to check the details if needed.

Another key aspect is the implementation of the initUI method in mainwindow.cpp as follows:

```
void MainWindow::initUI()
{
    this->resize(800, 600);
    // setup menubar
    fileMenu = menuBar()->addMenu("&File");
    viewMenu = menuBar()->addMenu("&View");

    // setup toolbar
    fileToolBar = addToolBar("File");
    viewToolBar = addToolBar("View");

    // main area for image display
    imageScene = new QGraphicsScene(this);
    imageView = new QGraphicsView(imageScene);
    setCentralWidget(imageView);

    // setup status bar
    mainStatusBar = statusBar();
    mainStatusLabel = new QLabel(mainStatusBar);
    mainStatusBar->addPermanentWidget(mainStatusLabel);
    mainStatusLabel->setText("Image Information will be here!");
}
```

As you can see, at this stage, we don't create every item and button for the menu and toolbar; we just set up the main skeleton. In the preceding code, the `imageScene` variable is a `QGraphicsSence` instance. Such an instance is a container for 2D graphical items. According to its design, it only manages graphics items but doesn't have a visual appearance. In order to visualize it, we should create an instance of the `QGraphicsView` class with it, which is why the `imageView` variable is there. In our application, we use these two classes to display images.

After implementing all the methods of the `MainWindow` class, it's time to compile the sources. Before doing this, a number of changes need to be made to the `ImageViewer.pro` project file, as follows:

1. We just write a new source file, and it should be known by qmake:

```
# in ImageViewer.pro
SOURCES += main.cpp mainwindow.cpp
```

2. The header file, `mainwindow.h`, has a special macro, `Q_OBJECT`, which indicates that it has something that cannot be dealt with by a standard C++ preprocessor. That header file should be correctly handled by a Qt-provided preprocessor named `moc`, the **Meta-Object Compiler**, to generate a C++ source file that contains some code relating to the Qt meta-object system. So, we should tell qmake to check this header file by adding the following line to `ImageViewer.pro`:

```
HEADERS += mainwindow.h
```

OK. Now that all of that is complete, let's run `qmake -makefile` and `make` again, and then run the new executable. You should see the following window:

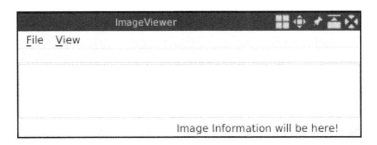

Well, so far so good. Now, let's go on to add the items that should appear in the menus as we intended. In Qt, each item in a menu is represented by an instance of QAction. Here, we take the action, which is to open a new image as an example. First, we declare a pointer to a QAction instance as a private member of our MainWindow class:

```
QAction *openAction;
```

Then, in the body of the initUI method, we create the action as a child widget of the main window by calling the new operator, and add it to the **File** menu as follows:

```
openAction = new QAction("&Open", this);
fileMenu->addAction(openAction);
```

You may notice that we create many Qt objects by calling the new operator, but never delete them. That is fine because all these objects are instances of QObject, or a subclass of it. Instances of QObject are organized in one or many object trees in the Qt library. When a QObject is created as the child of another object, the object will be added to its parent's children() list automatically. The parent object will take ownership of the child object. And, when the parent object is disposed of, its children will be deleted in its destructor automatically. In our application, we create most instances of QObject as children of the main window object, so we don't need to delete them.

Fortunately, buttons on the toolbar can also be represented by QAction, so we can add openAction directly to the file toolbar:

```
fileToolBar->addAction(openAction);
```

As mentioned previously, we have seven actions to create: open, save as, exit, zoom in, zoom out, previous image, and next image. All of them can be added in the same way as we added the open action. Also, given that many lines of code are required to add these actions, we can do a little refactoring of the code—create a new private method named createActions, insert all the code of the action into that method, and then call it in initUI.

All actions are now created in a separate method, `createActions`, after the refactoring. Let's compile the sources and see what the window looks like now:

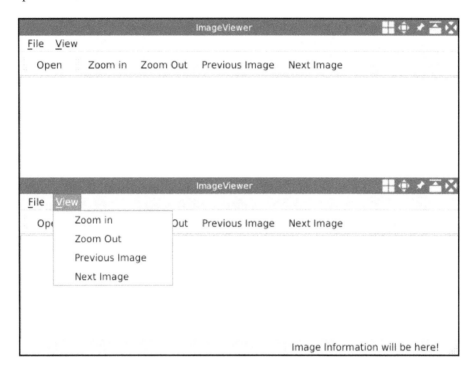

Great! The window looks just like the wireframe we designed, and we can now expand the menu by clicking on the items on the menu bar!

Implementing the functions for the actions

In the previous section, we added several actions to the menu and toolbar. However, if we click on these actions, nothing happens. That's because we have not written any handler for them yet. Qt uses a signal and slot connection mechanism to establish the relationship between events and their handlers. When users perform an operation on a widget, a signal of that widget will be emitted. Then, Qt will ascertain whether there is any slot connected with that signal. The slot will be called if it is found. In this section, we will create slots for the actions we have created in the preceding sections and make connections between the signals of the actions to these slots respectively. Also, we will set up some hotkeys for frequently used actions.

The Exit action

Take Exit action as an example. If users click it from the **File** menu, a signal named `triggered` will be emitted. So, let's connect this signal to a slot of our application instance in the `MainWindow` class's member function, `createActions`:

```
connect(exitAction, SIGNAL(triggered(bool)), QApplication::instance(),
SLOT(quit()));
```

The `connect` method takes four parameters: the signal sender, the signal, the receiver, and the slot. Once the connection is made, the slot on the receiver will be called as soon as the signal of the sender is emitted. Here, we connect the `triggered` signal of the Exit action with the `quit` slot of the application instance to enable the application to exit when we click on the Exit action.

Now, to compile and run, click the **Exit** item from the **File** menu. The application will exit as we expect if everything goes well.

Opening an image

The `quit` slot of `QApplication` is provided by Qt, but if we want to open an image when clicking on the open action, which slot should we use? In this scenario, there's no slot built-in for this kind of customized task. We should write a slot on our own.

To write a slot, first we should declare a function in the body of the class, `MainWindow`, and place it in a slots section. As this function is not used by other classes, we put it in a private slots section, as follows:

```
private slots:
    void openImage();
```

Then, we give this slot (also a member function) a simple definition for testing:

```
void MainWindow::openImage()
{
    qDebug() << "slot openImage is called.";
}
```

Now, we connect the `triggered` signal of the open action to the `openImage` slot of the main window in the body of the `createActions` method:

```
connect(openAction, SIGNAL(triggered(bool)), this, SLOT(openImage()));
```

Now, let's compile and run it again. Click the **Open** item from the **File** menu, or the **Open** button on the toolbar, and the `slot openImage is called.` message will be printed in the Terminal.

We now have a testing slot that works well with the open action. Let's change its body, as shown in the following code, to implement the function of opening an image from disk:

```
QFileDialog dialog(this);
dialog.setWindowTitle("Open Image");
dialog.setFileMode(QFileDialog::ExistingFile);
dialog.setNameFilter(tr("Images (*.png *.bmp *.jpg)"));
QStringList filePaths;
if (dialog.exec()) {
    filePaths = dialog.selectedFiles();
    showImage(filePaths.at(0));
}
```

Let's go through this code block line by line. In the first line, we create an instance of `QFileDialog`, whose name is `dialog`. Then, we set many properties of the dialog. This dialog is used to select an image file locally from the disk, so we set its title as **Open Image**, and set its file mode to `QFileDialog::ExistingFile` to make sure that it can only select one existing file, rather than many files or a file that doesn't exist. The name filter **Images (*.png *.bmp *.jpg)** ensures that only files with the extension mentioned (that is, `.png`, `.bmp`, and `.jpg`) can be selected. After these settings, we call the `exec` method of `dialog` to open it. This appears as follows:

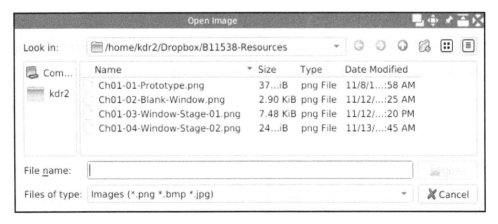

If the user selects a file and clicks the **Open** button, a non-zero value will be returned by `dialog.exec`. Then, we call `dialog.selectedFiles` to get the path of the files that are selected as an instance of `QStringList`. Here, only one selection is allowed; hence, there's only one element in the resulting list: the path of the image that we want to open. So, we call the `showImage` method of our `MainWindow` class with the only element to display the image. If the user clicks the **Cancel** button, a zero value will be returned by the `exec` method, and we can just ignore that branch because that means the user has given up on opening an image.

The `showImage` method is another private member function we just added to the `MainWindow` class. It is implemented as follows:

```
void MainWindow::showImage(QString path)
{
    imageScene->clear();
    imageView->resetMatrix();
    QPixmap image(path);
    imageScene->addPixmap(image);
    imageScene->update();
    imageView->setSceneRect(image.rect());
    QString status = QString("%1, %2x%3, %4
Bytes").arg(path).arg(image.width())
            .arg(image.height()).arg(QFile(path).size());
    mainStatusLabel->setText(status);
}
```

In the process of displaying the image, we add the image to `imageScene` and then update the scene. Afterward, the scene is visualized by `imageView`. Given the possibility that there is already an image opened by our application when we open and display another one, we should remove the old image, and reset any transformation (for example, scaling or rotating) of the view before showing the new one. This work is done in the first two lines. After this, we construct a new instance of `QPixmap` with the file path we selected, and then we add it to the scene and update the scene. Next, we call `setSceneRect` on `imageView` to tell it the new extent of the scene—it is the same size as the image.

At this point, we have shown the target image in its original size in the center of the main area. The last thing to do is display the information pertaining to the image on the status bar. We construct a string containing its path, dimensions, and size in bytes, and then set it as the text of `mainStatusLabel`, which had been added to the status bar.

Let's see how this image appears when it's opened:

Not bad! The application now looks like a genuine image viewer, so let's go on to implement all of its intended features.

Zooming in and out

OK. We have successfully displayed the image. Now, let's scale it. Here, we take zooming in as an example. With the experience from the preceding actions, we should have a clear idea as to how to do that. First, we declare a private slot, which is named zoomIn, and give its implementation as shown in the following code:

```
void MainWindow::zoomIn()
{
    imageView->scale(1.2, 1.2);
}
```

Easy, right? Just call the `scale` method of `imageView` with a scale rate for the width and a scale rate for the height. Then, we connect the `triggered` signal of `zoomInAction` to this slot in the `createActions` method of the `MainWindow` class:

```
connect(zoomInAction, SIGNAL(triggered(bool)), this, SLOT(zoomIn()));
```

Compile and run the application, open an image with it, and click on the **Zoom in** button on the toolbar. You will find that the image enlarges to 120% of its current size on each click.

Zooming out just entails scaling the `imageView` with a rate of less than `1.0`. Please try to implement it by yourself. If you find it difficult, you can refer to our code repository on GitHub (`https://github.com/PacktPublishing/Qt-5-and-OpenCV-4-Computer-Vision-Projects/tree/master/Chapter-01`).

With our application, we can now open an image and scale it for viewing. Next, we will implement the function of the `saveAsAction` action.

Saving a copy

Let's look back at the `showImage` method of `MainWindow`. In that method, we created an instance of `QPixmap` from the image and then added it to `imageScene` by calling `imageScene->addPixmap`. We didn't hold any handler of the image out of that function; hence, now we don't have a convenient way to get the `QPixmap` instance in the new slot, which we will implement for `saveAsAction`.

To solve this, we add a new private member field, `QGraphicsPixmapItem *currentImage`, to `MainWindow` to hold the return value of `imageScene->addPixmap` and initialize it with `nullptr` in the constructor of `MainWindow`. Then, we find the line of code in the body of `MainWindow::showImage`:

```
imageScene->addPixmap(image);
```

To save the returned value, we replace this line with the following one:

```
currentImage = imageScene->addPixmap(image);
```

Now, we are ready to create a new slot for `saveAsAction`. The declaration in the private slot section is straightforward, as follows:

```
void saveAs();
```

The definition is also straightforward:

```
void MainWindow::saveAs()
{
    if (currentImage == nullptr) {
        QMessageBox::information(this, "Information", "Nothing to
save.");
        return;
    }
    QFileDialog dialog(this);
    dialog.setWindowTitle("Save Image As ...");
    dialog.setFileMode(QFileDialog::AnyFile);
    dialog.setAcceptMode(QFileDialog::AcceptSave);
    dialog.setNameFilter(tr("Images (*.png *.bmp *.jpg)"));
    QStringList fileNames;
    if (dialog.exec()) {
        fileNames = dialog.selectedFiles();
        if(QRegExp(".+\\.(png|bmp|jpg)").exactMatch(fileNames.at(0)))
{
            currentImage->pixmap().save(fileNames.at(0));
        } else {
            QMessageBox::information(this, "Information", "Save error:
bad format or filename.");
        }
    }
}
```

First, we check whether `currentImage` is `nullptr`. If true, it means we haven't opened any image yet. So, we open a `QMessageBox` to tell the user there's nothing to save. Otherwise, we create a `QFileDialog`, set the relevant properties for it, and open it by calling its `exec` method. If the user gives the dialog a filename and clicks the open button on it, we will get a list of file paths that have only one element in it as our last usage of `QFileDialog`. Then, we check whether the file path ends with the extensions we support using a regexp matching. If everything goes well, we get the `QPixmap` instance of the current image from `currentImage->pixmap()` and save it to the specified path. Once the slot is ready, we connect it to the signal in `createActions`:

```
connect(saveAsAction, SIGNAL(triggered(bool)), this, SLOT(saveAs()));
```

To test this feature, we can open a PNG image and save it as a JPG image by giving a filename that ends with `.jpg` in the **Save Image As...** file dialog. Then, we open the new JPG image we just saved, using another image view application to check whether the image has been correctly saved.

Navigating in the folder

Now that we have completed all of the actions in relation to a single image, let's go further and navigate all the images that reside in the directory in which the current image resides, that is, `prevAction` and `nextAction`.

To know what constitutes the previous or next image, we should be aware of two things as follows:

- Which is the current one
- The order in which we count them

So, first we add a new member field, `QString currentImagePath`, to the `MainWindow` class to save the path of the current image. Then, we save the image's path while showing it in `showImage` by adding the following line to the method:

```
currentImagePath = path;
```

Then, we decide to count the images in alphabetical order according to their names. With these two pieces of information, we can now determine which is the previous or next image. Let's see how we define the slot for `prevAction`:

```cpp
void MainWindow::prevImage()
{
    QFileInfo current(currentImagePath);
    QDir dir = current.absoluteDir();
    QStringList nameFilters;
    nameFilters << "*.png" << "*.bmp" << "*.jpg";
    QStringList fileNames = dir.entryList(nameFilters, QDir::Files,
QDir::Name);
    int idx =
fileNames.indexOf(QRegExp(QRegExp::escape(current.fileName())));
    if(idx > 0) {
        showImage(dir.absoluteFilePath(fileNames.at(idx - 1)));
    } else {
        QMessageBox::information(this, "Information", "Current image
is the first one.");
    }
}
```

First, we get the directory in which the current image resides as an instance of `QDir`, and then we list the directory with name filters to ensure that only PNG, BMP, and JPG files are returned. While listing the directory, we use `QDir::Name` as the third argument to make sure the returned list is sorted by filename in alphabetical order. Since the current image we are viewing is also in this directory, its filename must be in the filename list. We find its index by calling `indexOf` on the list with a regexp, which is generated by `QRegExp::escape`, so that it can exactly match its filename. If the index is zero, this means the current image is the first one in this directory. A message box pops up to give the user this information. Otherwise, we show the image whose filename is at the position of `index` − `1` to complete the operation.

Before you test whether `prevAction` works, don't forget to connect the signal and the slot by adding the following line to the body of the `createActions` method:

```
connect(prevAction, SIGNAL(triggered(bool)), this, SLOT(prevImage()));
```

Well, it's not too hard, so attempt the work of `nextAction` yourself or just read the code for it in our code repository on GitHub.

Responding to hotkeys

At this point, almost all of the features are implemented as we intended. Now, let's add some hotkeys for frequently used actions to make our application much easier to use.

You may have noticed that, when we create the actions, we occasionally add a strange & to their text, such as `&File` and `E&xit`. Actually, this is a way of setting shortcuts in Qt. In certain Qt widgets, using & in front of a character will automatically create a mnemonic (a shortcut) for that character. Hence, in our application, if you press *Alt* + *F*, the **File** menu will be triggered, and while the **File** menu is expanded, we can see the Exit action on it. At this time, you press *Alt* + *X*, and the Exit action will be triggered to let the application exit.

Now, let's give the most frequently used actions some single key shortcuts to make using them more convenient and faster as follows:

- Plus (+) or equal (=) for zooming in
- Minus (-) or underscore (_) for zooming out
- Up or left for the previous image
- Down or right for the next image

To achieve this, we add a new private method named `setupShortcuts` in the `MainWindow` class and implement it as follows:

```
void MainWindow::setupShortcuts()
{
    QList<QKeySequence> shortcuts;
    shortcuts << Qt::Key_Plus << Qt::Key_Equal;
    zoomInAction->setShortcuts(shortcuts);

    shortcuts.clear();
    shortcuts << Qt::Key_Minus << Qt::Key_Underscore;
    zoomOutAction->setShortcuts(shortcuts);

    shortcuts.clear();
    shortcuts << Qt::Key_Up << Qt::Key_Left;
    prevAction->setShortcuts(shortcuts);

    shortcuts.clear();
    shortcuts << Qt::Key_Down << Qt::Key_Right;
    nextAction->setShortcuts(shortcuts);
}
```

To support multiple shortcuts for one action, for example, + and = for zooming in, for each action we make an empty `QList` of `QKeySequence`, and then add each shortcut key sequence to the list. In Qt, `QKeySequence` encapsulates a key sequence as used by shortcuts. Because `QKeySequence` has a non-explicit constructor with `int` arguments, we can add `Qt::Key` values directly to the list and they will be converted to instances of `QKeySequence` implicitly. After the list is filled, we call the `setShortcuts` method on each action with the filled list, and this way setting shortcuts will be easier.

Add the `setupShortcuts()` method call at the end of the body of the `createActions` method, then compile and run; now you can test the shortcuts in your application and they should work well.

Summary

In this chapter, we used Qt to build a desktop application for image viewing, from scratch. We learned how to design the user interface, create a Qt project from scratch, build the user interface, open and display images, respond to hotkeys, and save a copy of images.

In the next chapter, we will add more actions to the application to allow the user to edit the image with the functions provided by OpenCV. Also, we will add these editing actions in a more flexible way by using the Qt plugin mechanism.

Questions

Try these questions to test your knowledge of this chapter:

1. We use a message box to tell users that they are already viewing the first or last image while they are trying to see the previous one before the first image, or the next one after the last image. But there is another way to deal with this situation—disable `prevAction` when users are viewing the first image, and disable `nextAction` when users are viewing the last image. How is this implemented?

2. Our menu items or tool buttons only contain text. How could we add an icon image to them?

3. We use `QGraphicsView.scale` to zoom in or out of an image view, but how do you rotate an image view?

4. What does `moc` do? What actions do the `SIGNAL` and `SLOT` macros perform?

Editing Images Like a Pro
2

In `Chapter 1`, *Building an Image Viewer*, we built a simple application for image viewing with Qt from scratch. With that application, we can view an image from the local disk, zoom the view in or out, and navigate in the opening directory. In this chapter, we will continue with that application and add some features to allow users to edit the opening image. To achieve this goal, we will get the OpenCV library we mentioned at the beginning of this book involved. To make the application extensible, we will develop most of these editing features as plugins using the plugin mechanism of Qt.

The following topics will be covered in this chapter:

- Converting images between Qt and OpenCV
- Extending an application through Qt's plugin mechanism
- Modifying images using image processing algorithms provided by OpenCV

Technical requirements

Users are required to have the `ImageViewer` application, which we built in the previous chapter, running correctly. Our development in this chapter will be based on that application.

Also, some basic knowledge of OpenCV is required as a prerequisite. We will be using the latest version of OpenCV, that is, version 4.0, which was released in December 2018, when this book was being written. Since the new version is not yet included in the software repositories of many operator systems, such as Debian, Ubuntu, or Fedora, we will build it from the source. Please don't worry about this—we will cover the installation instructions briefly, later in this chapter.

All of the code for this chapter can be found in this book's GitHub repository at `https://github.com/PacktPublishing/Qt-5-and-OpenCV-4-Computer-Vision-Projects/tree/master/Chapter-02`.

Check out the following video to see the code in action: `http://bit.ly/2FhYLro`

The ImageEditor application

In this chapter, we will build an application that can be used to edit images, so we will name it `ImageEditor`. To edit an image with a GUI application, the first step is opening and viewing the image with that application, which is what we did in the previous chapter. Therefore, I decided to make a copy of the `ImageViewer` application and rename it `ImageEditor`, before adding the image editing features to it.

Let's start by copying the sources:

```
$ mkdir Chapter-02
$ cp -r Chapter-01/ImageViewer/ Chapter-02/ImageEditor
$ ls Chapter-02
ImageEditor
$ cd Chapter-02/ImageEditor
$ make clean
$ rm -f ImageViewer
```

With these commands, we copy the `ImageViewer` directory under the `Chapter-01` directory to `Chapter-02/ImageEditor`. Then, we can enter that directory, run `make clean` to clean all intermediate files that were generated in the compiling process, and remove the old target executable file using `rm -f ImageViewer`.

Now that we have a cleaned project, let's rename some of it:

- The project directory is named with the new project name `ImageEditor` in the copying process, so we don't need to do anything here.
- The Qt project file, `ImageViewer.pro`, should be renamed to `ImageEditor.pro`. You can do this in your file manager or in a Terminal.
- In the `ImageEditor.pro` file, we should rename the `TARGET` to `ImageEditor` by changing the `TARGET = ImageViewer` line to `TARGET = ImageEditor`.
- In the source file, `main.cpp`, we should change the window title by changing the `window.setWindowTitle("ImageViewer");` line to `window.setWindowTitle("ImageEditor");`.

Now that everything has been renamed, let's compile and run the new
`ImageEditor` application, which has been copied from `ImageViewer`:

```
$ qmake -makefile
$ make
g++ -c -pipe ...
# output truncated
# ...
$ ls
ImageEditor ImageEditor.pro main.cpp main.o mainwindow.cpp mainwindow.h
mainwindow.o Makefile moc_mainwindow.cpp moc_mainwindow.o moc_predefs.h
$ export LD_LIBRARY_PATH=/home/kdr2/programs/opencv/lib/
$ ./ImageEditor
```

You will see that the window is exactly the same as the window of `ImageViewer`, except
that it has a different window title, `ImageEditor`. Anyway, we have set our editor
application up, even though it has no feature for image editing now. We will add a simple
editing feature in the next chapter.

Blurring images using OpenCV

In the preceding section, we set up our editor application. In this section, we will add a
simple feature of image editing—an action (both on the menu and the toolbar) to blur the
image.

We will do this in two steps:

1. First, we will set up the UI and add the action, and then connect the action to a
   dummy slot.
2. Then, we will rewrite the dummy slot to blur the image, which will get the
   OpenCV library involved.

Adding the blur action

Most of the actions we will add in this chapter will be used to edit an image, so we should
categorize them in a new menu and toolbar. First, we will declare three members, that is,
the edit menu, the edit toolbar, and the blur action, in the private section of the
`mainwindow.h` header file:

```
QMenu *editMenu;
QToolBar *editToolBar;
QAction *blurAction;
```

Then, we will create them in the `MainWindow::initUI` and
`MainWindow::createActions` methods, respectively, as follows:

In `MainWindow::initUI`, this is executed as follows:

```
editMenu = menuBar()->addMenu("&Edit");
editToolBar = addToolBar("Edit");
```

In `MainWindow::createActions`, this is executed as follows:

```
blurAction = new QAction("Blur", this);
editMenu->addAction(blurAction);
editToolBar->addAction(blurAction);
```

Up until now, we have an edit menu and an edit toolbar with a blur action on both of them.
But, if the user clicks either the blur buttons on the toolbar or the blur items under the edit
menu, nothing will happen. This is because we haven't connected a slot to that action yet.
Let's give the action a slot now. First, we will declare a slot in the private slots section of
`mainwindow.h`, as follows:

```
// for editing
void blurImage();
```

Then, we will give it a dummy implementation in `mainwindow.cpp`:

```
void MainWindow::blurImage()
{
    qDebug() << "Blurring the image!";
}
```

Now that the slot is ready, it's time to connect the `triggered` signal of the blur action with
this slot at the end of the `mainwindow::createActions` method:

```
connect(blurAction, SIGNAL(triggered(bool)), this,
    SLOT(blurImage()));
```

When you compile and run the application, you will see the menu, toolbar, and the action.
If you trigger the action by clicking it, you will see the message `Blurring the image!`
being printed.

This is what the window and printed message look like:

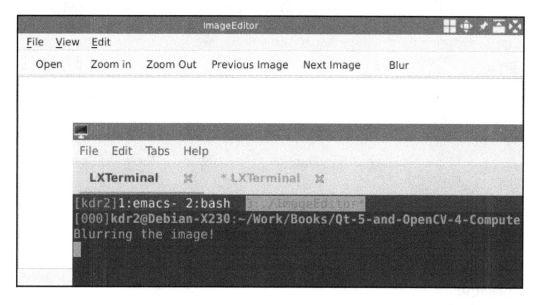

The UI part is now ready, which means that we can focus on how to blur the image by using OpenCV in the slot in the following sections.

Building and installing OpenCV from the source

In the preceding section, we installed a dummy slot for the blur action that does nothing but prints a simple message. Now, we are going to rewrite the implementation of that slot to do the real blurring work.

As we mentioned in the preceding sections, we will be using the OpenCV library, and, more precisely, the latest version (4.0) of it, to edit the images. So, before we start with our code, we will install the latest version of the OpenCV library and include it in our project.

OpenCV is a set of libraries, tools, and modules that contain classes and functions that are required for building computer vision applications. Its release files can be found on the release page of its official website: `https://opencv.org/releases.html`. Another thing we need to know is that OpenCV uses a modern build tool called CMake to construct its building system. This means that we must have CMake installed on our operating system to build OpenCV from source, and at least version 3.12 of CMake is required, so please ensure that your version of CMake is set up properly.

How to build a project, especially a large scale project, is a complex topic in the software engineering world. Many tools have been invented to cope with a variety of situations in relation to this topic in the vicissitude during the development of software engineering. From make to Autotools, from SCons to CMake, from Ninja to bazel—there's too many to talk about here. However, up until now, only two of them were introduced in our book: Qmake is the one that was developed by the Qt team and is dedicated to building Qt projects. CMake is another one that is widely adopted nowadays by many projects, including OpenCV.

In our book, we will try our best to keep the use of these tools simple and clear.

The OpenCV release page looks as follows:

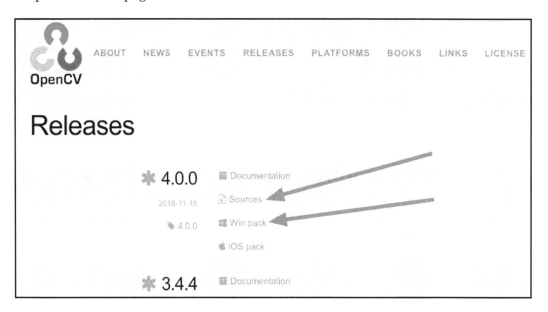

We can click the **Sources** link to download the ZIP package of its source to the local disk and then unzip it. We will build OpenCV by using CMake in a Terminal, so, we will open a Terminal and change its work directory to the directory of the unzipped source. Also, OpenCV doesn't allow you to build directly in the root directory of its source tree, so we should create a separate directory to build it.

Here are the instructions we used to build OpenCV in the Terminal:

```
$ cd ~/opencv-4.0.0 # path to the unzipped source
$ mkdir release # create the separate dir
$ cd release
$ cmake -D CMAKE_BUILD_TYPE=RELEASE -D
CMAKE_INSTALL_PREFIX=$HOME/programs/opencv ..
# ... output of cmake ...
# rm ../CMakeCache.txt if it tells you are not in a separate dir
$ make
# ... output of make ...
$ make install
```

The cmake ... line reads the CMakeLists.txt file in the root directory of the unzipped source and generates a makefile. The CMAKE_BUILD_TYPE variable we pass to the cmake command using -D specifies that we build OpenCV in the RELEASE mode. Likewise, the CMAKE_INSTALL_PREFIX variable specifies the path to where the OpenCV library will be installed. Here, I install OpenCV to $HOME/programs/opencv, that is, /home/kdr2/programs/opencv—you can change the value of CMAKE_INSTALL_PREFIX to change the destination directory if you so desire. After the cmake command ends in success, a file named Makefile will be generated. With the makefile, now we can run make and make install to compile and install the library.

If all the preceding instructions go well, your OpenCV version will be installed correctly. You can check this by browsing the installation directory:

```
$ ls ~/programs/opencv/
bin include lib share
$ ls ~/programs/opencv/bin/
opencv_annotation opencv_interactive-calibration opencv_version
opencv_visualisation setup_vars_opencv4.sh
$ ls -l ~/programs/opencv/lib/
# ...
lrwxrwxrwx 1 kdr2 kdr2 21 Nov 20 13:28 libopencv_core.so ->
libopencv_core.so.4.0
lrwxrwxrwx 1 kdr2 kdr2 23 Nov 20 13:28 libopencv_core.so.4.0 ->
libopencv_core.so.4.0.0
-rw-r--r-- 1 kdr2 kdr2 4519888 Nov 20 12:34 libopencv_core.so.4.0.0
# ...
lrwxrwxrwx 1 kdr2 kdr2 24 Nov 20 13:28 libopencv_imgproc.so ->
libopencv_imgproc.so.4.0
lrwxrwxrwx 1 kdr2 kdr2 26 Nov 20 13:28 libopencv_imgproc.so.4.0 ->
libopencv_imgproc.so.4.0.0
-rw-r--r-- 1 kdr2 kdr2 4714608 Nov 20 12:37 libopencv_imgproc.so.4.0.0
# ... output truncated
```

OpenCV is a modular library. It consists of two types of modules—the main modules and the extra modules.

The main modules are included in OpenCV by default when we build it from source, and they contain all of the core OpenCV functionality, along with the modules that are used for image processing tasks, filtering, transformation, and many more capabilities.

The extra modules include all of the OpenCV functionalities that are not included in the OpenCV library by default, and they mostly include additional computer vision-related functionalities.

If we look back at the contents of the `lib` directory under the OpenCV install path when we checked whether our OpenCV was installed correctly, we will find many files named in the pattern of `libopencv_*.so*`. Typically, each of these files corresponds to an OpenCV module. For instance, the `libopencv_imgproc.so` file is the `imgproc` module, which is used for image processing tasks.

Now that we have the OpenCV library installed, it's time to include it in our Qt project. Let's open our Qt project file, `ImageEditor.pro`, and add the following lines to it:

```
unix: !mac {
    INCLUDEPATH += /home/kdr2/programs/opencv/include/opencv4
    LIBS += -L/home/kdr2/programs/opencv/lib -lopencv_core -l
opencv_imgproc
    }
```

The `unix: !mac` directive means to use the configuration in the brackets next to it on any UNIX-like system except macOS. I am using this directive because I am using Debian GNU/Linux. The directives inside the brackets are the crucial part of importing the OpenCV library in the following lines:

- The first line tells the compiler where the header files of OpenCV that we will use in our code lie by updating the value of `INCLUDEPATH`.
- The second line tells the linker which OpenCV modules (shared objects) our application should link against, and where to find them. More concretely, `-lopencv_core -l opencv_imgproc` means that we should link our application against `libopencv_core.so` and `libopencv_imgproc.so`, and `-L...` means that the linker should find these lib files (shared objects) under the `/home/kdr2/programs/opencv/lib` directory.

On macOS or Windows, OpenCV is built and linked in another way, but not in each library file of a module. In that situation, all the modules are linked to one library, called `opencv_world`. We can pass `-DBUILD_opencv_world=on` to CMake to achieve the same effect on Linux:

```
# on mac
$ ls -l
-rwxr-xr-x 1 cheftin staff 25454204 Dec 3 13:47
libopencv_world.4.0.0.dylib
    lrwxr-xr-x 1 cheftin staff 27 Dec 3 13:36 libopencv_world.4.0.dylib ->
libopencv_world.4.0.0.dylib
    lrwxr-xr-x 1 cheftin staff 25 Dec 3 13:36 libopencv_world.dylib ->
libopencv_world.4.0.dylib

# on Linux with -D BUILD_opencv_world=on
$ ls -l
lrwxrwxrwx 1 kdr2 kdr2 22 Nov 29 22:55 libopencv_world.so ->
libopencv_world.so.4.0
    lrwxrwxrwx 1 kdr2 kdr2 24 Nov 29 22:55 libopencv_world.so.4.0 ->
libopencv_world.so.4.0.0
    -rw-r--r-- 1 kdr2 kdr2 57295464 Nov 29 22:09 libopencv_world.so.4.0.0
```

Building OpenCV in this way simplifies the linker options when we compile our source—we don't need to give a module list to the linker as we did with `-lopencv_core -lopencv_imgproc`. Telling the linker to link against `opencv_world` is enough. For macOS and Windows, we can put the following code into `ImageEditor.pro`:

```
unix: mac {
    INCLUDEPATH += /path/to/opencv/include/opencv4
    LIBS += -L/path/to/opencv/lib -lopencv_world
}

win32 {
    INCLUDEPATH += c:/path/to/opencv/include/opencv4
    LIBS += -lc:/path/to/opencv/lib/opencv_world
}
```

Although this way is easier, this book still uses separate modules to let you get a deep insight into the OpenCV modules we are learning about and using.

Qmake provides you with another way of configuring the third-party library, that is, through `pkg-config`, which is a facility for maintaining the meta information of libraries. Unfortunately, according to https://github.com/opencv/opencv/issues/13154, OpenCV deprecated the support of `pkg-config` starting from version 4.0. This means that we need to use a more direct and flexible way to configure OpenCV in our Qt project rather than using the `pkg-config` way.

Blurring images

Finally, we have the OpenCV library installed and configured. Now, let's try to use it to blur the image in the slot that's connected to our blur action.

First, we will add the following lines to the beginning of the `mainwindow.cpp` file so that we can include the OpenCV header file:

```
#include "opencv2/opencv.hpp"
```

The preparation is now done, so let's focus on the implementation of the slot method. Like any slot that intends to operate on a single open image, before doing anything, we need to check whether there is an image open at the current time:

```
if (currentImage == nullptr) {
    QMessageBox::information(this, "Information", "No image to
edit.");
    return;
}
```

As you can see, we prompt a message box and return immediately from the function if there is no image open.

After we make sure that there is an image open at the current time in our application, we know that we can obtain the open image as an instance of `QPixmap`. But how can we blur the image, which is in the form of a `QPixmap` using OpenCV? The answer is, we can't. Before we do any manipulation on an image with OpenCV, we must have the image in the form of how OpenCV holds an image, which is typical as an instance of the `Mat` class. The `Mat` class in OpenCV means **matrix**—any image is, in fact, a matrix with a given width, height, number of channels, and depth. In Qt, we have a similar class called `QImage`, which is used to hold the matrix data of an image. This means that we have an idea of how to blur `QPixmap` using OpenCV—we need to convert the `QPixmap` into a `QImage`, construct a `Mat` using `QImage`, blur the `Mat`, then convert the `Mat` back to `QImage` and `QPixmap`, respectively.

We have to do quite a bit of work in terms of conversion. Let's discuss this by going through the following lines of code:

```
QPixmap pixmap = currentImage->pixmap();
QImage image = pixmap.toImage();
```

This snippet is quite straightforward. We obtain the data of the current image as an instance of QPixmap, and then convert it into a QImage instance by calling its toImage method.

The next step is to convert QImage into Mat, but things get a little complex here. The image we are opening may be in any format—it might be a monochrome image, a grayscale image, or a color image with different depths. To blur it, we must know its format, so we convert it into a normal format with an 8-bit depth and three channels, despite its original format. This is represented by QImage::Format_RGB888 in Qt, and CV_8UC3 in OpenCV. Let's now see how we can do the conversion and construct the Mat object:

```
image = image.convertToFormat(QImage::Format_RGB888);
cv::Mat mat = cv::Mat(
    image.height(),
    image.width(),
    CV_8UC3,
    image.bits(),
    image.bytesPerLine());
```

Finally, it's a scrutable piece of code. Now that we have the Mat object, let's blur it:

```
cv::Mat tmp;
cv::blur(mat, tmp, cv::Size(8, 8));
mat = tmp;
```

The blur function is provided by OpenCV in its imgproc module. It blurs an image using the normalized box filter with a kernel. The first argument is the image we want to blur, while the second argument is where we want to place the blurred image. We use a temporary matrix to store the blurred image and assign it back to the original one after the blurring finishes. The third argument is the size of the kernel. Here, the kernel is used to tell OpenCV how to change the value of any given pixel by combining it with different amounts of neighboring pixels.

Now that we have the blurred image as an instance of `Mat`, we have to convert it back into an instance of `QPixmap` and show it on our scene and view:

```
QImage image_blurred(
    mat.data,
    mat.cols,
    mat.rows,
    mat.step,
    QImage::Format_RGB888);
pixmap = QPixmap::fromImage(image_blurred);
imageScene->clear();
imageView->resetMatrix();
currentImage = imageScene->addPixmap(pixmap);
imageScene->update();
imageView->setSceneRect(pixmap.rect());
```

The new part of the preceding code for us is constructing the `QImage` object, `image_blurred`, from the `mat` object, and converting the `QImage` object into a `QPixmap` using the `QPixmap::fromImage` static method. Although this is new, it's clear enough. The rest of this code isn't new to us— it's the same code we use in the `showImage` method of the `MainWindow` class.

Now that we've displayed the blurred image, we can update the message on the status bar to tell users that this image they are viewing is an edited one, and not the original image they've opened:

```
QString status = QString("(editted image), %1x%2")
    .arg(pixmap.width()).arg(pixmap.height());
mainStatusLabel->setText(status);
```

At this point, we've finished the `MainWindow::blurImage` method. Let's rebuild our project by issuing the `qmake -makefile` and `make` commands in our Terminal, and then run the new executable.

If you installed OpenCV in a path that isn't `/usr` or `/usr/local`, like me, you may encounter a problem while running the executable:

```
$ ./ImageEditor
./ImageEditor: error while loading shared libraries:
libopencv_core.so.4.0: cannot open shared object file: No such file or
directory
```

This is because our OpenCV libraries are not in the library search path of the system. We can add its path to the library search path by setting the LD_LIBRARY_PATH environment variable on Linux, and DYLD_LIBRARY_PATH on macOS:

```
$ export LD_LIBRARY_PATH=/home/kdr2/programs/opencv/lib/
$ ./ImageEditor
```

When opening an image with our app, we get the following output:

After clicking the **Blur** button on the toolbar, it appears as follows:

We can see that our image has been successfully blurred.

QPixmap, QImage, and Mat

In the preceding section, we added a new feature to blur an image that's opened in our ImageEditor app. While blurring the image, we converted the image from `QPixmap` to `QImage` to `Mat`, and then converted it backward after blurring it using OpenCV. There, we did the work, but didn't say much about these classes. Let's talk about them now.

QPixmap

QPixmap is a class that's provided by the Qt library, and it is intended to be used when we need to display images on a screen. That's exactly how we used it in our project—we read an image in as an instance of it and added the instance to QGraphicsSence to display it.

There are many ways to create instances of QPixmap. Like we did in Chapter 1, *Building an Image Viewer*, and the previous sections of this chapter, we can instantiate it with the path of an image file:

```
QPixmap map("/path/to/image.png");
```

Alternatively, we can instantiate an empty QPixmap and then load data into it afterward:

```
QPixmap map;
map.load("/path/to/image.png");
```

With an instance holding an image in it, we can save the image in it to a file by calling its save method, just like we did in the slot for our *save as* action:

```
map.save("/path/to/output.png");
```

Finally, we can convert a QPixmap method into a QImage method by calling its toImage method:

```
//...
QImage image = map.toImage();
```

QImage

While QPixmap is mainly for displaying images in Qt, QImage is designed and optimized for I/O, and for direct pixel access and manipulation. With this class, we can get information about images, such as its size, whether it has an alpha channel, whether it is a grayscale image and the color of any pixels in it.

QImage is designed for direct pixel access and manipulation, and it provides functions to do image processing, such as pixel manipulation and transformations. After all, the Qt library isn't a library that's dedicated to image processing, and so the features it provides in this domain can't slake our requirements in this chapter. Therefore, we will be using OpenCV to do the image processing after we convert QImage objects into Mat objects.

Then, the question is, how can we convert between these three data types, that is, `QImage`, `QPixmap`, and `Mat`? We talked about how to convert a `QPixmap` into a `QImage` in the previous section, but let's now look at how to convert it back:

```
QPixmap pixmap = QPixmap::fromImage(image);
```

As you can see, this is a simple process—you just call the `fromImage` static method of the `QPixmap` class with the `QImage` object as the only argument.

If you are interested in the details of the other features of `QImage`, you can refer to its documentation at `https://doc.qt.io/qt-5/qimage.html`. In the following section, we will talk about how to convert `QImage` into `Mat`, and vice versa.

Mat

The `Mat` class is one of the most important classes in the OpenCV library, and its name is short for **matrix**. In the sphere of computer vision, any image is, as we mentioned previously, a matrix with a given width, height, number of channels, and depth. Therefore, OpenCV uses the `Mat` class to represent images. In fact, the `Mat` class is an n-dimensional array that can be used to store single or multiple channels of data with any given data type, and it contains many members and methods to create, modify, or manipulate it in many ways.

The `Mat` class has many constructors. For example, we can create an instance of it that has a width (columns) of 800, and a height (rows) of 600, with three channels that contain 8-bit unsigned int values, as follows:

```
Mat mat(600, 800, CV_8UC3);
```

The third argument of this constructor is the `type` of that matrix; OpenCV predefines many values that can be used for it. These predefined values have a pattern in their names so that we can know about the type of the matrix when we see the name, or we can guess the name we should use when the nature of the matrix is determined.

This pattern is called `CV_<depth><type>C<channels>`:

- `<depth>` can be replaced by 8, 16, 32, or 64, which represent the number of bits used to store each element in the pixels
- `<type>` needs to be replaced with `U`, `S`, or `F` for the unsigned integer, signed integer, and floating point values, respectively
- `<channel>` should be the number of channels

So, in our code, CV_8UC3 means the declared image has 8 as its depth, each element of its pixels are stored in an 8-bit unsigned int, and it has three channels. In other words, each pixel has 3 elements in it and CV_8UC3 occupies 24 bits (depth * channels).

We can also fill the image with some data while constructing it. For example, we can fill it with constant color, as follows:

```
int R = 40, G = 50, B = 60;
Mat mat(600, 800, CV_8UC3, Scalar(B, G, R));
```

In the preceding code, we created the same image that we created in the previous example, but filled it with constant color, RGB(40, 50, 60), which is specified by the fourth argument.

It's important to note that the default order of colors in OpenCV is BGR, not RGB, which means a swapped B and R value. Therefore, we represent the constant color as Scalar(B, G, R) instead of Scalar(R, G, B) in the code. This is important if we read images using OpenCV, but manipulate them using another library that uses a different order for the colors, or vice versa, especially when our manipulation treats each channel of the images separately.

That is what happens in our application—we load the images with Qt and convert them into the OpenCV Mat data structure, and then process it and convert it back into QImage. However, as you can see, while blurring the image, we didn't swap the red and blue channels to resort to the color order. That's because the blur function operates symmetrically on the channels; there's no interference between channels, so the color order is not important in this situation. We can omit the channel swapping if we do the following:

- We convert QImage to Mat, and then process the Mat and convert it back to QImage
- All the manipulation during the processing period that we do on Mat is symmetric on the channels; that is, there's no interference between channels
- We don't show the images during the processing period; we only show them after they are converted back to QImage

In such a situation, we can simply ignore the problem of the order of colors. This will be applied to most of the plugins we will write later. However, in some situations, you can't just simply ignore this. For example, if you read an image using OpenCV, convert it into an instance of `QImage`, and then show it in Qt, the following code will show an image whose red and blue channels have been swapped:

```
cv::Mat mat = cv::imread("/path/to/an/image.png");
QImage image(
    mat.data,
    mat.cols,
    mat.rows,
    mat.step,
    QImage::Format_RGB888
);
```

You should swap the R and B channels before converting it into a `QImage`:

```
cv::Mat mat = cv::imread("/path/to/an/image.png");
cv::cvtColor(mat, mat, cv::COLOR_BGR2RGB);
QImage image(
    mat.data,
    mat.cols,
    mat.rows,
    mat.step,
    QImage::Format_RGB888
);
```

Remember that if we use a process that doesn't treat the color channels symmetrically using OpenCV, we must ensure that the color order is BGR before doing that.

Now that we've discussed the order of colors, we will go back to the topic of creating `Mat` objects. We just learned that we can fill a `Mat` object with a constant color while creating it, but, in our application, we should create a `Mat` object that holds the same image of the given `QImage` object. Let's look back to see how we did this:

```
// image is the give QImage object
cv::Mat mat = cv::Mat(
    image.height(),
    image.width(),
    CV_8UC3,
    image.bits(),
    image.bytesPerLine()
);
```

Besides the first three arguments that we have already talked about, we pass the data pointer that's held by the `QImage` object and returned by its `bits` method as the fourth argument. We also pass another extra argument, that is, the number of bytes per row of the image, to let OpenCV know how to deal with the image padding bytes, and how to store it in memory in an efficient way.

As we stated previously, there are too many constructors of the `Mat` class to talk about here; we can even create `Mat` objects with much higher dimensions. You can refer to the documentation at `https://docs.opencv.org/4.0.0/d3/d63/classcv_1_1Mat.html` to get a full list of its constructors. We won't talk about them much more in this chapter.

Now that we have some knowledge of how to convert image objects between Qt and OpenCV, we will move on to how to edit images using OpenCV in the following sections.

Adding features using Qt's plugin mechanism

In the previous section, we added a new menu and toolbar named **Edit** to our application and added an action to both of them to blur the opening image. Let's recall the progress of adding this feature.

First, we added the menu and toolbar, and then the action. After the action was added, we connected a new slot to the action. In the slot, we got the opening image as an instance of `QPixmap` and converted it into a `QImage` object, and then a `Mat` object. The crucial editing work began here—we used OpenCV to modify the `Mat` instance to get the editing work done. Then, we converted `Mat` back into `QImage` and `QPixmap` accordingly to show the edited image.

Now, if we want to add another editing feature to our app, what should we do? Of course, just repeating the preceding process of adding the blurring action is fine, but it's not efficient. If we imagine that we just added another editing action to our app in the same way we added the blurring action, we will find that most of the work or code is the same. We are repeating ourselves. That's not only a bad developing pattern, but also boring work.

To resolve this issue, we should go through the repeated process carefully, break it into steps, and then find which steps are exactly the same and which ones vary.

By doing so, we can find out the key points of adding a different editing feature:

- The names of the actions are different for different editing features.
- The operations on the `Mat` instance are different for different editing features.

All the other steps or logic are the same in the process of adding different editing actions besides the previous two. That is, when we want to add a new editing feature, we only have to do two things. First, we name it, and then we figure out a way to do the editing operation on the `Mat` instance by using OpenCV. Once these two things are clear, the new editing feature is determined. What we should do next is integrate the new feature into the application.

So, how do we integrate it into the application? We will do this using Qt's plugin mechanism, and each editing feature will be a plugin.

The plugin interface

The Qt plugin mechanism is a powerful method that makes Qt applications more extensible. As we discussed previously, we will use this mechanism to abstract a way in which we can add new editing features easily. Once we're finished, we only need to pay attention to the name of the editing feature and the operation on the `Mat` instance while adding a new editing feature.

The first step is to figure out an interface in order to provide a common protocol between the application and the plugins so that we can load and call the plugins despite how they are implemented. In C++, an interface is a class with pure virtual member functions. For our plugins, we take care of the action name and the operation to `Mat`, so we declare our interface in `editor_plugin_interface.h`, as follows:

```
#ifndef EDITOR_PLUGIN_INTERFACE_H
#define EDITOR_PLUGIN_INTERFACE_H

#include <QObject>
#include <QString>
#include "opencv2/opencv.hpp"

class EditorPluginInterface
{
public:
    virtual ~EditorPluginInterface() {};
```

```
        virtual QString name() = 0;
        virtual void edit(const cv::Mat &input, cv::Mat &output) = 0;
    };


    #define EDIT_PLUGIN_INTERFACE_IID "com.kdr2.editorplugininterface"
    Q_DECLARE_INTERFACE(EditorPluginInterface, EDIT_PLUGIN_INTERFACE_IID);

    #endif
```

We use the `ifndef`/`define` idiom (the first two lines and the last line) to ensure that this header file will be included once in the source files. Following the first two lines, we include some header files that are provided by Qt and OpenCV to introduce the relevant data structures. Then, we declare a class named `EditorPluginInterface`, which is our interface class. In the class, besides a virtual empty destructor, we can see two pure virtual member functions: the `name` and the `edit` function. The `name` function returns a `QString`, which will be the name of the editing action. The `edit` function takes two references of `Mat` as its input and output function, and is used for the editing operation. Each plugin will be a subclass of this interface, and the implementation of these two functions will determine the action name and the editing operation.

After the class declaration, we define a unique identifier string called `com.kdr2.editorplugininterface` as the ID of the interface. This ID must be unique in the application scope, that is, if you write other interfaces, you must use different IDs for them. Then, we use the `Q_DECLARE_INTERFACE` macro to associate the class name of the interface with the defined unique identifier so that Qt's plugin system can recognize the plugins of this interface before loading them.

At this point, the interface for editing feature has been figured out. Now, let's write a plugin to implement this interface.

Eroding images with ErodePlugin

To write a Qt plugin, we should start a new Qt project from scratch. In the previous editing feature, we simply blurred an image by calling the `blur` function from OpenCV. Considering that our main purpose is to introduce the plugin mechanism of the Qt library, we will still use a simple function from the OpenCV library to make a simple edit to keep this part clear. Here, we will call the `erode` function from the OpenCV library to erode the objects in an image.

Let's name the plugin `ErodePlugin` and create the project from scratch:

```
$ ls
ImageEditor
$ mkdir ErodePlugin
$ ls
ErodePlugin ImageEditor
$ cd ErodePlugin
$ touch erode_plugin.h erode_plugin.cpp
$ qmake -project
$ ls
erode_plugin.h erode_plugin.cpp ErodePlugin.pro
```

First, in a Terminal, we change directory to the parent directory of our `ImageEditor` project, create a new directory named `ErodePlugin`, and enter that directory. Then, we create two empty source files, `erode_plugin.h` and `erode_pluigin.cpp`. We will write our source in these two files later. Now, we run `qmake -project` in the Terminal, which will return a Qt project file called `ErodePlugin.pro`. Since this project is a Qt plugin project, its project file has many different settings. Let's have a look at it now:

```
TEMPLATE = lib
TARGET = ErodePlugin
COPNFIG += plugin
INCLUDEPATH += . ../ImageEditor
```

At the very beginning of the project file, we use `lib` rather than `app` as the value of its `TEMPLATE` setting. The `TARGET` setting is no different—we just use the project name as its value. We also add a special line, `CONFIG += plugin`, to tell `qmake` that this project is a Qt plugin project. Finally, in the last line of the previous code block, we add the root directory of our `ImageEditor` project as one item of the include paths of this project so that the compiler can find the interface header file, `editor_plugin_interface.h`, that we had placed in the `ImageEditor` project in the last section while compiling the plugin.

In this plugin, we also need OpenCV to implement our editing feature, so we need to add the OpenCV library's information—more precisely, the library path and include a path of the library, in the settings of our Qt plugin project, as we did in the `ImageEditor` project:

```
unix: !mac {
    INCLUDEPATH += /home/kdr2/programs/opencv/include/opencv4
    LIBS += -L/home/kdr2/programs/opencv/lib -lopencv_core -l
opencv_imgproc
}

unix: mac {
    INCLUDEPATH += /path/to/opencv/include/opencv4
```

```
        LIBS += -L/path/to/opencv/lib -lopencv_world
    }

    win32 {
        INCLUDEPATH += c:/path/to/opencv/include/opencv4
        LIBS += -lc:/path/to/opencv/lib/opencv_world
    }
```

At the end of the project file, we add the header file and the C++ source file to the project:

```
HEADERS += erode_plugin.h
SOURCES += erode_plugin.cpp
```

Now that the project file for our plugin is complete, let's start writing our plugin. Just like we designed, writing a plugin for a new editing feature is just to provide an implementation of the `EditorPluginInterface` interface we abstracted in the previous section. Therefore, we declare a subclass of that interface in `erode_plugin.h`:

```
#include <QObject>
#include <QtPlugin>

#include "editor_plugin_interface.h"

class ErodePlugin: public QObject, public EditorPluginInterface
{
    Q_OBJECT
    Q_PLUGIN_METADATA(IID EDIT_PLUGIN_INTERFACE_IID);
    Q_INTERFACES(EditorPluginInterface);
public:
    QString name();
    void edit(const cv::Mat &input, cv::Mat &output);
};
```

As you can see, after including the necessary header files, we declare a class named `ErodePlugin` that inherits from both `QObject` and `EditorPluginInterface`. The latter is the interface we defined in `editor_plugin_interface.h` in the previous section. Here, we are making the plugin implementation a subclass of `QObject` because that's the requirement of the Qt meta-object system and plugin mechanism. In the body of the class, we add more information using some macros defined by the Qt library:

```
Q_OBJECT
Q_PLUGIN_METADATA(IID EDIT_PLUGIN_INTERFACE_IID);
Q_INTERFACES(EditorPluginInterface);
```

We introduced the Q_OBJECT macro in the last chapter; it's concerned with the Qt meta-object system. The Q_PLUGIN_METADATA(IID EDIT_PLUGIN_INTERFACE_IID) line declares the metadata for this plugin and this is where we declare the unique identifier of the plugin interface we defined in editor_plugin_interface.h as its IID metadata. Then, we use the Q_INTERFACES(EditorPluginInterface) line to tell Qt that it is the EditorPluginInterface interface that this class is trying to implement. With the previous information being clear, the Qt plugin system knows everything about this project:

- It's a Qt plugin project, so the target of the project will be a library file.
- The plugin is an instance of EditorPluginInterface, whose IID is EDIT_PLUGIN_INTERFACE_IID, so a Qt application could tell this and load this plugin.

Now, we can focus on how to implement the interface. First, we declare the two pure vital functions in the interface:

```
public:
    QString name();
    void edit(const cv::Mat &input, cv::Mat &output);
```

Then, we implement them in the erode_plugin.cpp file. For the name function, this is simple—we just return a QString, Erode, as the name of the plugin (also the name of the editing action):

```
QString ErodePlugin::name()
{
    return "Erode";
}
```

For the edit function, we implement it as follows:

```
void ErodePlugin::edit(const cv::Mat &input, cv::Mat &output)
{
    erode(input, output, cv::Mat());
}
```

This is simple too—we just call the erode function, which is provided by the OpenCV library. What this function does is called image erosion. It is one of the two base operators in the area of mathematical morphology. Erosion is the process of shrinking the image's foreground or 1-valued objects. It smooths object boundaries and removes peninsulas, fingers, and small objects. We will see the effect of this after we load this plugin in our application in the next section.

OK. Most of the work for our plugin project is done, so let's compile it. The way we compile it is the same way we compile a normal Qt application:

```
$ qmake -makefile
$ make
g++ -c -pipe -O2 ...
# output trucated
ln -s libErodePlugin.so.1.0.0 libErodePlugin.so
ln -s libErodePlugin.so.1.0.0 libErodePlugin.so.1
ln -s libErodePlugin.so.1.0.0 libErodePlugin.so.1.0
$ ls -l *.so*
lrwxrwxrwx 1 kdr2 kdr2 23 Dec 12 16:24 libErodePlugin.so ->
libErodePlugin.so.1.0.0
lrwxrwxrwx 1 kdr2 kdr2 23 Dec 12 16:24 libErodePlugin.so.1 ->
libErodePlugin.so.1.0.0
lrwxrwxrwx 1 kdr2 kdr2 23 Dec 12 16:24 libErodePlugin.so.1.0 ->
libErodePlugin.so.1.0.0
-rwxr-xr-x 1 kdr2 kdr2 78576 Dec 12 16:24 libErodePlugin.so.1.0.0
$
```

First, we run qmake -makefile to generate the Makefile, and then we compile the source by executing the make command. Once the compiling process is finished, we check the output files by using ls -l *.so* and find many shared object files. These are the plugin files we will load into our application.

While checking the output files, you may find that there are many files with extensions such as 1.0.0. These kinds of strings tell us about the version number of the library files. Most of these files are aliases (in the form of symbol links) of one real library file. When we load the plugin in the next section, we will make a copy of the real library file without its version number.

If you are using a platform that differs from GNU/Linux, your output files may differ too: on Windows, the files will be named something like ErodePlugin.dll, and on macOS, the files will be named something like libErodePlugin.dylib.

Loading the plugin into our application

In the previous sections, we abstracted an interface for the editing feature of our application, and then implemented a plugin that satisfied that interface by applying the erode function from the OpenCV library to our opening image. In this section, we will load that plugin into our application so that we can use it to erode our image. After that, we will look at a new action named Erode, which can be found under the edit menu and on the edit toolbar. If we trigger the action by clicking on it, we will see what Erode does on an image.

So, let's load the plugin! First, we modify the project file of our ImageEditor project and add the header file that contains the plugin interface to the list of the HEADERS setting:

```
HEADERS += mainwindow.h editor_plugin_interface.h
```

Then, we include this file in our mainwindow.cpp source file. We will also use another data structure named QMap to save the list of all the plugins we will have loaded, so we include the header file of QMap too:

```
#include <QMap>

#include "editor_plugin_interface.h"
```

Then, in the body of the declaration of the MainWindow class, we declare two member functions:

- void loadPlugins(): This is used to load all the plugins that appear in a certain directory.
- void pluginPerform(): This is a common slot that will be connected to all the actions that are created by the loaded plugins. In this slot, we should distinguish which action is triggered, which causes this slot to be invoked, and then we find the plugin related to that action and perform its editing operation.

After adding these two member functions, we add a member field of the QMap type to register all the loaded plugins:

```
QMap<QString, EditorPluginInterface*> editPlugins;
```

The keys of this map will be the names of the plugins, and the values will be the pointers to the instance of the loaded plugins.

All the work in the header file has been completed, so let's implement the `loadPlugins` function to load our plugins. First, we should include the necessary header files in `mainwindow.cpp`:

```
#include <QPluginLoader>
```

Then, we will provide the implementation of the `loadPlugins` member function, as follows:

```cpp
void MainWindow::loadPlugins()
{
    QDir pluginsDir(QApplication::instance()->applicationDirPath() +
"/plugins");
    QStringList nameFilters;
    nameFilters << "*.so" << "*.dylib" << "*.dll";
    QFileInfoList plugins = pluginsDir.entryInfoList(
        nameFilters, QDir::NoDotAndDotDot | QDir::Files, QDir::Name);
    foreach(QFileInfo plugin, plugins) {
        QPluginLoader pluginLoader(plugin.absoluteFilePath(), this);
        EditorPluginInterface *plugin_ptr =
dynamic_cast<EditorPluginInterface*>(pluginLoader.instance());
        if(plugin_ptr) {
            QAction *action = new QAction(plugin_ptr->name());
            editMenu->addAction(action);
            editToolBar->addAction(action);
            editPlugins[plugin_ptr->name()] = plugin_ptr;
            connect(action, SIGNAL(triggered(bool)), this,
SLOT(pluginPerform()));
            // pluginLoader.unload();
        } else {
            qDebug() << "bad plugin: " << plugin.absoluteFilePath();
        }
    }
}
```

We assume that there is a sub-directory named `plugins` in the directory where our executable resides. The directory that contains the executable can be fetched by simply calling `QApplication::instance()->applicationDirPath()`, and then we append the `/plugins` string to the end of it to generate the plugins directory. As we mentioned in the previous section, our plugins are library files whose names end with `.so`, `.dylib`, or `.dll`, according to the operating system we are using. Then, we list all the files with these extension names in the plugins directory.

After listing all the potential plugin files as a QFileInfoList, we iterate over that list to try and load each plugin with foreach. foreach is a macro defined by Qt and implements a for loop. Inside the loop, each file is an instance of QFileInfo. We get its absolute path by calling its abstractFilePath method and then construct an instance of QPluginLoader on that path.

Then, we have a number of crucial steps to go over. First, we call the instance method on the QPluginLoader instance. If the target plugin has been loaded, a pointer to a QObject will be returned, otherwise 0 will be returned. We then cast the return pointer to a pointer to our plugin interface type, that is, EditorPluginInterface*. If that pointer is non-zero, that will be an instance of a plugin! Then, we create a QAction, with its name being the name of the loaded plugin, that is, the result of plugin_ptr->name(). Do you remember what it is? This is the name function in ErodePlugin where we return the Erode string:

```
QString ErodePlugin::name()
{
    return "Erode";
}
```

Now that the Erode action has been created, we will add it to both the edit menu and the edit toolbar by calling their addAction methods with that action. Then, we register the loaded plugin in our editPlugins map:

```
editPlugins[plugin_ptr->name()] = plugin_ptr;
```

We will use this map to find the plugin by its name later, in the common slot of all the actions that have been created by the plugins.

Finally, we will connect a slot with the action:

```
connect(action, SIGNAL(triggered(bool)), this,
    SLOT(pluginPerform()));
```

You may be curious that this line of code is in the loop and that we connect the triggered signal of all the actions to the same slot; is this OK? Yes, we have a way to distinguish between which action is triggered in the slot, and then we can perform an operation according to that. Let's see how this is done. In the implementation of the pluginPerform slot, we check whether there is an image open:

```
if (currentImage == nullptr) {
    QMessageBox::information(this, "Information", "No image to
edit.");
    return;
}
```

Then, we find the action it just triggered so that it sends the signal and invokes the slot by calling the `sender()` function, which is provided by the Qt library. The `sender()` function returns a pointer to a `QObject` instance. Here, we know that we only connected instances of `QAction` to this slot, so we can cast the returned pointer to a pointer of `QAction` safely by using `qobject_cast`. Now, we know which action has been triggered. Then, we get the text of the action. In our application, the text of the action is the name of the plugin that created that action. By using this text, we can find a certain plugin from our register map. This is how we do this:

```
QAction *active_action = qobject_cast<QAction*>(sender());
EditorPluginInterface *plugin_ptr =
editPlugins[active_action->text()];
    if(!plugin_ptr) {
        QMessageBox::information(this, "Information", "No plugin is
found.");
        return;
    }
```

After we get the plugin pointer, we check whether it exists. If it doesn't, we simply show a message box to the users and return from the slot function.

At this point, we have the plugin that the user has triggered by its action, so now we can look at the editing operation. This piece of code is very similar to the one in the `blurImage` slot function. First, we get the opening image as a `QPixmap` and then convert it into `QImage` and `Mat` in turn. Once it becomes an instance of `Mat`, we can apply the `edit` function of the plugin to it, that is, `plugin_ptr->edit(mat, mat);`. Following the editing operation, we convert the edited `Mat` back into `QImage` and `QPixmap`, respectively, and then show the `QPixmap` on the graphics scene and update the information on the status bar:

```
QPixmap pixmap = currentImage->pixmap();
QImage image = pixmap.toImage();
image = image.convertToFormat(QImage::Format_RGB888);
Mat mat = Mat(
    image.height(),
    image.width(),
    CV_8UC3,
    image.bits(),
    image.bytesPerLine());

plugin_ptr->edit(mat, mat);

QImage image_edited(
    mat.data,
    mat.cols,
```

```
            mat.rows,
            mat.step,
            QImage::Format_RGB888);
    pixmap = QPixmap::fromImage(image_edited);
    imageScene->clear();
    imageView->resetMatrix();
    currentImage = imageScene->addPixmap(pixmap);
    imageScene->update();
    imageView->setSceneRect(pixmap.rect());
    QString status = QString("(editted image), %1x%2")
        .arg(pixmap.width()).arg(pixmap.height());
    mainStatusLabel->setText(status);
```

The two new functions have been added, so the last thing we need to do is call the `loadPlugins` function in the constructor of the `MainWindow` class by adding the following line to the end of `MainWindow::MainWindow(QWidget *parent)`:

```
    loadPlugins();
```

Now that we've loaded and set up the plugin from the `plugins` sub-directory in the directory where our executable resides, let's compile the application and test it.

First, in a Terminal, change the directory to the root of the `ImageEditor` project, and issue the `qmake -makefile` and `make` commands. Wait for these commands to finish. Then, start our app by running the `./ImageEditor` command; you will see the following output:

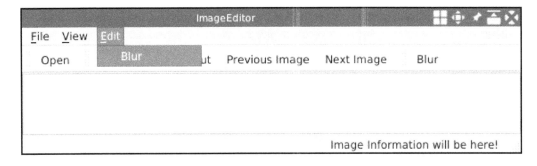

Don't forget to set the `LD_LIBRARY_PATH` or
`DYLD_LIBRARY_PATH` environment variable to the `lib` directory of
OpenCV on Linux or macOS before running the application.

Oh, nothing changed—we can't find our `Erode` action under the edit menu or on the edit
toolbar. This is because we didn't copy our `Erode` plugin file to our `plugins` directory.
Let's do this now:

```
$ ls
ImageEditor ImageEditor.pro plugins ...
$ ls -l ../ErodePlugin/*.so*
lrwxrwxrwx 1 kdr2 kdr2 23 Dec 12 16:24
../ErodePlugin/libErodePlugin.so -> libErodePlugin.so.1.0.0
lrwxrwxrwx 1 kdr2 kdr2 23 Dec 12 16:24
../ErodePlugin/libErodePlugin.so.1 -> libErodePlugin.so.1.0.0
lrwxrwxrwx 1 kdr2 kdr2 23 Dec 12 16:24
../ErodePlugin/libErodePlugin.so.1.0 -> libErodePlugin.so.1.0.0
-rwxr-xr-x 1 kdr2 kdr2 78576 Dec 12 16:24
../ErodePlugin/libErodePlugin.so.1.0.0
$ cp ../ErodePlugin/libErodePlugin.so.1.0.0 plugins/libErodePlugin.so
$ ls plugins/
libErodePlugin.so
$
```

If you are using macOS, after you compile the project, you will find a
directory named `ImageEditor.app` instead of an
`ImageEditor` executable. This is because, on macOS, each application is a
directory with `.app` as its extension name. The real executable file is at
`ImageEditor.app/Contents/MacOS/ImageEdtior`, so, on macOS, our
plugins directory is `ImageEditor.app/Contents/MacOS/plugins`. You
should create that directory and copy the plugin file there.

Let's run our application again:

Now, we can see the **Erode** action under both the **Edit** menu and on the **Edit** toolbar. Let's open an image to see what **Erode** does.

This is an image that's been opened by our application before we've done anything to it:

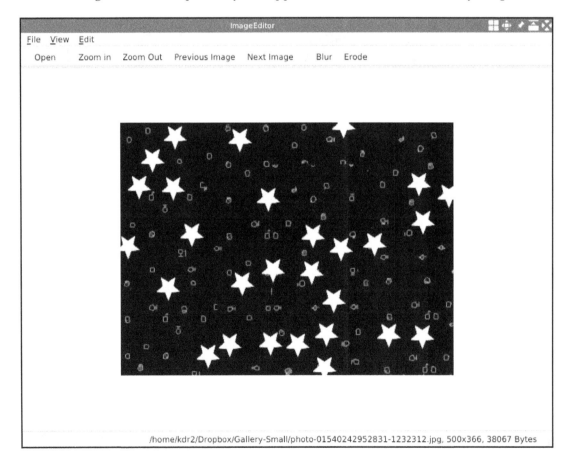

After we click on the **Erode** action, we get the following output:

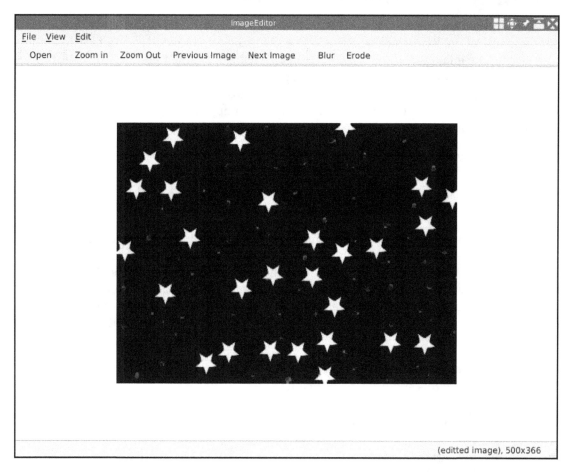

As you can see, the dark part of the image is enlarged and the white objects are shrunk after the **Erode** action is clicked. This is because the dark part of the image is treated as the background by OpenCV and it erodes the objects (the light parts) in the image.

We've successfully added a new editing feature using the plugin mechanism provided by the Qt library. The salient point of this section is to introduce that plugin mechanism, but not the feature of the image editing, so we only used an `erode` function to implement the editing feature in order to simplify image editing. Now that the plugin mechanism has been introduced, we can move on to the OpenCV library and the image editing feature that uses that library.

Editing images like a pro

In the preceding section, we looked at how we can add image editing features as plugins for our application. By doing this, we don't need to take care of the user interface, opening and closing the images, and the hotkeys. Instead, we have to add a new editing feature, which we do by writing a subclass of the `EditorPluginInterface` interface and implementing its pure virtual functions, and then compile it into a plugin file (a shared library file) and copy it into the plugin directory of our application. In this section, we will talk about image editing using OpenCV.

First, let's start with sharpening images.

Sharpening images

Image sharpening is a common feature that is implemented by many famous image editing software, such as GIMP and Photoshop. The principle of sharpening an image is that we subtract a smoothed version of an image from the original version to get the difference between these two versions, and then add that difference to the original image. We can get the smoothed version by applying the Gaussian smoothing filter to a copy of the image. We will see how to do that using OpenCV later, but the first step here is to create a new Qt plugin project.

Since we created a Qt plugin project named `ErodePlugin` in the previous section, creating another project like this shouldn't be difficult.

First, we create the directory and the necessary files in a Terminal:

```
$ ls
ErodePlugin ImageEditor
$ mkdir SharpenPlugin
$ ls
ErodePlugin ImageEditor SharpenPlugin
$ cd SharpenPlugin
$ touch sharpen_plugin.h sharpen_plugin.cpp
$ qmake -project
$ ls
sharpen_plugin.h sharpen_plugin.cpp SharpenPlugin.pro
```

Then, we edit the `SharpenPlugin.pro` project file and set up its configuration:

```
TEMPLATE = lib
TARGET = SharpenPlugin
COPNFIG += plugin
INCLUDEPATH += . ../ImageEditor
unix: !mac {
    INCLUDEPATH += /home/kdr2/programs/opencv/include/opencv4
    LIBS += -L/home/kdr2/programs/opencv/lib -lopencv_core -l
opencv_imgproc
}

unix: mac {
    INCLUDEPATH += /path/to/opencv/include/opencv4
    LIBS += -L/path/to/opencv/lib -lopencv_world
}

win32 {
    INCLUDEPATH += c:/path/to/opencv/include/opencv4
    LIBS += -lc:/path/to/opencv/lib/opencv_world
}

HEADERS += sharpen_plugin.h
SOURCES += sharpen_plugin.cpp
```

Most of the content of this project file is the same as the project file of
our `ErodePlugin` plugin project, except for the settings of TARGET, HEADERS, and
SOURCES. The changes in these three settings are easy and self-explanatory in terms of their
keys and values.

Now, let's take a look at the source files. The first is the header file, `sharpen_plugin.h`:

```
#include <QObject>
#include <QtPlugin>

#include "editor_plugin_interface.h"

class SharpenPlugin: public QObject, public EditorPluginInterface
{
    Q_OBJECT
    Q_PLUGIN_METADATA(IID EDIT_PLUGIN_INTERFACE_IID);
    Q_INTERFACES(EditorPluginInterface);
public:
    QString name();
    void edit(const cv::Mat &input, cv::Mat &output);
};
```

This is the same as the `erode_plugin.h` header file we wrote in the ErodePlugin project, except we are using a different class name, `SharpenPlugin`, here. We make the class a descendant of both `QObject` and `EditorPluginInterface`. In the body of the class, we use several Qt macros to provide the necessary information to the metaobject and plugin system of the Qt library and then declare the two methods that we must implement to satisfy the `EditorPluginInterface` interface.

We are done with the project file and the header file. As you can see, most of their content is the same as what we had in the ErodePlugin project, except for some name changes, including the project name, target name, and filenames.

Now, it's time to look at the implementation of the methods in `sharpen_plugin.cpp`. Not surprisingly, the only changes to it are the changes to the names and the changes to the body of the methods. First let's look at the `name` method:

```
QString SharpenPlugin::name()
{
    return "Sharpen";
}
```

Here, we change the class name to `SharpenPlugin` in the first line, and then return the `Sharpen` string as its name and label. That is pretty simple. Now, let's move on to the `edit` method:

```
void SharpenPlugin::edit(const cv::Mat &input, cv::Mat &output)
{
    int intensity = 2;
    cv::Mat smoothed;
    GaussianBlur(input, smoothed, cv::Size(9, 9), 0);
    output = input + (input - smoothed) * intensity;
}
```

While only changing the class name in the first line, we change a lot in the body of this method to do the sharpening work. First, we define two variables. The `intensity` variable is an integer that will indicate how intensively we will sharpen the image, while `smoothed` is an instance of `cv::Mat` that will be used to hold the smoothed version of the image. Then, we call the `GaussianBlur` function to smooth the image that is passed to our method as a `cv::Mat` instance and store the smoothed version in our `smoothed` variable.

In image processing, Gaussian blur is an algorithm that is widely adopted, especially when you are going to reduce the noise or detail of images. It is named after Carl Friedrich Gauss, a great mathematician and scientist, because it uses the Gaussian function to blur images. It is also occasionally referred to as Gaussian smoothing.

You can find out more about this algorithm at `http://homepages.inf.ed.ac.uk/rbf/ HIPR2/gsmooth.htm`. In OpenCV, we use the `GaussianBlur` function to achieve this effect. This function accepts many arguments, as most OpenCV functions do. The first and second ones are the input and output images. The third argument is a `cv::Size` object that represents the size of the kernel. The fourth one is a variable of the double type, which represents the Gaussian kernel standard deviation in the X direction. It also has two extra arguments that have default values. We use its default values in our code to keep the method easy to understand, but you can refer to the documentation of the `GaussianBlur` function at `https://docs.opencv.org/4.0.0/d4/d86/group__imgproc__ filter.html` to find out more.

After we get the smoothed version of the original image, we can find the nice distinction between the original version and the smoothed version by subtracting the smoothed version from the original version, which is `input - smoothed`. The subtraction operation in this expression is called the element-wise matrix operation in OpenCV. Element-wise matrix operations are mathematical functions and algorithms in computer vision that work on individual elements of a matrix—in other words, pixels of an image. It's important to note that element-wise operations can be parallelized, which fundamentally means that the order in which the elements of a matrix are processed is not important. By doing this subtraction, we get the distinction—it's also a `cv::Mat` instance, so you can show it in your application if you want to view it. Since this distinction is very slight, you will see a black image if you show it, though it isn't completely black—it has a few non-block pixels in it. To sharpen our original image, we can just superimpose this distinction matrix onto the original image one or more times by using the additional element-wise operation. In our code, the count of the times is the `intensity` variable we have defined. First, we multiply the `intensity` scalar by the distinction matrix (this is an element-wise operation as well, between a scalar and a matrix), and then add the result to the original image matrix:

```
input + (input - smoothed) * intensity
```

Finally, we assign the resulting matrix to the output variable, a reference to `cv::Mat`, to return the sharpened image in the out parameter way.

All the code is ready, so let's compile our plugin in the Terminal:

```
$ qmake -makefile
$ make
g++ -c -pipe -O2 ...
# output truncated
$ ls -l *so*
lrwxrwxrwx 1 kdr2 kdr2 25 Dec 20 11:24 libSharpenPlugin.so ->
libSharpenPlugin.so.1.0.0
lrwxrwxrwx 1 kdr2 kdr2 25 Dec 20 11:24 libSharpenPlugin.so.1 ->
```

```
libSharpenPlugin.so.1.0.0
    lrwxrwxrwx 1 kdr2 kdr2 25 Dec 20 11:24 libSharpenPlugin.so.1.0 ->
libSharpenPlugin.so.1.0.0
    -rwxr-xr-x 1 kdr2 kdr2 78880 Dec 20 11:24 libSharpenPlugin.so.1.0.0
    $ cp libSharpenPlugin.so.1.0.0
../ImageEditor/plugins/libSharpenPlugin.so
    $
```

After we've compiled the plugin and copied it to the plugin directory of the `ImageEditor` application, we can run the application to test our new plugin:

```
$ cd ../ImageEditor/
$ export LD_LIBRARY_PATH=/home/kdr2/programs/opencv/lib/
$ ./ImageEditor
```

If all goes well, you will see the **Sharpen** action under both the **Edit** menu and the **Edit** toolbar. Let's see what an image looks like after opening it:

Now, let's see what the image looks like after we sharpen it by clicking the **Sharpen** action that's provided by our new plugin:

We can see the obvious difference between them. Please feel free to play around with the `intensity` variable and the parameters of the `GaussianBlur` function to achieve your favorite outcome.

Cartoon effect

In the preceding section, we added a new editing feature so that we can sharpen images in our application. In this section, we will add a new editing feature so that we can create an interesting cartoon effect for an image. In order to achieve this cartoon effect, we need to do two things: first, we need to make the image have a cartoon look, so we need to find a way to reduce its color palette; then, we will detect the edges in the image and produce bold silhouettes along with them. After that, we will merge the resulting images of these steps and then get a new image that has the cartoon effect implemented.

Fortunately, all of this can be done by using the OpenCV library. So, let's start our new plugin project, which we will call `CartoonPlugin`. The steps for creating the plugin project and the directory structure of the project are very similar to what we did previously, so we won't show you how to create the project step by step here in order to keep this chapter concise.

To create the project, we will create a new directory named `CartoonPlugin`, and then create the project file and the source files in the directory. The directory should appear as follows:

```
$ ls
cartoon_plugin.cpp cartoon_plugin.h CartoonPlugin.pro
$
```

You can copy the project file from one of our previous plugin projects and change the values of the `TARGET`, `HEADERS`, and `SOURCES` settings to the proper values for this project. Since the content of the source files is also very similar to the ones in the previous projects, you can use the sources files in any of our finished plugin projects as the templates to simplify the development process—just copy the files, change their filenames, the plugin class name in them, and the implementation of the `name` and `eidt` methods.

We use `CartoonPlugin` as the plugin class name in this project, and `return "Cartoon";` in the `CartoonPlugin::name` method. Now, all we need to do is implement the `CartoonPlugin::edit` method. Let's move on to this crucial part now.

The first task is to reduce the color palette. To achieve this, we can resort to the bilateral filter that's provided by the OpenCV library. Although the bilateral filter works very well and gives a common RGB image a cartoon look and feel by smoothing the flat regions and keeping the sharp edges, it is much slower than other smoothing algorithms (for example, the Gaussian blur algorithm we used in the previous section) by several orders of magnitude. However, in our application, speed is important—to keep the code easy to understand, we won't create a separate worker thread to do the editing work. If the editing process is too slow, it will freeze the UI of our application—that is, when editing, our application won't be interactive and the UI won't be updated.

Luckily, we have two approaches to speed up this period, thereby shortening the freezing time:

1. Down-scale the original image and then apply the filter to that down-scaled version.
2. Instead of applying a large bilateral filter to the image once, we can apply a small bilateral filter multiple times.

Let's look at how we can do this:

```cpp
int num_down = 2;
int num_bilateral = 7;

cv::Mat copy1, copy2;

copy1 = input.clone();
for(int i = 0; i < num_down; i++) {
    cv::pyrDown(copy1, copy2);
    copy1 = copy2.clone();
}

for(int i = 0; i < num_bilateral; i++) {
    cv::bilateralFilter(copy1, copy2, 9, 9, 7);
    copy1 = copy2.clone();
}

for(int i = 0; i < num_down; i++) {
    cv::pyrUp(copy1, copy2);
    copy1 = copy2.clone();
}
```

First, we define two `Mat` class objects, `copy1` and `copy2`, and assign a clone of the `input` to `copy1`.

Then, we use `cv::pyrDown` to scale down `copy1` repeatedly (two times through `int num_down = 2;`). In this loop, we operate on the two defined matrices, `copy1` and `copy2`. Because the `cv::pyrDown` function doesn't support in-place operations, we must use a matrix that's different from the input matrix for the output. To achieve the repeated operation, we should assign a clone of the resulting matrix's `copy2` to `copy1` after each operation.

After the scaling down operation, we get a down-sampled version of the original image in `copy1`. Now, like the process of scaling down, we apply a small bilateral filter to `copy1` repeatedly (seven times through `int num_bilateral = 7;`). This function doesn't support in-place either, so we use `copy1` as its input image, and `copy2` as its output image. The last three arguments we pass to the `cv::bilateralFilter` function specifies the diameter of the pixel neighborhood, whose value is 9, the filter sigma in the color space, whose value is also 9, and the filter sigma in the coordinate space, whose value is 7, respectively. You can refer to http://homepages.inf.ed.ac.uk/rbf/CVonline/LOCAL_COPIES/MANDUCHI1/Bilateral_Filtering.html to find out how these values are used in the filter.

After reducing the color palette, we should scale up the down-sampled image to its original size. This is done by calling `cv::pyrUp` on `copy1` the same amount of times we had called `cv::pyrDown` on it.

Because the size of the resulting image is computed as `Size((input.cols + 1) / 2, (input.rows + 1) / 2)` while scaling down, and is computed as `Size(input.cols * 2, (input.rows * 2)` while scaling up, the size of the `copy1` matrix may not be the same as the original image. It may be equal or a few pixels larger than, the original one. Here, we should resize `copy1` to the size of the original image if it isn't the same as the original image in terms of dimensions:

```
if (input.cols != copy1.cols || input.rows != copy1.rows) {
    cv::Rect rect(0, 0, input.cols, input.rows);
    copy1(rect).copyTo(copy2);
    copy1 = copy2;
}
```

At this point, we have got a copy of the original image that has its color palette reduced and dimensions unchanged. Now, let's move on and detect the edges and produce some bold silhouettes. There are many facilities offered by OpenCV for detecting edges. Here, we choose the `cv::adaptiveThreshold` function and call it with `cv::THRESH_BINARY` as its threshold type to perform edge detection. In the adaptive thresholding algorithm, instead of using a global value as the threshold, it uses a dynamic threshold, which is determined by the pixels in a small region around the current pixel. In this way, we can detect the most prominent features in each small region from which we calculate the threshold. These features are exactly the places where we should draw bold and black outlines around the objects in the image. At the same time, the adaptive algorithm also has its weakness—it is prone to be influenced by noise. Therefore, it is better to apply a median filter to the image before detecting the edge since the median filter will set the value of each pixel to the median value of all the pixels around it, which can reduce noise. Let's look at how we can do this:

```
cv::Mat image_gray, image_edge;

cv::cvtColor(input, image_gray, cv::COLOR_RGB2GRAY);
cv::medianBlur(image_gray, image_gray, 5);

cv::adaptiveThreshold(image_gray, image_gray, 255,
    cv::ADAPTIVE_THRESH_MEAN_C, cv::THRESH_BINARY, 9, 2);

cv::cvtColor(image_gray, image_edge, cv::COLOR_GRAY2RGB);
```

First, we convert the input image into a grayscale image by calling the cvtColor function, and then have cv::COLOR_RGB2GRAY as the color space conversion code as its third argument. This function doesn't work in-place either, so we use another matrix, image_gray, which is different from its input matrix, as the output matrix. After this, we get a grayscale version of the original image in the image_gray matrix. Then, we call cv::medianBlur to apply the median filter to the grayscale image. As you can see, in this function call, we use the image_gray matrix as both its input and output matrices. This is because this function supports in-place operations; it can do its work on the data of the input matrix in-place; that is, it reads data from the input, does the computing, and writes the results into the input matrix without interfering with anything else when it comes to the image.

After applying the median filter, we call cv::adaptiveThreshold on the grayscale image to detect the edges in the image. We do this in-place on the grayscale image, so, after this operation, the grayscale image becomes a binary image that only contains the edges. Then, we convert the binary edges into an RGB image and store it in the image_edge matrix by calling cvtColor.

Now that the color palette has reduced and the edge images are ready, let's merge them by using a bit-wise and operation and assign it to the output matrix in order to return them:

```
output = copy1 & image_edge;
```

At this point, all the development work is complete. Now, it's time to compile and test our plugin:

```
$ make
g++ -c -pipe -O2 -Wall ...
# output truncated
$ cp libCartoonPlugin.so.1.0.0
../ImageEditor/plugins/libCartoonPlugin.so
$ ls ../ImageEditor/plugins/
libCartoonPlugin.so libErodePlugin.so libSharpenPlugin.so
$ export LD_LIBRARY_PATH=/home/kdr2/programs/opencv/lib/
$ ../ImageEditor/ImageEditor
```

After starting our application and opening an image with it, we get the following output:

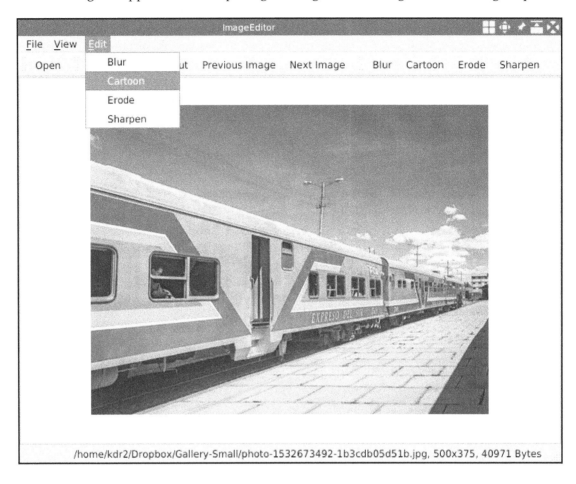

Let's click on the **Cartoon** action and see what happens:

This isn't bad—you can play around with the parameters of all the filter functions to tune the cartoon effect yourself if you want to.

In this section, we have used many filter functions provided by OpenCV. While calling these functions, I pointed out that the medianBlur function supports in-place operation, and the bilateralFilter function doesn't. What does this mean and how do we know whether a function supports in-place operations?

As we mentioned previously, if a function supports in-place operation, this means that this function can read from the input image, do the computing, and then write the result to a matrix, which can either be the one we used as the input matrix or one that differs from the input one. When we use one matrix as both its input and output, the function still works well and puts the results into the input matrix without corrupting the data. If a function doesn't support in-place operation, then you must use a matrix that's different from the input matrix as its output, otherwise, the data may become corrupted. Actually, in the implementation of OpenCV, it makes an assertion to ensure that the input and output are not the same matrices or different matrices sharing the same data buffer in such functions that don't support in-place operation. If a function supports in-place operation, we can use this to improve the performance of our programs, because this manner can save memory. Since OpenCV is well-documented, we can refer to the documentation to find out whether a function supports in-place operation. Let's look at the documentation of the medianBlur function we just used:

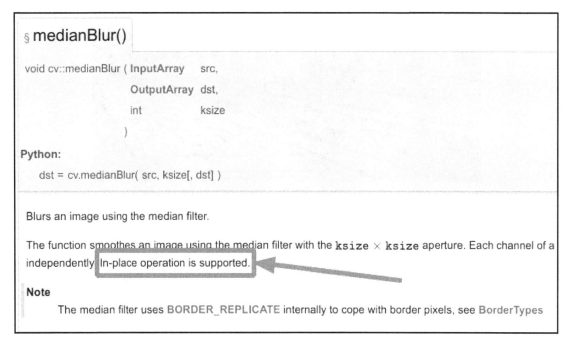

In the preceding screenshot, I have highlighted the line that says that this function supports in-place operation. Some (but not all) functions that don't support in-place operation also have a statement explicitly stating that; for example, the bilateralFilter() function, which we also used in this section:

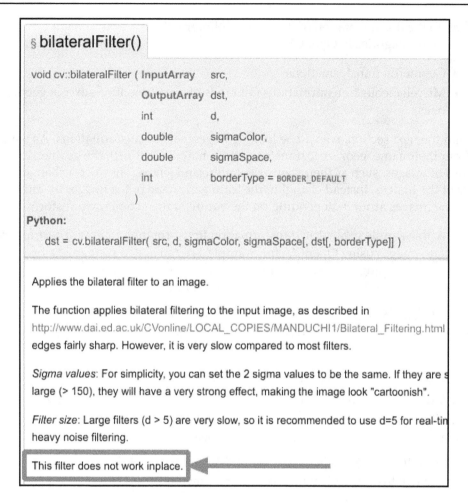

§ bilateralFilter()

```
void cv::bilateralFilter ( InputArray    src,
                           OutputArray   dst,
                           int           d,
                           double        sigmaColor,
                           double        sigmaSpace,
                           int           borderType = BORDER_DEFAULT
                         )
```

Python:
```
dst = cv.bilateralFilter( src, d, sigmaColor, sigmaSpace[, dst[, borderType]] )
```

Applies the bilateral filter to an image.

The function applies bilateral filtering to the input image, as described in http://www.dai.ed.ac.uk/CVonline/LOCAL_COPIES/MANDUCHI1/Bilateral_Filtering.html edges fairly sharp. However, it is very slow compared to most filters.

Sigma values: For simplicity, you can set the 2 sigma values to be the same. If they are s large (> 150), they will have a very strong effect, making the image look "cartoonish".

Filter size: Large filters (d > 5) are very slow, so it is recommended to use d=5 for real-tin heavy noise filtering.

This filter does not work inplace.

It's worth noting that if the documentation says that a function supports in-place operation, then it does. If the documentation says nothing about whether a function supports in-place operation, it's best to assume that it doesn't support in-place operation.

Rotating images

We have added many editing features as plugins in the previous sections, all of which are utilizing image filters provided by OpenCV. From this section on, we will add some features that utilize the transformation capabilities of the OpenCV library.

According to the documentation of the OpenCV library, there are two image transformation categories in OpenCV:

- Geometric transformations
- Miscellaneous transformations (all kinds of transformations except geometric ones)

In this and the next section, we will be looking at geometric transformations. As we can guess from their name, geometric transformations mainly deal with the geometric properties of images, such as their size, orientation, and shape. They don't change the contents of the images, instead changing the form and shape of the images by moving the pixels of the images around, depending on the nature of the geometric transformation.

Let's start with a simple geometric transformation first—rotating images. There are many ways to rotate images using OpenCV; for example, we can apply a composite operation of transposing and flipping on a matrix, or we can do an affine transformation with a proper transformation matrix. We will use the latter method in this section.

It's time to start a new hands-on project in order to develop the rotation plugin. We can do this by using a previous plugin project as a template. Here is a list of the important points of this process:

1. Use `RotatePlugin` as the project name.
2. Create the project file and source files (a `.h` file and a `.cpp` file).
3. Change the relevant settings in the project file.
4. Use `RotatePlugin` as the plugin class name.
5. Return `Rotate` as the plugin name in the `name` method.
6. Change the implementation of the `edit` method.

Every step is very straightforward, except for the last one. So, let's skip the first five steps and go straight to the last step—this is how we implement the `edit` method in this plugin:

```
void RotatePlugin::edit(const cv::Mat &input, cv::Mat &output)
{
    double angle = 45.0;
    double scale = 1.0;
    cv::Point2f center = cv::Point(input.cols/2, input.rows/2);
    cv::Mat rotateMatrix = cv::getRotationMatrix2D(center, angle, scale);

    cv::Mat result;
    cv::warpAffine(input, result,
        rotateMatrix, input.size(),
```

```
        cv::INTER_LINEAR, cv::BORDER_CONSTANT);
    output = result;
}
```

As we mentioned previously, we use an affine transformation to do the rotation, which is achieved by calling the `cv::warpAffine` function that's provided by the OpenCV library. This function does not support in-place operation, so we will define a new temporary matrix, `result`, to store the output.

 When we call the `edit` method of each plugin in the ImageEditor application, we use one matrix as the input and the output arguments, that is, `plugin_ptr->edit(mat, mat);`, so, in the implementation of the plugin's edit method, the argument input and output are actually the same matrices. This means we can't pass them to a function that doesn't support in-place operation.

The `warpAffine` function takes a matrix called the transformation matrix as its third argument. This transformation matrix contains the data that describes how the affine transformation should be done. It's a little complex to write this transformation matrix by hand, so OpenCV provides functions to generate it. To generate a transformation matrix for rotation, we can use the `cv::getRotationMatrix2D` function by giving it a point as the axis point, an angle, and a scale rate.

In our code, we use the center point of the input image as the axis point of the rotation and use a positive number, 45, to represent the fact that the rotation will be turning 45 degrees counterclockwise. Since we only want to rotate the image, we use 1.0 as the scale rate. With these arguments ready, we get `rotateMatrix` by calling the `cv::getRotationMatrix2D` function and then pass it to `cv::warpAffine` in the third position.

The fourth argument of `cv::warpAffine` is the size of the output image. We use the size of the input image here to ensure that the size of the image doesn't change during the editing process. The fifth argument is the interpolation method, so we simply use `cv::INTER_LINEAR` here. The sixth argument is the pixel extrapolation method for the borders of the output image. We use `cv::BORDER_CONSTANT` here so that, after the rotation, if some areas are not covered by the original image, they will be filled with a constant color. We can specify this color as the seventh argument, otherwise, it will use black by default.

Since the code is now clear, let's compile and test the plugin:

```
$ make
g++ -c -pipe -O2 -Wall ...
# output truncated
$ cp libRotatePlugin.so.1.0.0
../ImageEditor/plugins/libRotatePlugin.so
$ ls ../ImageEditor/plugins/
libCartoonPlugin.so libErodePlugin.so libRotatePlugin.so
libSharpenPlugin.so
$ export LD_LIBRARY_PATH=/home/kdr2/programs/opencv/lib/
$ ../ImageEditor/ImageEditor
```

After opening an image, we should get the following output:

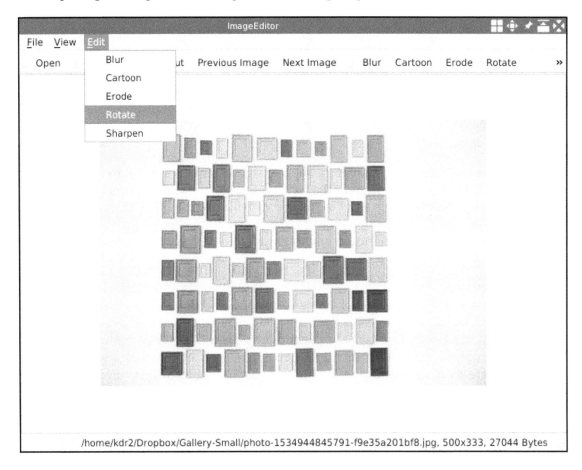

Let's click on the **Rotate** action and see what happens:

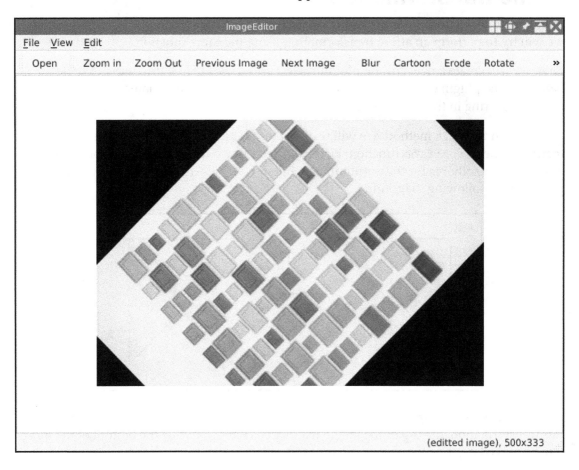

As we can see, the image turns 45 degrees counterclockwise, as we expected. Feel free to change the value of the center point, the angle, and the scale to see what happens.

Affine transformation

In the previous section, we successfully rotated images using `warpAffine`. In this section, we will try to perform an affine transformation using the same function.

First, we will create a new editing plugin project and use `AffinePlugin` as the project name and the plugin class name, and then use `Affine` as the action name (that is, we will return this string in the `name` method).

This time, in the `edit` method, we will use another method to obtain the transformation matrix for the `warpAffine` function. First, we prepare two triangles—one is for the input image, and the other is for the output image. In our code, we use the triangles that are shown in the following diagram:

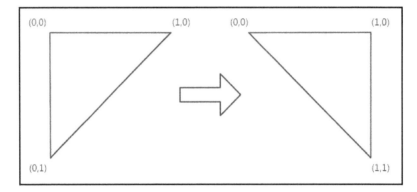

The left one is for the input, while the right one is for the output. We can easily see that, in this transformation, the top of the image will not be changed, while the bottom of the image will be moved right by the same distance as the image's width.

In the code, we will use an array of three `Point2f` class to represent each triangle and then pass them to the `getAffineTransform` function to obtain the transformation matrix. Once we get the transformation matrix, we can call the `warpAffine` function, as we did in our `RotatePlugin` project. This is how we do this in code:

```
void AffinePlugin::edit(const cv::Mat &input, cv::Mat &output)
{

    cv::Point2f triangleA[3];
    cv::Point2f triangleB[3];

    triangleA[0] = cv::Point2f(0 , 0);
    triangleA[1] = cv::Point2f(1 , 0);
```

```
        triangleA[2] = cv::Point2f(0 , 1);

        triangleB[0] = cv::Point2f(0, 0);
        triangleB[1] = cv::Point2f(1, 0);
        triangleB[2] = cv::Point2f(1, 1);

        cv::Mat affineMatrix = cv::getAffineTransform(triangleA,
triangleB);
        cv::Mat result;
        cv::warpAffine(
            input, result,
            affineMatrix, input.size(), // output image size, same as
input
            cv::INTER_CUBIC, // Interpolation method
            cv::BORDER_CONSTANT // Extrapolation method
            //BORDER_WRAP // Extrapolation method
        );

        output = result;
    }
```

Now that we've finished the development, let's compile the project, copy the plugin, and then run the ImageEditor application:

```
$ make
g++ -c -pipe -O2 -Wall ...
# output truncated
$ cp libAffinePlugin.so.1.0.0
../ImageEditor/plugins/libAffinePlugin.so
$ ls ../ImageEditor/plugins/
libAffinePlugin.so libCartoonPlugin.so libErodePlugin.so
libRotatePlugin.so libSharpenPlugin.so
$ export LD_LIBRARY_PATH=/home/kdr2/programs/opencv/lib/
$ ../ImageEditor/ImageEditor
```

This is what our application looks like after opening an image:

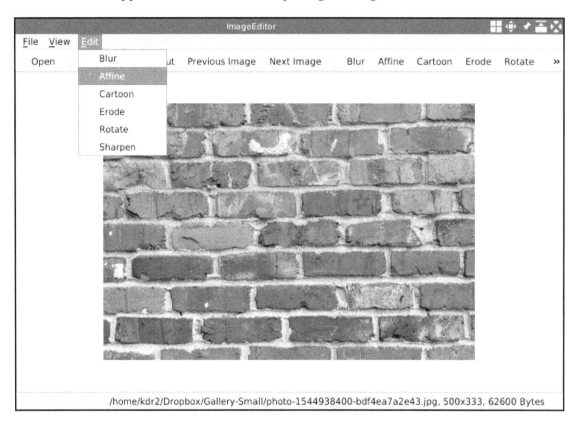

This is the effect we get after triggering the **Affine** action:

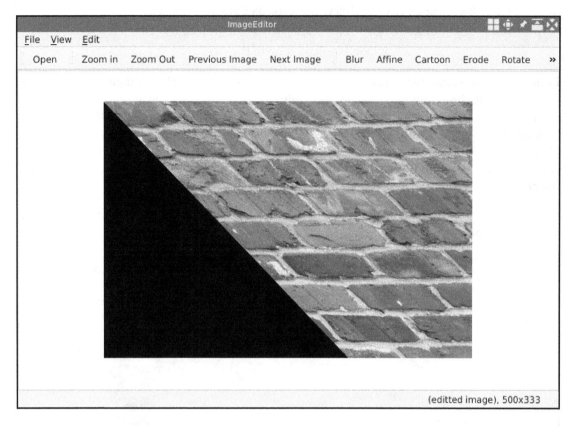

Hooray! The image transforms in the same way that was shown in the preceding diagram.

You may notice that, in this code, we use BORDER_CONSTANT as the border type as well, so after the image moves obliquely, its bottom left corner is filled by a constant color, which is black by default. Besides filling the borders by a constant color, there are many other ways to interpolate the borders. The following list shows all the methods from the OpenCV document:

- BORDER_CONSTANT: Interpolates as iiiiii|abcdefgh|iiiiiii with a specified i
- BORDER_REPLICATE: Interpolates as aaaaaa|abcdefgh|hhhhhhh
- BORDER_REFLECT: Interpolates as fedcba|abcdefgh|hgfedcb
- BORDER_WRAP: Interpolates as cdefgh|abcdefgh|abcdefg
- BORDER_REFLECT_101: Interpolates as gfedcb|abcdefgh|gfedcba

- BORDER_TRANSPARENT: Interpolates as uvwxyz|abcdefgh|ijklmno
- BORDER_REFLECT101: This is the same as BORDER_REFLECT_101
- BORDER_DEFAULT: This is the same as BORDER_REFLECT_101
- BORDER_ISOLATED: Don't look outside of the ROI

In the explanation clauses of this list, |abcdefgh| means the original image, and the letters surrounding it show how the interpolation will be done. For example, if we use the BORDER_WRAP value, the interpolation will be cdefgh|abcdefgh|abcdefg; that is, it will be using the right-hand side of the image to fill the left border, and using the left-hand side of the image to fill the right border. As a special case, BORDER_TRANSPARENT leaves the corresponding pixels in the destination matrix untouched and doesn't use a color from the input image.

If we use BORDER_WRAP in our AffinePlugin plugin, the image will look like this after the transformation:

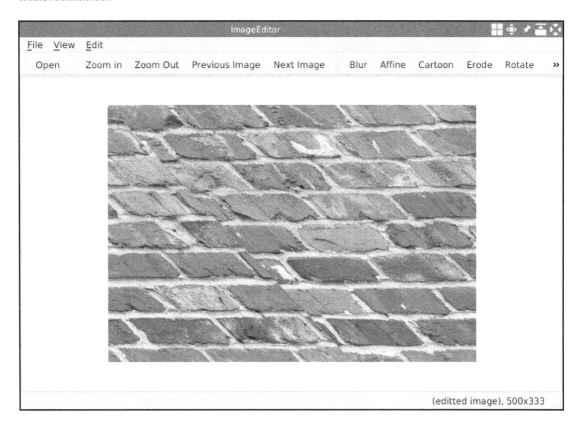

The effects of all the border interpolation types are not demonstrated here, so please try them for yourself if you are interested.

In this and the preceding section, we learned about how to use the affine transformation to transform images. Besides this way of transforming images, there are many ways in which we can do the geometric transformation. All of these ways are provided by OpenCV and include resizing, perspective transformation, remapping, and many miscellaneous transformations, such as color space converting. These geometric transformations are scrutable, and you can find their documentation at `https://docs.opencv.org/4.0.0/da/d54/group__imgproc__transform.html`. In terms of miscellaneous transformations, we used one of them, `cv::adaptiveThreshold`, in our `CartoonPlugin` plugin. The full documentation for this category of transformation can be found at `https://docs.opencv.org/4.0.0/d7/d1b/group__imgproc__misc.html`. You can fiddle with all of these transformations in our plugin project or in your own plugins to learn more about them.

Summary

In this chapter, we remade the desktop application for image viewing that we built in `Chapter 1`, *Building an Image Viewer*, to make an image editor application. Then, we added a simple editing feature to blur images. At the same time, we learned about how to install and set up OpenCV for Qt applications, the data structures related to image processing both in Qt and OpenCV, and how to process images using OpenCV.

Afterward, we learned about the plugin mechanism of the Qt library and abstracted out a way to add editing features to our applications in a more flexible and convenient way as plugins. As an example of this, we wrote our first plugin to erode images.

Then, we moved our attention to the OpenCV library to discuss how to edit images like a pro—we made numerous plugins to edit images, to sharpen images, to make cartoon effects, to rotate, to execute affine transformations, and so on.

In the next chapter, we will learn about how to deal with videos with OpenCV and Qt, and we will build a simple security application at home that's facilitated by motion analysis technology.

Questions

Try out these questions to test your knowledge of this chapter:

1. How do we know if an OpenCV function supports in-place operation or not?
2. How can we add a hotkey for each action we added as a plugin?
3. How can we add a new action to discard all the changes to the current image in our application?
4. How can we resize images using OpenCV?

Home Security Applications
3

In `Chapter 2`, *Editing Images Like a Pro*, we learned about the plugin mechanism of the Qt library and many image filters and transformations from the OpenCV library by building our own image editor application. In this chapter, we will move on from working with images to working with videos. We will build a new application with which we can do many things with the webcam of a PC, such as play video that's been captured from it in real time, record portions of video from its video feed, calculate its **frames per second** (**FPS**), detect motion by doing motion analysis on its video feed in real time, and more.

The following topics will be covered in this chapter:

- Designing and creating the **user interface** (**UI**)
- Handling cameras and videos
- Recording videos
- Calculating the FPS in real time
- Motion analysis and movement detection
- Sending notifications to a mobile in a desktop application

Technical requirements

As we saw in the previous chapters, you are required to have Qt version 5 (at least) installed and have basic knowledge of C++ and Qt programming. Also, the latest version of OpenCV (4.0) should be correctly installed. Besides the core and `imgproc` modules, the video and `videoio` modules of OpenCV will also be used in this chapter. Following the previous chapters, these requirements must be already met.

In this chapter, we will show you how to handle cameras, so you need to have a webcam, either a built-in one or an external one, which can be accessed from your computer.

A basic knowledge of multi-threading is also a requirement of this chapter.

All the code for this chapter can be found in this book's GitHub repository at `https://github.com/PacktPublishing/Qt-5-and-OpenCV-4-Computer-Vision-Projects/tree/master/Chapter-03`.

Check out the following video to see the code in action: `http://bit.ly/2Fj4BJ8`

The Gazer application

In order to delve into camera handling, video processing, and motion analysis, we will develop a brand new application. Besides learning about these topics, we will also get an application that has many pragmatic features: being able to record video through a webcam, monitor for our home security, and notify us on our mobile if a suspicious motion is detected. Let's clarify its features, which are as follows:

- Open a webcam and play the video that's been captured from it in real time
- Record video from the webcam by clicking on a start/stop button
- Show a list of saved videos
- Detect motion, save video, and send notifications to our mobile phone if suspicious motion is detected
- Show some information about the cameras and the application's status

After these features have been clarified, we can design the UI. Again, we will use the open source GUI prototyping tool that we used in `Chapter 1`, *Building an Image Viewer*, Pencil, to draw the wireframe of the prototype of our application, as shown in the following diagram:

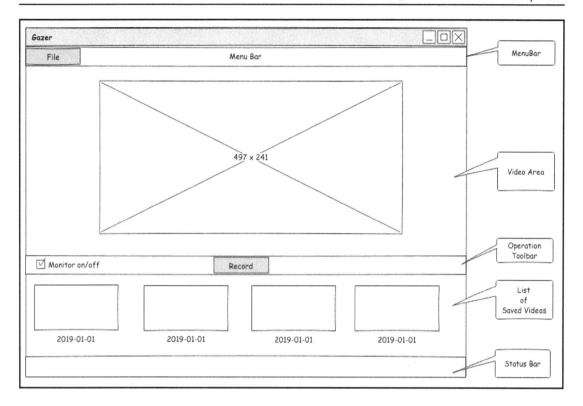

As you see in the preceding wireframe, we divide the whole window into five parts: the menu bar, the main area where we will play the video, the operation area where the operation buttons lie, a horizontal list in which the thumbnails of saved video will be placed, and the status bar.

You can find the source file of this design from our code repository on GitHub at `https://github.com/PacktPublishing/Qt-5-and-OpenCV-4-Computer-Vision-Projects`. The file resides in the root directory of the repository and is called `WireFrames.epgz`. Don't forget that it should be opened using the Pencil application. The wireframe is on *page 2* of this file.

Starting the project and setting up the UI

OK, we now know what the application will look like, so let's roll up our sleeves and set up the UI with Qt!

Name the project and the `Gazer` application. Now, let's create the project in our Terminal:

```
$ mkdir Gazer/
$ cd Gazer/
$ touch main.cpp
$ ls
main.cpp
$ qmake -project
$ ls
Gazer.pro main.cpp
$
```

Next, let's edit the `Gazer.pro` project file. First, we need to set up the application information and modules from the Qt library we will use:

```
TEMPLATE = app
TARGET = Gazer
INCLUDEPATH += .

QT += core gui multimedia
greaterThan(QT_MAJOR_VERSION, 4): QT += widgets
```

We are now very familiar with qmake and the project file of a Qt project, so I don't need to explain this piece of code line by line here. The only point we should note is that we include the multimedia module of the Qt library, which we will use later on.

Then, we will set up the configuration of the OpenCV library:

```
unix: !mac {
    INCLUDEPATH += /home/kdr2/programs/opencv/include/opencv4
    LIBS += -L/home/kdr2/programs/opencv/lib -lopencv_core -
lopencv_imgproc -lopencv_video -lopencv_videoio
}

unix: mac {
    INCLUDEPATH += /path/to/opencv/include/opencv4
    LIBS += -L/path/to/opencv/lib -lopencv_world
}

win32 {
    INCLUDEPATH += c:/path/to/opencv/include/opencv4
    LIBS += -lc:/path/to/opencv/lib/opencv_world
}
```

We append the video and `videoio` modules of the OpenCV library to the end of the value of the `LIBS` key since we will be using these modules to process the video in our project. Another point you should note is that you should change the paths in this piece of code to your real OpenCV installation path.

Finally, let's set up the headers and sources:

```
HEADERS += mainwindow.h
SOURCES += main.cpp mainwindow.cpp
```

While we are setting three source files here, including the header file, we now have only one empty `main.cpp` file. Don't worry about this—we have done lots of work of this kind before in our previous projects, so let's do some copying, pasting, and changing:

1. Copy the `main.cpp` file to our `Gazer` project from any of our previous projects, for example, the `ImageViewer` project from `Chapter 1`, *Building an Image Viewer* and keep its content unchanged.

2. Copy the `mainwindown.h` file to our `Gazer` project from one of our previous projects, open the file, and delete all the lines in the class body except for the line of the `Q_OBJECT` macro, the constructor, and the destructor. The class body should look like this after the change:

```
class MainWindow : public QMainWindow
{
    Q_OBJECT

public:
    explicit MainWindow(QWidget *parent=nullptr);
    ~MainWindow();
}
```

3. Create the `mainwindow.cpp` source file as an empty file and add the implementations of the constructor and destructor to it:

```
MainWindow::MainWindow(QWidget *parent) :
    QMainWindow(parent)
{
}

MainWindow::~MainWindow()
{
}
```

You can now compile and run our application, but what you will see when you run it will be a blank window.

To set up the full UI as we designed, we should add several Qt widgets to the blank window. First, we will declare a `QMenu` method and three `QAction` methods for that menu in a private section of the body of the `MainWindow` class:

```
private:
    QMenu *fileMenu;

    QAction *cameraInfoAction;
    QAction *openCameraAction;
    QAction *exitAction;
```

Next is the main area with which we will display the video. The video will be captured frame by frame using the OpenCV library, and each frame is an image itself. To play the video, we can display the frame within a certain area as soon as it is captured. Therefore, we still use `QGraphicsSence` and `QGraphicsView` to display the frames one by one to achieve the effect of playing the video:

```
    QGraphicsScene *imageScene;
    QGraphicsView *imageView;
```

Then, there's the buttons on the operation area, the horizontal list for saved videos, and the status bar:

```
    QCheckBox *monitorCheckBox;
    QPushButton *recordButton;

    QListView *saved_list;

    QStatusBar *mainStatusBar;
    QLabel *mainStatusLabel;
```

The checkbox in the first line we declared will be used to tell us whether the security monitor status is turned on or not. If it's checked, our application will perform motion detection and send a notification when something happens; otherwise, the application will only work as a camera player. The push button will be used to start or stop recording a video.

In the header file, we just declared these widgets, but to arrange these widgets into their right positions, as we designed in our prototype wireframe, we should resort to the Qt layout system. With the help of the Qt layout system, the child widgets of a parent widget can be arranged automatically so that all the available space will be used properly by the child widgets. The layout system will also take care of the arrangement of all the widgets and ensure that it's managed when the parent widgets of the managed widgets have their size or position changed, or when the managed widgets themselves have changes made to their size or position.

For this layout system, Qt provides many classes that are all derived from the QLayout class. Let's look at some examples:

- A QHBoxLayout class arranges widgets from left to right order in a horizontal row.
- A QVBoxLayout class arranges widgets from the top to bottom order in a vertical column.
- A QGridLayout class arranges widgets that can occupy multiple cells in a two-dimensional grid.
- A QFormLayout class arranges widgets in a two-column grid, with each row having two widgets arranged in a descriptive label field.

For the design of our application, Gazer, we can use a QGridLayout class, which has multiple rows and only one column. According to my rough estimate, the proportion of the height of these three parts (the main area, the operation area, and the list of the saved videos) is about 12:1:4. Therefore, we can make a 17 x 1 QGridLayout class to arrange the widgets we have designed and declared.

With the knowledge of the layout system introduced, let's set up the full UI we designed. First, we declare two private methods, initUI and createActions, in the body of the MainWindow class:

```
private:
    void initUI();
    void createActions();
```

Then, we go to the mainwindow.cpp source file to implement them. Let's look at void MainWindow::initUI() first. In this method, we set the main window of our application to a proper size and create the file menu at the beginning:

```
this->resize(1000, 800);
// setup menubar
fileMenu = menuBar()->addMenu("&File");
```

Then, we set the center area of the window:

```
QGridLayout *main_layout = new QGridLayout();
imageScene = new QGraphicsScene(this);
imageView = new QGraphicsView(imageScene);
main_layout->addWidget(imageView, 0, 0, 12, 1);
```

In this piece of code, we create a new instance of the `QGridLayout` class that will have 17 x 1 as its size, as we had planned previously. Then, we create instances of `QGraphicsSence` and `QGraphicsView`, which will be used to display images and, hence, play videos. The last line, which is very new to us, shows how we add a widget to a layout. We call the `addWidget` method of the `QGridLayout` instance with five arguments: the first one is the widget that we want to add to the layout, and the following four numbers describe a rectangle (the start row, the start column, the number of rows it spans, and the number of columns it spans) that the added widget will occupy. In our code, `QGraphicsView` will occupy the first 12 rows of the grid layout.

The following video playing area is the operation area. We have two widgets, a checkbox, and a push button in this area. Therefore, we need a new layout to arrange them. We will also select `QGridLayout` to do the arrangement here. This means that we will nest another grid layout in the main grid layout:

```
QGridLayout *tools_layout = new QGridLayout();
main_layout->addLayout(tools_layout, 12, 0, 1, 1);

monitorCheckBox = new QCheckBox(this);
monitorCheckBox->setText("Monitor On/Off");
tools_layout->addWidget(monitorCheckBox, 0, 0);

recordButton = new QPushButton(this);
recordButton->setText("Record");
tools_layout->addWidget(recordButton, 0, 1, Qt::AlignHCenter);
tools_layout->addWidget(new QLabel(this), 0, 2);
```

In the first two lines of the preceding code, we create a new grid layout called `tools_layout`, and then add it to the main grid layout. With `12, 0, 1, 1` as its position rectangle, this child layout only occupies a single row in the main grid layout, that is, the 13th row. After the child layout is in its position, let's create the children widgets and add them in. The widgets should be arranged horizontally in one single row, so the layout will have `1xN` as its size. As we mentioned previously, we have two widgets that will be placed to the operation area, but as we designed, we want to align the most important widget—the record push button—to the center in the horizontal direction. To do so, we append a placeholder, a blank `QLable` method, to `tools_layout`. We now have three widgets in the layout; the record push button is the second one, that is, the middle one.

In the preceding code, it's obvious that we create the widgets, set their texts, and add them to the layout. It's worth noting that when we call the addWidget method of the grid layout object, we use only three arguments instead of using five, like when we called it on the main layout object. That's because that there's no row spanning or column spanning for any widget in this layout—giving only the row index and the column index is enough to locate a single cell for the widget. Also, when we add the push button, we use an extra alignment argument, Qt::AlignHCenter, to ensure that the button is not only in the middle cell but also in the center of that cell.

Beneath the operation area is a list of saved videos. Qt provides a widget called QListView that we can use directly here, so we just create the object and add it to our main layout:

```
// list of saved videos
saved_list = new QListView(this);
main_layout->addWidget(saved_list, 13, 0, 4, 1);
```

Remember the 12:1:4 proportion? Here, we make the list widget occupy four rows in the main grid layout, which starts from the 14th row.

Up until now, all the widgets in the main layout are in their position. It's time to add the main layout to our main window. Here, we can't directly call this->setLayout(main_layout); because the main window has its own way to manage its content. As you may recall from the projects we had completed in the previous chapters, you will realize that we called setCentralWidget in the main window to set its content in these projects. Here, we can create a new widget that will have the main grid layout as its layout, and then set this widget as the central widget of the main window:

```
QWidget *widget = new QWidget();
widget->setLayout(main_layout);
setCentralWidget(widget);
```

The next thing we need to look at is the status bar and actions:

```
// setup status bar
mainStatusBar = statusBar();
mainStatusLabel = new QLabel(mainStatusBar);
mainStatusBar->addPermanentWidget(mainStatusLabel);
mainStatusLabel->setText("Gazer is Ready");

createActions();
```

As you see in the preceding code, besides the status bar, at the tail end of the initUI method, we call MainWindow::createActions to create the actions in the **File** menu. The implementation of the createActions method is simple—in it, we create instances of QActions, and then add them to the **File** menu. I haven't explained the code line by line here because we have done this kind of thing many times in the previous projects. For the exit action, we connect the quit slot of the application to its triggered signal; for other actions, we don't have any slot for them at this point but will provide one in the following sections.

Now, we call the initUI method in the constructor of the MainWindow class. Finally, we have the full UI set up, so let's compile and run the application to see what it looks like:

As you can see, with the help of the layout system provided by Qt, we have the designed UI perfectly implemented. If you want to learn more about this powerful layout system, you can refer to its documentation at https://doc.qt.io/qt-5/layout.html.

Accessing cameras

In the preceding section, we set up the UI of our application. In this section, we will play the video feed that's provided by a camera from a personal computer.

Before accessing a camera, we should find out some information about it—if we use OpenCV, we need the index of the camera that we want to capture a video from; if we use Qt, we need the device name of it. For a typical laptop, it usually has one default built-in webcam whose index is 0, but its name is platform or environment dependent. If we have multiple webcams for a computer, usually both of their indices and names are platform or environment dependent. To determine this information, we can turn to the QCameraInfo class from the Qt library.

Listing cameras with Qt

By using the QCameraInfo class from the Qt library, we can easily obtain the available cameras on the current computer. It has a static method named availableCameras that returns a list of QCameraInfo objects.

Now, we are going to add a slot for cameraInfoAction to do this work. First, we declare a private slot in the body of the MainWindow class in the mainwindow.h file:

```
private slots:
    void showCameraInfo();
```

Then, we give its implementation, as follows:

```
void MainWindow::showCameraInfo()
{
    QList<QCameraInfo> cameras = QCameraInfo::availableCameras();
    QString info = QString("Available Cameras: \n");

    foreach (const QCameraInfo &cameraInfo, cameras) {
        info += " - " + cameraInfo.deviceName() + ": ";
        info += cameraInfo.description() + "\n";
    }
    QMessageBox::information(this, "Cameras", info);
}
```

In this piece of code, we obtain the camera information list, build a human-readable string with all the cameras in the list, and show it with a prompt message box.

Finally, we connect this slot to the `triggered` signal of `cameraInfoAction` in the `MainWindow::createActions` method:

```
        connect(cameraInfoAction, SIGNAL(triggered(bool)), this,
    SLOT(showCameraInfo()));
```

OK, let's compile and run the `Gazer` application. Now, click the **Camera Information** item under the **File** menu and see what information is provided:

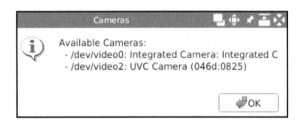

My laptop has a built-in webcam and an external one attached to a USB port, so the application shows two cameras while it is running on my computer: **/dev/video0** and **/dev/video2**. I am using GNU/Linux on my laptop, and, on this platform, the device names are in the pattern of `/dev/video<N>`, where `<N>` is the index of the camera. If you are using other operating systems, the information you see may be different from mine.

In this context, the word **available** in the **Available Cameras** phrase means a camera is properly attached and driven on the computer and that it must be not busy, that is, not used by any application. If a camera is being used by any application, it will not be included in the return list of the `QCameraInfo::availableCameras` method.

Capturing and playing

We have gotten the information of the webcams in the preceding section, so let's capture and play the video feed from a chosen webcam using OpenCV.

It is very easy to capture a video using OpenCV. The following is an example:

```
#include <iostream>
#include "opencv2/opencv.hpp"

using namespace std;
using namespace cv;

int main() {
```

```
VideoCapture cap(0);
if(!cap.isOpened()) {
    return -1;
}

while(1) {
    Mat frame;
    cap >> frame;

    if (frame.empty())
        break;

    imshow( "Frame", frame );

    char c = (char)waitKey(25);
    if(c==27) // ESC
        break;
}

cap.release();
destroyAllWindows();

return 0;
}
```

In the preceding code, first, we create an instance of `VideoCapture` with the index of the default webcam, and then test whether the camera is successfully opened. If it is opened, we enter an infinite loop. In the loop, we read an image from the `VideoCapture` instance to a `Mat` instance. As the loop progresses, consecutive images will be read from the webcam and they will compose a video. In terms of video processing, each of these consecutive images is usually called a frame. That's why we use the name `frame` in the previous code. After a frame is read, we check whether it's empty. If true, we break the infinite loop; otherwise, we show it by calling the `imshow` function. Then, we wait up to 25 milliseconds for a key press. If the *Esc* key is pressed during the waiting, we break the loop; otherwise, the infinite loop will keep going. After the loop ends, we free the resources we allocated, such as releasing the camera, destroying the windows that are used to show images, and more.

As you can see, capturing video using OpenCV is very straightforward. But when we start to integrate this feature into a real-world GUI application, things will get a little complicated. Do you remember that we built a feature to generate a cartoon effect of an image in the *Cartoon effect* section of Chapter 2, *Editing Images Like a Pro*? In order to achieve that feature, we employ some algorithms that are much slower. Running a slow task in the GUI thread will freeze the UI during the running period of the task. To avoid making the application too complicated, in that case, we resort to the way of optimizing the algorithms to shorten the running time of the task, hence shortening the frozen period of the GUI. But in the current case of capturing video, we must keep capturing frames at all times as long as the camera is opened by the user since we have no way to optimize this in the time dimension. If we capture the video in the GUI thread, the UI will be frozen all the time. So, in order to keep the interface of the application responsive, we must capture the video in another thread that differs from the GUI thread.

The Qt library offers many different technologies to deal with multithreading in applications. The QThread class is the most straightforward and fundamental facility. It is simple, yet powerful and flexible. In this section, we will mostly use this class to separate the capturing task into a new thread.

To do the video capturing in another thread, the first thing we need to do is define a new class derived from the QThread class. We name this class CaptureThread and declare it in the capture_thread.h file.

Let's take a look at the header file. At the beginning and the end of this file are the include-once macro definitions and the header file including directives:

```
#ifndef CAPTURE_THREAD_H
#define CAPTURE_THREAD_H

#include <QString>
#include <QThread>
#include <QMutex>

#include "opencv2/opencv.hpp"

// ... the class declaration goes here.

#endif // CAPTURE_THREAD_H
```

In the middle is the class declaration:

```
class CaptureThread : public QThread
{
    Q_OBJECT
public:
```

```
        CaptureThread(int camera, QMutex *lock);
        CaptureThread(QString videoPath, QMutex *lock);
        ~CaptureThread();
        void setRunning(bool run) {running = run; };

    protected:
        void run() override;

    signals:
        void frameCaptured(cv::Mat *data);

    private:
        bool running;
        int cameraID;
        QString videoPath;
        QMutex *data_lock;
        cv::Mat frame;
    };
```

The class is derived from the QThread class, as we mentioned previously, and in the first line of its body, we use the Q_OBJECT macro to tell the meta-object system of the Qt library to take care of this class.

Then, we declare two constructors and a destructor in the public section. The first constructor accepts an integer, which is the index of the target webcam, and a pointer of QMutex, which will be used to protect data in a race condition. The second constructor accepts a string that will be treated as a path to a video file and a QMutex pointer. With this constructor, we can use a video file to emulate a webcam. There's also a public method called setRunning, which is used to set the running status of the capturing thread.

Next is the protected section. In this section, we declare a method named run. The override keyword indicates that this method is a virtual method and that it is overriding a method with the same name as one of its base class' methods. The run method of QThread is the starting point for a thread. When we call the start method of a thread, its run method will be called after the new thread is created. We will do the capturing work in this method later.

Then, we declare a signal whose name is frameCapture, which takes a pointer to a Mat object as its only argument. This signal will be emitted each time a frame is captured from the webcam. If you are interested in this signal, you can connect a slot to it.

Finally, in the private section, we declare many member fields:

- running for the thread state
- cameraID for the camera index
- videoPath for the path of the video that is used to emulate a webcam
- data_lock for protecting data in race conditions
- frame for storing the currently captured frame

That's it in terms of class declaration. Now, let's move on to the method implementations in the capture_thread.cpp file. First up are the constructors and the destructor. All of them are straightforward, and just provide information on things such as field initialization:

```
CaptureThread::CaptureThread(int camera, QMutex *lock):
    running(false), cameraID(camera), videoPath(""), data_lock(lock)
{
}

CaptureThread::CaptureThread(QString videoPath, QMutex *lock):
    running(false), cameraID(-1), videoPath(videoPath),
data_lock(lock)
{
}

CaptureThread::~CaptureThread() {
}
```

Then comes the most important part—the implementation of the run method:

```
void CaptureThread::run() {
    running = true;
    cv::VideoCapture cap(cameraID);
    cv::Mat tmp_frame;
    while(running) {
        cap >> tmp_frame;
        if (tmp_frame.empty()) {
            break;
        }
        cvtColor(tmp_frame, tmp_frame, cv::COLOR_BGR2RGB);
        data_lock->lock();
        frame = tmp_frame;
        data_lock->unlock();
        emit frameCaptured(&frame);
    }
    cap.release();
    running = false;
}
```

This method is called immediately after the thread is created, and when it returns, the lifespan of the thread will finish. Therefore, we set the running status to true when we enter this method and set the running status to false before returning from the method. Then, like the example we gave at the beginning of this section, we create an instance of the `VideoCapture` class using the camera index and create an instance of `Mat` to save the captured frame. Afterward is the infinite loop. In the loop, we capture a frame and check whether it's empty. We are using OpenCV to capture the frames, so the color order of the capture frames is BGR instead of RGB. Considering we will display the frames using Qt, we should convert the frames into new ones with RGB as their color order. That's what the call to the `cvtColor` function does.

After the preparation of the captured frame is done, we assign it to the `frame` class member, and then we emit the `frameCapture` signal with a pointer that points to the `frame` member field that we just modified. If you are interested in this signal, you can connect a slot to it. In the connected slot, you will have the pointer to this `frame` member as its argument. In other words, you can read from or write to this `frame` object freely in the connected slot. Considering that the connected slot will run in another thread that differs from the capturing thread in all probability, the `frame` member is very likely modified by two different threads at the same time, and this behavior may corrupt the data in it. In order to prevent this kind of situation from happening, we use `QMutex` to ensure that there is only one thread that is accessing the `frame` member field at any time. The `QMutex` instance we used here is the `QMutex *data_lock` member field. We call its `lock` method before assigning it to the `frame` member, and call its `unlock` method after the assignment.

If someone sets the `running` status to false (usually in another thread), the infinite loop will break, and then we do some cleaning work after that, such as releasing the `VideoCapture` instance and ensuring that the running flag is set to false.

At this point, all the work of the capturing thread is done. Next, we need to integrate it with our main window. So, let's get started.

First, we add some private member fields to our `MainWindow` class in the `mainwindow.h` header file:

```
cv::Mat currentFrame;

// for capture thread
QMutex *data_lock;
CaptureThread *capturer;
```

The `currentFrame` member is used to store the frame that's captured by the capturing thread. `capturer` is the handle to the capturing thread, which we are using to do the video capturing work when the user opens a camera. The `QMutext` object, `data_lock`, is used to protect the data of `CaptureThread.frame` in the race conditions. It will be used in both the GUI thread and the capturing thread. Then, in the constructor of the `MainWindow` class, we initialize the `data_lock` field after the call to the `initUI` method:

```
initUI();
data_lock = new QMutex();
```

Next, let's go back to the `mainwindow.h` header file and add two more private slots in the class declaration:

```
void openCamera();
void updateFrame(cv::Mat*);
```

The `openCamera` slot is used to create a new capturing thread and will be called when the **Open Camera** action in the file menu is triggered. First, we connect this slot to the `triggered` signal of the **Open Camera** action in the `createActions` method:

```
connect(openCameraAction, SIGNAL(triggered(bool)), this,
    SLOT(openCamera()));
```

Then, we go to the implementation of the `openCamera` slot:

```
int camID = 2;
capturer = new CaptureThread(camID, data_lock);
connect(capturer, &CaptureThread::frameCaptured, this,
    &MainWindow::updateFrame);
capturer->start();
mainStatusLabel->setText(QString("Capturing Camera
%1").arg(camID));
```

In the preceding code, we create a new instance of our `CaptureThread` class with a given camera index and the `QMutex` object we created in the constructor of the `MainWindow` class, and then assign it to the `capturer` member field.

Then, we connect the `frameCaptured` signal of `capturer` to the `updateFrame` slot of our main window, so that when the `CaptureThread::frameCaptured` signal is emitted, the `MainWindow::updateFrame` slot (method) will be called with the same argument that's used when the signal is emitted.

Now that this preparation is done, we can start the capturing thread by calling the `start` method of the `CaptureThread` instance, known as `capturer`. Incidentally, we tell the user that a certain camera is opened by showing some text in the status bar.

 As I've mentioned already, I have two webcams on my laptop, and I am using the second one, whose index is 2. You should change the value of the `camID` variable to the correct camera index according to your choice. In common cases, the value 0 should be used for the default webcam.

Now, the capturing thread has started, and it will keep on capturing frames from the camera and emitting the `frameCaptured` signal. Let's fill our `updateFrame` slot of the main window to respond to the emitted signals:

```
void MainWindow::updateFrame(cv::Mat *mat)
{
    data_lock->lock();
    currentFrame = *mat;
    data_lock->unlock();

    QImage frame(
        currentFrame.data,
        currentFrame.cols,
        currentFrame.rows,
        currentFrame.step,
        QImage::Format_RGB888);
    QPixmap image = QPixmap::fromImage(frame);

    imageScene->clear();
    imageView->resetMatrix();
    imageScene->addPixmap(image);
    imageScene->update();
    imageView->setSceneRect(image.rect());
}
```

In this slot, as we mentioned previously, we have a pointer to the frame that's captured by `CaptureThread` as the argument. In the slot body, we assign that captured frame to the `currentFrame` field of the main window class. In this assignment expression, we read from the captured frame and then do the assignment. So, in order to avoid getting corrupted data, we use the `data_lock` mutex to ensure the reading will not occur while the capturing thread is writing to its `frame` field.

After getting the captured frame, we show it with the graphics scene and view, just like we did in our image editor application that we built in Chapter 2, *Editing Images Like a Pro*.

All the points are connected together now—the user clicks the **Open Camera** action; the triggered signal of that action is then emitted; the openCamera slot is called; the capturing thread is created and it starts to capture frames from the camera; as the frames are consecutively captured, the frameCaptured signal is continuously emitted; the updateFrame slot of the main window is then called for each captured frame; and, as a result, the graphics view in the main area of our main window will show these captured consecutive frames one after one quickly, and the end user will see the video playing.

But there is still a glitch in our code: if the user clicks the **Open Camera** action multiple times, more than one capturing thread will be created and they will run simultaneously. This isn't a situation we want. So, before starting a new thread, we must check whether there's already one running and, if there is, we should stop it before starting a new one. To do so, let's add the following code at the beginning of the openCamera slot:

```
if(capturer != nullptr) {
    // if a thread is already running, stop it
    capturer->setRunning(false);
    disconnect(capturer, &CaptureThread::frameCaptured, this,
&MainWindow::updateFrame);
    connect(capturer, &CaptureThread::finished, capturer,
&CaptureThread::deleteLater);
}
```

In the preceding code, we set the running status of the CaptureThread instance, that is, capturer, to false to break its infinite loop if we find it's not null. Then, we disconnect the connected signals and slots of it and connect a new slot, deleteLater, of itself to its finished signal. After the infinite loop ends and the run method returns, the thread will go to the end of its lifetime, and its finished signal will be emitted. Because of the connection from the finished signal to the deleteLater slot, the deleteLater slot will be called once the thread ends. As a result, the Qt library will delete this thread instance when the control flow of the program returns to the event loop of the Qt library.

Now, let's update the Gazer.pro project file so that we can add our new header files and source files to our application:

```
HEADERS += mainwindow.h capture_thread.h
SOURCES += main.cpp mainwindow.cpp capture_thread.cpp
```

Then, we will need to compile and run the application:

```
$ qmake -makefile
$ make
g++ -c -pipe -O2 -Wall -W...
# output truncated
$ echo $LD_LIBRARY_PATH
```

```
/home/kdr2/programs/opencv/lib/
$ ./Gazer
# the application is running now.
```

After the application starts up, click the **Open Camera** action in the **File** menu to see the view from the perspective of our camera. The following is the view outside my office from my webcam:

Threading and the performance of real-time video processing

In this section, we will get multithreading technology involved in our application. This is for the following two purposes:

- To avoid the main thread (the GUI thread) being frozen
- To avoid a potential performance decrease in video processing

First, as we mentioned previously, running a slow task in the GUI thread will freeze the UI during the running period of the task. Capturing a video from a camera and processing it is an ongoing process; it's endless and will freeze the GUI forever until we close the camera. Therefore, we must separate the main thread and the video capturing thread.

On the other hand, the work of video processing, especially video processing in real time, is a CPU-intensive and time-sensitive task. Capture a frame, process it, and display it—all the work must be done as soon as possible.

One key point of this are the algorithms we use to process each frame. They must be performant enough. If they are too slow, while new frames are generated by the camera, the program is still busy processing the previously captured frame, so it has no chance to read the new frames. That will cause the new frames to be lost.

Another key point is if there is more than one thread that is sharing the data of the frames and, at the same time, locks are used to keep the data safe, the locks must not block the threads for too long. For example, in our application, in the capturing thread, let's say we use the following lock:

```
while(running) {
    data_lock->lock(); // notice here,
    cap >> tmp_frame;
    if (tmp_frame.empty()) {
        data_lock->unlock(); // and here,
        break;
    }
    cvtColor(tmp_frame, tmp_frame, cv::COLOR_BGR2RGB);
    frame = tmp_frame;
    data_lock->unlock(); // and here.
    emit frameCaptured(&frame);
}
```

If we move more lines to the scope that is guarded by the lock, and then recompile and run the application, you will feel the lag of the frames or frame lost. That's because, with this change, the UI thread should wait a long time in the updateFrame slot.

Capturing and playing with Qt

In the preceding section, we showed you how to capture a video from a webcam using OpenCV. The Qt library also provides many facilities for playing with multimedia in its Qt Multimedia module, including ones that allow us to capture a video from a webcam. In this section, we will have a go at using these facilities to capture a video from the webcam instead of using OpenCV.

To capture a video using Qt, we can simply use an instance of the QCamera class with a QCameraViewfinder object instead of the QGraphicsSence and QGraphicsView objects. Let's see their declarations in the mainwindow.h header file:

```
#ifdef GAZER_USE_QT_CAMERA
    QCamera *camera;
    QCameraViewfinder *viewfinder;
#endif
```

As you can see, the variable declarations are surrounded by an ifdef/endif block in our code. This ensures that only when the GAZER_USE_QT_CAMERA macro is defined while the application is being compiled, the code regarding capturing video using Qt will be used. Otherwise, our application still captures video using OpenCV.

Then, in the implementation of the initUI method in the mainwindow.cpp file, we create and configure the QCamera and QCameraViewfinder objects that we just declared:

```
#ifdef GAZER_USE_QT_CAMERA
    QList<QCameraInfo> cameras = QCameraInfo::availableCameras();
    // I have two cameras and use the second one here
    camera = new QCamera(cameras[1]);
    viewfinder = new QCameraViewfinder(this);
    QCameraViewfinderSettings settings;
    // the size must be compatible with the camera
    settings.setResolution(QSize(800, 600));
    camera->setViewfinder(viewfinder);
    camera->setViewfinderSettings(settings);
    main_layout->addWidget(viewfinder, 0, 0, 12, 1);
#else
    imageScene = new QGraphicsScene(this);
    imageView = new QGraphicsView(imageScene);
    main_layout->addWidget(imageView, 0, 0, 12, 1);
#endif
```

In the preceding code, we first test whether the GAZER_USE_QT_CAMERA macro is defined in the compiling time. If it is defined, we will use Qt to capture a video from the camera—first, we fetch the information of all the available cameras and choose one of them to create the QCamera object.

Then, we create QCameraViewfinder and QCameraViewfinderSettings. The object is used to configure the viewfinder object. In our code, we use it to set the resolution of the viewfinder. The value of the resolution here must be compatible with the camera. My camera is a Logitech C270, and from its specifications page (https://support.logitech. com/en_us/product/hd-webcam-c270/specs) we can see it supports the resolutions of 320 x 240, 640 x 480, and 800 x 600. I am using 800 x 600 in the code. After the settings and the viewfinder are ready, we set them to our camera object by calling its setViewfinder and setViewfinderSettings methods. Then, we add the viewfinder to our main grid layout of the main window and make it occupy the first 12 rows.

If the GAZER_USE_QT_CAMERA macro is not defined, the code in the #else branch will be used, that is, we still use the graphics scene and the graphics view to play the video that's been captured by the webcam.

Now that the changes in the widgets have been made, we are going to change the openCamera slot:

```
#ifdef GAZER_USE_QT_CAMERA
void MainWindow::openCamera()
{
    camera->setCaptureMode(QCamera::CaptureVideo);
    camera->start();
}
#else
// The original implementation which uses QThread and OpenCV
#endif
```

The version of openCamera that is using Qt is defined if the GAZER_USE_QT_CAMERA macro is defined. This version is simple—it sets the capturing mode of the camera, and then calls the start method of the camera. No explicit things about threading need to be handled since the QCamera class will handle it for us.

Finally, we update our Gazer.pro project file and add the following lines to it:

```
# Using OpenCV or QCamera
DEFINES += GAZER_USE_QT_CAMERA=1
QT += multimediawidgets
```

The `DEFINES += GAZER_USE_QT_CAMERA=1` line will define the `GAZER_USE_QT_CAMERA` macro as 1 during compile time, while the next line, `QT += multimediawidgets`, includes the `multimediawidgets` Qt module in our project. After the project file is updated, we can compile and run our application. Compile it, start it, and click the **Open Camera** action—you will see the video in the main area of our application. The following is a screenshot of the application while it is running on my computer:

As you see in the preceding screenshot, it almost has the same effect as when we use OpenCV, except that `QCameraViewfinder` has a black background. As you can see, using Qt to capture the video is much easier than using OpenCV. However, we will still use OpenCV in our project instead of Qt because one of the features of our application, motion detection, is beyond the domain of the Qt library. Qt is mainly a GUI library or framework, while OpenCV is dedicated to the domain of computer vision, which includes image and video processing. We must use the right tools to do the right things in development, so we will take advantage of these two libraries to build our application.

In the remaining part of this chapter, we will have the lines we just added to the project file commented out and we will keep using OpenCV to handle the video processing work:

```
# Using OpenCV or QCamera
# DEFINES += GAZER_USE_QT_CAMERA=1
# QT += multimediawidgets
```

> When you compile the application, if no source file was changed, only the project file will be updated, so nothing will happen. You should run the `make clean` command to clean up the project and then run the `make` command to compile it.

Calculating the FPS

In the previous sections, we learned how to capture and play video using the video and `videoio` modules of OpenCV and the multimedia facilities provided by Qt. As I mentioned previously, in the rest of this chapter, we will process video by using the OpenCV library, and not the multimedia module of the Qt library. The Qt library will only be used for the UI.

Before saving the videos we captured from the webcams, let's discuss an important indicator of videos and cameras, the FPS, though, sometimes, it is called **frame rate** or **frame frequency**. For a camera, its FPS means how many frames we can capture from it in one second. If this number is too small, the user will perceive each frame individually instead of perceiving the consecutive frames like a motion. On the other hand, if this number is too large, it means that lots of frames will flood in during a short space of time, which may explode our video processing program if the program is not performant enough. Usually, for a film or an animation, the FPS is **24**. This is a fair number and is suitable for the human eyes to perceive frames as motions, and also friendly enough for a common video processing program.

With the knowledge of the previous FPS, we can easily calculate the FPS of a given camera—read a certain number of frames from it and measure the time this capturing process used. Then, the FPS can be calculated by diving the number of frames by the used time. Doesn't this sound easy? Let's do this in our application now.

In order to avoid the UI freezing, we will do the calculation in the video capturing thread and notify the main thread with a signal after the calculation is done. So, let's open the `capture_thread.h` header file and add some fields and methods to the `CaptureThread` class. First, we will add two fields to the private section:

```
// FPS calculating
bool fps_calculating;
float fps;
```

The `fps_calculating` field of the `bool` type is used to indicate whether the capturing thread is doing, or should do, an FPS calculation or not. Another field called `fps` is used to save the calculated FPS. We initialize them to `false` and `0.0` in the constructors in the `capture_thread.cpp` source file:

```
fps_calculating = false;
fps = 0.0;
```

Then, we add some methods:

- The `startCalcFPS` method is used to trigger an FPS calculation. When the user wants to calculate the FPS of their camera, this method will be directly called in the UI thread. In this method, we simply set the `fps_calculating` field to `true`. Since this method is a simple inline method, we don't need to give an implementation in the `.cpp` file.
- The `void fpsChanged(float fps)` method lies in the signals section, so it is a signal. When the FPS calculation is done, this signal will be emitted with the calculated value of the FPS. Since this method is a signal, `moc` will take care of its implementation.
- A private method, called `void calculateFPS(cv::VideoCapture &cap)`, which is used to calculate the FPS.

The third method, `calculateFPS`, is the only one that needs an implementation in the `.cpp` file. Let's look at its method body in the `capture_thread.cpp` file:

```
void CaptureThread::calculateFPS(cv::VideoCapture &cap)
{
    const int count_to_read = 100;
    cv::Mat tmp_frame;
    QTime timer;
```

```
timer.start();
for(int i = 0; i < count_to_read; i++) {
        cap >> tmp_frame;
}
int elapsed_ms = timer.elapsed();
fps = count_to_read / (elapsed_ms / 1000.0);
fps_calculating = false;
emit fpsChanged(fps);
}
```

In its body, we decide to read 100 frames from the camera, which is passed in as the only argument. Before the reading starts, we create an instance of QTimer and start it to time the reading process. When the for loop is executed, the reading process is done and we use the timer.elapsed() expression to obtain the elapsed time in milliseconds. Then, the FPS is calculated by dividing the frame count by the elapsed time in seconds. In the end, we set the fps_calculating flag to false and emit the fpsChanged signal with the calculated FPS.

The last thing for the capturing thread is calling the calculateFPS method in the infinite loop in the run method when the fps_calculating field is set to true. Let's add the following code to the end of that infinite loop:

```
if(fps_calculating) {
    calculateFPS(cap);
}
```

OK, the work of the capturing thread has finished, so let's go to the UI thread to provide an action that will be used to trigger the FPS calculation and show the calculated FPS on the status bar of the main window when the calculation is done.

In the mainwindow.h header file, we will add a new QAction method and two slots:

```
private slots:
    // ....
    void calculateFPS();
    void updateFPS(float);
//...
private:
    //...
    QAction *calcFPSAction;
```

The action will be added to the file menu. When it is clicked, the newly added `calculateFPS` slot will be called. This is done by the following code in the `createActions` method:

```
calcFPSAction = new QAction("&Calculate FPS", this);
fileMenu->addAction(calcFPSAction);
// ...
connect(calcFPSAction, SIGNAL(triggered(bool)), this,
SLOT(calculateFPS()));
```

Now, let's see the `calculateFPS` slot when the action is triggered:

```
void MainWindow::calculateFPS()
{
    if(capturer != nullptr) {
        capturer->startCalcFPS();
    }
}
```

This is straightforward—if the capturing thread object is not null, we call its `startCalcFPS` method to tell it to calculate the FPS in the infinite loop in its run method. If the calculation is finished, the `fpsChanged` signal of the capturing thread object will be emitted. In order to receive the emitted signal, we must connect it to a slot. This is done by the code in the `MainWindow::openCamera` method, in which we create the capturing thread. After the capturing thread is created, we connect the signal to a slot immediately:

```
if(capturer != nullptr) {
    // ...
    disconnect(capturer, &CaptureThread::fpsChanged, this,
&MainWindow::updateFPS);
    }
    // ...
    connect(capturer, &CaptureThread::fpsChanged, this,
&MainWindow::updateFPS);
    capturer->start();
    // ...
```

As you can see, besides connecting the signal and the slot, we also disconnect them when we stop a capturing thread. The connected slot is also a newly added one in this section. Let's look at its implementation:

```
void MainWindow::updateFPS(float fps)
{
    mainStatusLabel->setText(QString("FPS of current camera is
%1").arg(fps));
}
```

It's simple; here, we construct `QString` and set it on the status bar.

All work is done, so we can now compile our application and run it to calculate the FPS of our webcam. This is the result of my external webcam, the **Logitech C270**:

The result says that the **FPS of the current camera is 29.80**. Let's check this on its home page at `https://support.logitech.com/en_us/product/hd-webcam-c270/specs`:

Image Capture (4:3 SD)	320x240, 640x480 1.2 MP, 3.0 MP
Image Capture (16:9 W)	360p, 480p, 720p
Video Capture (4:3 SD)	320x240, 640x480, 800x600
Video Capture (16:9 W)	360p, 480p, 720p,
Frame Rate (max)	30fps @ 640x480
Video Effects (VFX)	N/A

On that web page, the provider says its FPS is 30. Our result is very close.

We must open the webcam before calculating its frame rate. So, in our application, please click the **Open Camera** action before clicking the **Calculate FPS** action. Another thing that is worth noting is that all the frames we captured during the frame rate calculation are discarded so that we see the last frame captured before the calculation is frozen on the UI during that period.

The FPS that's calculated in this way is a theoretical upper limit—it is of our hardware, not of our application (the software). If you want to get the FPS of our application, you can count the frames and time elapsed in the loop in the `run` method and use that data to work out the FPS.

Saving videos

In the preceding section, we learned how to access the cameras attached to our computer, as well as getting the information of all the cameras, playing the video that was captured from a camera in real time, and calculating the frame rate of a camera. In this section, we will learn how to record videos from the camera.

The principle of recording videos is simple: while we are capturing frames from a camera, we compress each frame in a certain way and write it to a video file. The `VideoWriter` class in the `videoio` module of the OpenCV library provides a convenient way to do this, and we will use it to record videos in this section.

Before we start with the work of recording videos, we should do some preparation work for our application, for example, where to save the video and how to name each video file. To resolve these prerequisites, we will create an assistant class named `Utilities` in a new header file called `utilities.h`:

```
class Utilities
{
 public:
    static QString getDataPath();
    static QString newSavedVideoName();
    static QString getSavedVideoPath(QString name, QString postfix);
};
```

As I omit the lines of the `ifndef/define` idiom and the `#include` directives, the class declaration is very clear; we have three static methods in it:

- The `QString getDataPath()` method returns the directory in which we will save the video files.
- The `QString newSavedVideoName()` method generates a new name for the video that will be saved.
- The `QString getSavedVideoPath(QString name, QString postfix)` method accepts a name and a postfix (the extension name) and returns the absolute path of the video file with the given name.

Let's look at their implementations in the `utilities.cpp` source file.

In the `getDataPath` method, we use the `QStandardPaths` class offered by Qt to obtain the standard location, which is used to save videos and movies by calling the `QStandardPaths::standardLocations` static method with `QStandardPaths::MoviesLocation` and picking up the first element in the returning list. On my laptop, a Linux box, this path is `/home/<USERNAME>/Videos/`. If you are using a different operating system, the path will be `/Users/<USERNAME>/Movies` on macOS or `C:\Users\<USERNAME>\Videos` on Windows. Then, we create a subdirectory called **Gazer** in that video directory and return the absolute path of the new directory. Here is the code:

```
QString Utilities::getDataPath()
{
    QString user_movie_path =
QStandardPaths::standardLocations(QStandardPaths::MoviesLocation)[0];
    QDir movie_dir(user_movie_path);
    movie_dir.mkpath("Gazer");
    return movie_dir.absoluteFilePath("Gazer");
}
```

In the `newSavedVideoName` method, we use the date and time when the method is called to generate a new name. The time is formatted in the `yyyy-MM-dd+HH:mm:ss` pattern, which contains most of the fields of a date and time from the year to the second:

```
QString Utilities::newSavedVideoName()
{
    QDateTime time = QDateTime::currentDateTime();
    return time.toString("yyyy-MM-dd+HH:mm:ss");
}
```

In the `QString getSavedVideoPath(QString name, QString postfix)` method, we just simply return a new string, which is made by concatenating the given name and postfix with a dot, and then appending the concatenated string and a preceding slash to the string returned by `getDataPath`:

```
    return QString("%1/%2.%3").arg(Utilities::getDataPath(), name,
postfix);
```

OK, the preparation of video saving locations is done, so let's move on to the `CaptureThread` class and start the video saving work.

First, we add an enum type in the public section of the `CaptureThread` class:

```
enum VideoSavingStatus {
                STARTING,
                STARTED,
                STOPPING,
                STOPPED
};
```

We will do the video saving in the capturing thread. This enum type will be used to indicate the status of the video saving work in that thread. I will introduce the values of this enum later.

Then, we add some member fields to the `CaptureThread` class in its private section:

```
// video saving
int frame_width, frame_height;
VideoSavingStatus video_saving_status;
QString saved_video_name;
cv::VideoWriter *video_writer;
```

The `frame_width` and `frame_height` variables are quite self-explanatory in terms of their names, and they will be used when we create the video writer. While the `video_saving_status` field is the indicator of the video saving status that we have mentioned, the `saved_video_name` field will hold the name of video that is being saved. The final one, `cv::VideoWriter *video_writer`, is the video writer in which we will write the captured frames. It will help us save the frames to the target video files. These members should be initialized in the constructors:

```
frame_width = frame_height = 0;
video_saving_status = STOPPED;
saved_video_name = "";
video_writer = nullptr;
```

Next are the declarations of the new methods, signals, and slots:

```
public:
    // ...
    void setVideoSavingStatus(VideoSavingStatus status)
{video_saving_status = status; };
    // ...
signals:
    // ...
    void videoSaved(QString name);
    // ...
private:
    // ...
    void startSavingVideo(cv::Mat &firstFrame);
    void stopSavingVideo();
```

The `setVideoSavingStatus` inline method is used to set the video saving status. The `videoSaved` signal will be emitted with the name of a saved video file once the recording is stopped and the video file is completely saved. Due to the fact that it is an inline method defined in the header file or signal method, which is taken care of by the Qt meta-object system, we don't need to provide implementations for them in the `.cpp` file for these two methods. The `startSavingVideo` and `stopSavingVideo` methods are called when the video saving work is about to start or stop; let's take a look at their implementations in the `capture_thread.cpp` source file:

```
void CaptureThread::startSavingVideo(cv::Mat &firstFrame)
{
    saved_video_name = Utilities::newSavedVideoName();

    QString cover = Utilities::getSavedVideoPath(saved_video_name,
"jpg");
    cv::imwrite(cover.toStdString(), firstFrame);
```

```
        video_writer = new cv::VideoWriter(
            Utilities::getSavedVideoPath(saved_video_name,
"avi").toStdString(),
            cv::VideoWriter::fourcc('M','J','P','G'),
            fps? fps: 30,
            cv::Size(frame_width, frame_height));
        video_saving_status = STARTED;
    }
```

As you can see, the `startSavingVideo` method accepts a reference to a frame as its argument. That frame is the first frame that we will save in the video. In the method body, first, we generate a new name for the video, and then we get a path with that name and the `jpg` string as the postfix. Obviously, with `jpg` as the extension name, that path is for an image rather than a video file. Yes, we first save the first frame of the video to an image by calling the `imwrite` function, and this image will be used as the cover of the current video being saved on the UI. As the cover image is saved, we create the instance of the `VideoWriter` class with a proper video file path that's generated by our `Utilities` class. Besides the file path, we also need several arguments to create the video writer:

- A 4-character piece of codec that's used to compress the frames. Here, we use `VideoWriter::fourcc('M','J','P','G')` to obtain a motion-jpeg codec and then pass it to the writer constructor.
- The frame rate of the video file. It should be the same as the cameras. We use the FPS calculation of the camera if there is one; otherwise, we use the default value, `30`, which is from the specifications of my camera.
- The size of the video frame. We will initialize the variables that are used to construct the size arguments in the `run` method of the `CaptureThread` class later.

After the video writer is created, we set `video_saving_status` to `STARTED`.

Before we go into the implementation of the `stopSavingVideo` method, we should go to the `run` method of the `CaptureThread` class to do some updates. First, after we open the camera, and before we enter the infinite loop, we get the width and height of the video frames and assign them to the corresponding class members:

```
        frame_width = cap.get(cv::CAP_PROP_FRAME_WIDTH);
        frame_height = cap.get(cv::CAP_PROP_FRAME_HEIGHT);
```

Then, in the infinite loop, we add the following code after the frame is captured and before the captured frame is converted into the RGB color order image:

```
if(video_saving_status == STARTING) {
    startSavingVideo(tmp_frame);
}
if(video_saving_status == STARTED) {
    video_writer->write(tmp_frame);
}
if(video_saving_status == STOPPING) {
    stopSavingVideo();
}
```

In this piece of code, we check the value of the `video_saving_status` field:

- If it is set to `STARTING`, we call the `startSavingVideo` method. In that method, we save the current frame as the cover image, create the video writer, and set `video_saving_status` to `STARTED`.
- If it is set to `STARTED`, we write the captured frame to the video file.
- If it is set to `STOPPING`, we call the `stopSavingVideo` method to do some cleaning work.

Now, let's go back to `stopSavingVideo` and take a look at the cleaning work:

```
void CaptureThread::stopSavingVideo()
{
    video_saving_status = STOPPED;
    video_writer->release();
    delete video_writer;
    video_writer = nullptr;
    emit videoSaved(saved_video_name);
}
```

The cleaning work is rather straightforward—we set `video_saving_status` to `STOPPED`, release and delete the video writer, set the video writer to null, and then we emit the `VideoSaved` signal.

Up until now, we've finished all the video saving work in the capturing thread. Now, we are going to integrate it with the UI. So, let's open the `mainwindow.h` file and add some slots and fields:

```
private slots:
    // ...
    void recordingStartStop();
    void appendSavedVideo(QString name);
    //...
```

```
private:
    // ...
    QStandardItemModel *list_model;
```

The `list_model` field is used to provide data for the `QListView` object, `saved_list`. The `QListView` class is designed to follow the model/view pattern. In this pattern, the model that holds the data is separated from the view, which is in charge of representing the data. Therefore, we need a model to provide the data for it. In the body of the `MainWindow::initUI()` method, we add some code to set up the list for displaying the saved videos after we create `saved_list`:

```
// list of saved videos
saved_list = new QListView(this);
saved_list->setViewMode(QListView::IconMode);
saved_list->setResizeMode(QListView::Adjust);
saved_list->setSpacing(5);
saved_list->setWrapping(false);
list_model = new QStandardItemModel(this);
saved_list->setModel(list_model);
main_layout->addWidget(saved_list, 13, 0, 4, 1);
```

We set its view mode to `QListView::IconMode` to ensure that its items will be laid out using the `LeftToRight` flow with a large size. Then, we set its resize mode to `QListView::Adjust` to ensure that its items will be laid out every time the view is resized. The setting of spacing and wrapping are to ensure there are proper spaces between the items and that all the items will be placed in one row, no matter how many of them there are. After the list view is set up, we create the model and set it to the view.

The list view is set up, so let's move on to the slots. The `recordingStartStop` slot is for the `recordButton` push button. It is implemented as follows:

```
void MainWindow::recordingStartStop() {
    QString text = recordButton->text();
    if(text == "Record" && capturer != nullptr) {
        capturer->setVideoSavingStatus(CaptureThread::STARTING);
        recordButton->setText("Stop Recording");
    } else if(text == "Stop Recording" && capturer != nullptr) {
        capturer->setVideoSavingStatus(CaptureThread::STOPPING);
        recordButton->setText("Record");
    }
}
```

We check the text of the `recordButton` button and the capturing thread object. If the text is "Record" and the capturing thread is not null, we set the video saving status of the capturing thread to `CaptureThread::STARTING` to tell it to start the recording and set the text of `recordButton` to `Stop Recording`; if the text is `Stop Recording` and the capturing thread is not null, we set the video saving status of the capturing thread to `CaptureThread::STOPPING` to tell it to stop the recording and set the text of the `recordButton` back to `Record`. When this implementation is given, we can connect this slot to the `clicked` signal of `recordButton` once the button is created in the `MainWindow::initUI` method:

```
connect(recordButton, SIGNAL(clicked(bool)), this,
SLOT(recordingStartStop()));
```

Now, by clicking the **Record** button, we can start or stop recording a video. But in the main thread, how do we know that the recording has finished? Yes, we emit a signal when a video file is completely saved—the `CaptureThread::videoSaved` signal. The new `MainWindow::appendSavedVideo` slot is for this signal. Let's look at the implementation of this slot:

```
void MainWindow::appendSavedVideo(QString name)
{
    QString cover = Utilities::getSavedVideoPath(name, "jpg");
    QStandardItem *item = new QStandardItem();
    list_model->appendRow(item);
    QModelIndex index = list_model->indexFromItem(item);
    list_model->setData(index, QPixmap(cover).scaledToHeight(145),
Qt::DecorationRole);
    list_model->setData(index, name, Qt::DisplayRole);
    saved_list->scrollTo(index);
}
```

The slot is called with the video name, which is brought when the `CaptureThread::videoSaved` signal is emitted. In the method body, we generate the path of the cover image for the saved video by using our `Utilities` class. Then, we create a new `QStandardItem` object and append it to the model of the list view, `list_model`. A `QStandardItem` item is an item with a standard icon image and a string. Its icon is too small for our UI design, so we use an empty item as a placeholder, and then set a big image as the decoration data in its position later. To do so, after the empty item is appended, we find its index in the model, and then call the model's `setData` method to set a `QPixmap` object, which is constructed from the cover image and scaled to its proper size in the position that's indicated by the found index for the `Qt::DecorationRole` role. Similarly, we set the video name as the display data for the `Qt::DisplayRole` role in the same position. Finally, we tell the list view to scroll to the index of the newly added item.

The `MainWindow::appendSavedVideo` slot has been completed, so let's connect it to the `videoSaved` signal of the capturing thread in the `MainWindow::openCamera` method after the thread is created:

```
connect(capturer, &CaptureThread::videoSaved, this,
&MainWindow::appendSavedVideo);
```

Don't forget to disconnect them while stopping the existing capturing thread in the same method:

```
disconnect(capturer, &CaptureThread::videoSaved, this,
&MainWindow::appendSavedVideo);
```

Well, almost everything is done except for one thing: when we start our application, there may be many video files that were saved by our application the last time it ran. Therefore, we need to populate these files and let them show in the bottom list view. I have created a new method named `MainWindow::populateSavedList` to do this, and there's no new knowledge in its implementation, as you can see from the following list:

- Listing the video directory and finding all the cover files, which are for the work we did in `Chapter 2`, *Editing Images Like a Pro*, while we were loading plugins
- Appending each cover image to the bottom list view, which is what the `MainWindow::appendSavedVideo` method we just wrote does

I won't paste and explain the code of this method here; try to implement it by yourself. If help is needed, feel free to refer to the code in our accompanying GitHub repository.

Now, all the work regarding the code is done. Before compiling our application, we need to update our project file:

- Add the new source files.
- Add the `opencv_imgcodecs` OpenCV module to the `LIBS` setting, since the `imwrite` function we used to save the cover images is offered by that module.

The following code is what the changed lines of the project file look like the following:

```
# ...
    LIBS += -L/home/kdr2/programs/opencv/lib -lopencv_core -
lopencv_imgproc -lopencv_imgcodecs -lopencv_video -lopencv_videoio
    # ...
    # Input
    HEADERS += mainwindow.h capture_thread.h utilities.h
    SOURCES += main.cpp mainwindow.cpp capture_thread.cpp utilities.cpp
```

Finally, it's time to compile and run our application! The following screenshot shows what the application looks like after recording several video files:

In order to keep this chapter and the project simple and concise, we haven't provided a feature to play the saved videos in our application. If you want to play them, just use your favorite video player.

Motion analysis with OpenCV

In the previous sections, we built a complete application for playing and saving videos with our cameras. But for a **home security application**, that's not enough. We must know the situation at our home while something is happening there. This will be done by using the motion detection feature that's provided by OpenCV.

Motion detection with OpenCV

Usually, motion detection is done by the segmentation of background and foreground content in images. Because of that, while detecting motion, we usually assume that the background part of the given scene that appears in our camera is static and will not change over consecutive frames of the video. By analyzing these consecutive frames, we can extract the background of that scene in some way, and so the foreground can also be extracted. If some objects are found in the foreground, we can assume that motion is detected.

But this assumption is not always right in the real world—the sun rises and sets, the lights are on and off, and the shadows appear, move, and disappear. Any changes of these kind might change the background, so our algorithms depend on that assumption. Therefore, using fixed mounted cameras and controlled lighting conditions is always a prerequisite for building an accurate background/foreground segmentation system.

To make the implementation of our application simple, we will also assume that our webcams are fixed or mounted somewhere that has a stable lighting condition when it is in charge of the security of our home.

 In the territory of computer vision, the terminology background/foreground extraction, background subtraction, and background/foreground segmentation refers to the same technology that we are discussing. In this book, I will use them interchangeably.

In OpenCV, many algorithms are provided to do the background segmentation. Most of them are implemented as the subclasses of the BackgroundSubtractor class in the video module. We can find the class hierarchy at https://docs.opencv.org/4.0.0/d7/df6/ classcv_1_1BackgroundSubtractor.html. The following screenshot from that web page shows the relevant classes:

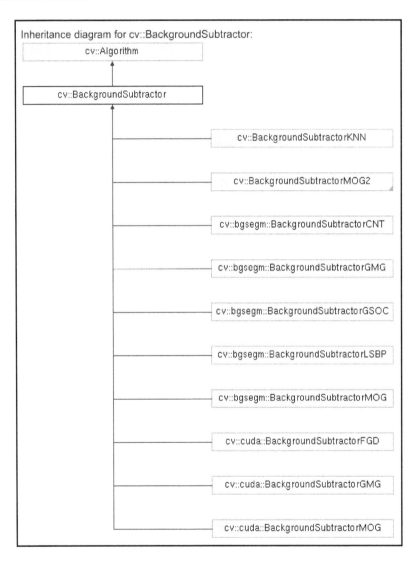

As we can see, there are 10 classes, of which 2 are in the OpenCV main module (the video module). The classes in the `cv::bgsegm` namespace are in the `bgsegm` extra module, while the classes in the `cv::cuda` namespace are in the `cudabgsegm` extra module. If you want to use the algorithms from the extra modules, you must ensure that these modules are properly configured while you build the OpenCV library. To do so, you should prepare the source directory of the extra module from `https://github.com/opencv/opencv_contrib`, and then pass the directory with the `-DOPENCV_EXTRA_MODULES_PATH` option to CMake while building OpenCV. In this section, we will use the `BackgroundSubtractorMOG2` class from the main OpenCV modules to keep things easy to learn. However, you are free to try any other algorithm implementations by yourself.

Let's start our work. First, we will open the `capture_thread.h` header file and add some new fields and methods:

```
public:
    // ...
    void setMotionDetectingStatus(bool status) {
        motion_detecting_status = status;
        motion_detected = false;
        if(video_saving_status != STOPPED) video_saving_status =
STOPPING;
    };
    // ...
private:
    void motionDetect(cv::Mat &frame);
    // ...
private:
    // ...
    // motion analysis
    bool motion_detecting_status;
    bool motion_detected;
    cv::Ptr<cv::BackgroundSubtractorMOG2> segmentor;
```

Let's look at the three fields first:

- `bool motion_detecting_status` is used to indicate whether our application is in charge of the security of our home. If true, the motion feature will be turned on; otherwise, our application is just a camera video player.
- `bool motion_detected` is used to save the state of whether the motion is detected in the last frame that's captured by the webcam.
- `cv::Ptr<cv::BackgroundSubtractorMOG2> segmentor`, obviously, is the subtractor instance that's used to detect motions in our video.

Now, let's look at the new methods:

- The `setMotionDetectingStatus` method is used to turn the motion detection feature on and off. Besides setting the value of the `motion_detecting_status` feature switch, we also reset the `motion_detected` flag and stop the video recording work if there is one. Please note this is an inline method, so we don't need implementation in other files.
- The `motionDetect` method will be called in the video capturing infinite loop on each frame to detect motions if the motion detection feature switch is turned on.

Now, let's go to the source file, `capture_thread.cpp`, to see what changes should be done there. First, we initialize the feature switch to false in the constructor:

```
motion_detecting_status = false;
```

Then, in the `CaptureThread::run` method, we create the subtractor instance after the camera is opened:

```
segmentor = cv::createBackgroundSubtractorMOG2(500, 16, true);
```

Three arguments are used to create the subtractor:

- This algorithm uses a sampling technique across the history of the pixels to create a sampled background image. The first argument is called `history` and we pass `500` as its value. This is used to define the number of previous frames that are used for sampling the background image.
- The second one, whose name is `dist2Threshold`, is the threshold of squared distance between a pixel's current value and its corresponding pixel value in the sampled background image.
- The third one, `detectShadows`, is used to determine whether the shadows are going to be detected during background segmentation or not.

After the subtractor is created, we call the new `motionDetect` method in the infinite loop:

```
if(motion_detecting_status) {
    motionDetect(tmp_frame);
}
```

This method call must be placed before the code of the video recording work because once we detect motion, we will turn on the video recording. The current frame should be in the recorded video.

For this class, the last thing is the implementation of the `motionDetect` method. This is the crucial part of the motion detection feature, so let's go through it in detail:

```
cv::Mat fgmask;
segmentor->apply(frame, fgmask);
if (fgmask.empty()) {
        return;
}
```

At the beginning of the method, in the preceding code, we create a new `Mat` instance to save the foreground mask. Then, we call the `apply` method of the `segmentor` subtractor with the captured frame and the foreground mask. Since this method is called on each captured frame, the subtractor will know about the scene and extract the background and foreground. After that, `fgmask` will be a grayscale image with the background filled black and the foreground part filled with non-block pixels.

Now that we have a grayscale foreground mask, let's do some image processing on it to remove noises and emphasize the objects that interest us:

```
cv::threshold(fgmask, fgmask, 25, 255, cv::THRESH_BINARY);

int noise_size = 9;
cv::Mat kernel = cv::getStructuringElement(cv::MORPH_RECT,
cv::Size(noise_size, noise_size));
cv::erode(fgmask, fgmask, kernel);
kernel = cv::getStructuringElement(cv::MORPH_RECT,
cv::Size(noise_size, noise_size));
cv::dilate(fgmask, fgmask, kernel, cv::Point(-1,-1), 3);
```

In the preceding code, we use the `threshold` function to filter out the pixels with values that are too small. This step will remove the dark noises from our foreground mask. Then, we perform an operation, typically called image opening, which erodes then dilates the mask with a certain kernel size. This step will remove the noise of whose size is less than the kernel size. We can adjust the value of `noise_size` to cope with different scenarios; for example, use a small value for long distance motion detection and a big value for close-up motion detection.

With the noises removed, we can find the contours of objects in the foreground mask by calling the `findContours` method:

```
vector<vector<cv::Point> > contours;
cv::findContours(fgmask, contours, cv::RETR_TREE,
cv::CHAIN_APPROX_SIMPLE);
```

More than one contour may be found, and each contour is described by a series of points. Once we find one or more contours in the mask, we can assume that motion is detected:

```
bool has_motion = contours.size() > 0;
if(!motion_detected && has_motion) {
    motion_detected = true;
    setVideoSavingStatus(STARTING);
    qDebug() << "new motion detected, should send a
notification.";
} else if (motion_detected && !has_motion) {
    motion_detected = false;
    setVideoSavingStatus(STOPPING);
    qDebug() << "detected motion disappeared.";
}
```

In the preceding code, if no motion is detected in the last frame but one or more are detected in the current frame, we can say that a new motion is detected; then, we can start to record video from the camera and tell someone that something is happening. On the other hand, when there is no motion being detected in the current frame but one or more are detected in the last one, we can say that the motion has gone and, hence, we stop the video recording.

Finally, we find a bounding rectangle for each contour we find in the mask and then draw it on the capture frame to emphasize what we found:

```
cv::Scalar color = cv::Scalar(0, 0, 255); // red
for(size_t i = 0; i < contours.size(); i++) {
    cv::Rect rect = cv::boundingRect(contours[i]);
    cv::rectangle(frame, rect, color, 1);
}
```

OK, the work of motion detection is done. Considering that this process is a bit abstract, we can save the captured frame, the extracted foreground mask, the mask with noises removed, and the frame with rectangles drawn to our hard disk as images. The following diagram shows the images I saved when a small dumpster passed among several vehicles:

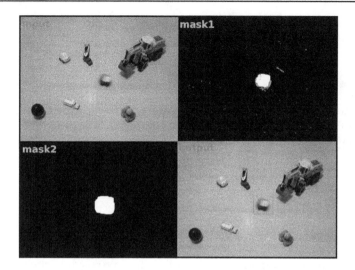

The preceding diagram contains four labeled images corresponding to the stages we mentioned:

- **input** is the origin captured frame.
- **mask1** is the foreground mask that's extracted by our subtractor.
- **mask2** is the foreground mask with noises removed.
- **output** is the frame with rectangles drawn.

Hopefully, with these images, you can easily understand how motion detection works.

The work in the capturing thread is done, so let's move on to the UI. Remember the checkbox we placed on the operation area of the main window? It's time to add a slot for it. In the `mainwindow.h` header file, we declare a new slot in the private slots section for it:

```
private slots:
    // ...
    void updateMonitorStatus(int status);
```

Then, we implement it in the `mainwindow.cpp` source file:

```
void MainWindow::updateMonitorStatus(int status)
{
    if(capturer == nullptr) {
        return;
    }
    if(status) {
        capturer->setMotionDetectingStatus(true);
        recordButton->setEnabled(false);
```

```
    } else {
        capturer->setMotionDetectingStatus(false);
        recordButton->setEnabled(true);
    }
}
```

In this slot, we return from the method immediately if the capturing thread is null; otherwise, we set the motion detecting status of the capturing thread on or off, according to the new status of the checkbox. Also, if motion detecting is turned on, we disable the recording button to avoid having the manually started recording process interfering with the automatically started one when motions are detected. Once this slot is ready, we can connect it to the checkbox after the creation of that checkbox in the initUI method:

```
connect(monitorCheckBox, SIGNAL(stateChanged(int)), this,
    SLOT(updateMonitorStatus(int)));
```

Besides this slot, there are some other trivial things to do regarding the status of the monitor status checkbox and the recording button:

- In the slot of the recording button, in the MainWindow::recordingStartStop method, we should disable the checkbox while starting to recording a video and enable it while the recording process is stopped. This is also to avoid having the manually started recording process interfering with the auto started one when motions are detected.
- In the MainWindow::openCamera method, after a new capturing thread is created, we should make sure that the checkbox is unchecked and that the **Record** button is enabled with its text as Record.

I haven't pasted the code of these changes here because they are very trivial—you should be able to do them by yourself or directly refer to the code in our code repository if you need help.

Now, the motion detecting feature is complete, so we can compile the application and try it. The following screenshot shows how it works on my scene of toy vehicles:

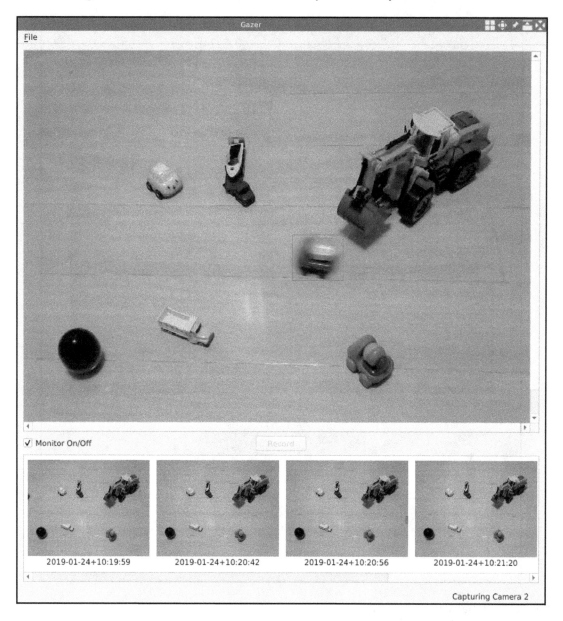

The toy vehicles are a close-up scene. For a long distance scene, which, for me, is outside my office, I change `noise_size` to 4. I get the following output:

You can see many rectangles around the people who are walking in the park and the cars that are being driven on the road across the park.

Sending notifications to our mobile phone

In the preceding section, we finished the motion detecting feature. But when it detects motion, besides saving a video of that motion, it only prints a message. As a home security application, this isn't enough. We need to know when motion has been detected, regardless of where we are or what we are doing. In this section, we will do this by sending notifications to our mobile phone through the IFTTT service.

IFTTT is a platform that connects many useful services. You can connect two chosen services by creating an IFTTT applet, one called **this** and another called **that**. If an event occurs on the side of **this**, the service will be triggered. This is what **IFTTT** means: **if this then that**.

To use IFTTT to send notifications, we need an IFTTT account, which can be made at `https://ifttt.com`. With an account, we can create an applet with a webhook as its **this** service and the mobile phone notification service as the **that** service. Let's create the applet step by step. There are eight steps in total to create an applet; the following screenshot shows the first four:

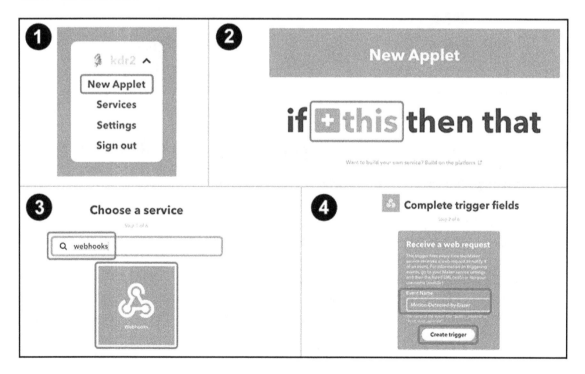

Here are the last four steps:

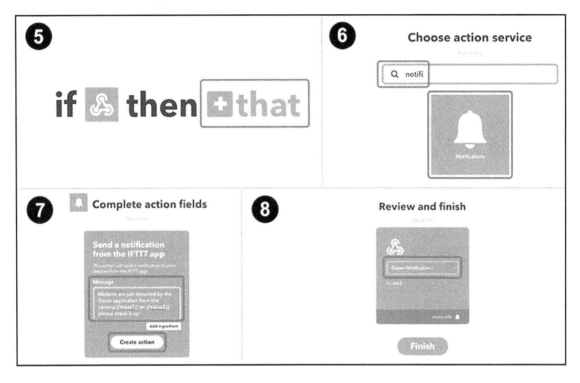

We need to take some actions at every step:

1. Log in, click your username in the top-right, and then click **New Applet** in the drop-down menu.
2. Click on the blue **+this** link.
3. On the **Choose a service** page, type `webhooks` into the textbox and click on the **Webhooks** square. Then, select **Receive a web request** on the next page.
4. On the **Complete trigger fields** page, type `Motion-Detected-by-Gazer` as the event name, and then click the **Create trigger** button.
5. Click the **+that** link on the new page.
6. On the **Choose action service** page, type `notifi` in the textbox and select the **Notifications** square, and then choose **Send a notification from the IFTTT app** on the next page.

7. On the **Complete action fields** page, you will find a text area. Type `Motions are just detected by the Gazer application from the camera {{Value1}} on {{Value2}}, please check it up!` into the text area and click the **Create action** button.

8. On the **Review and finish** page, name the applet and click on the **Finish** button. I named it `Gazer Notification`, but you can choose any name you want.

Now that the applet has been created, let's find the endpoint of the webhook on IFTTT:

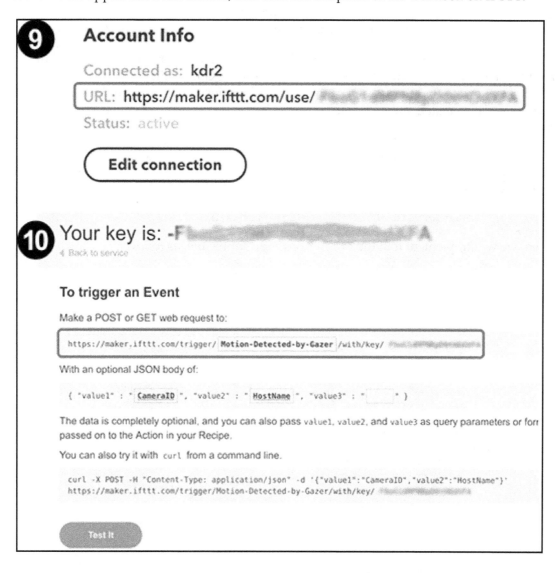

Go to the settings page of the webhook service on IFTTT. You can find the page by visiting `https://ifttt.com/services/maker_webhooks/settings` in your browser. On this page, you will find information like *step 9* shows in the previous screenshot. Copy the URL on that page and visit it—you will be navigated to a page like the one *step 10* shows. This page shows us how can we trigger the webhook. You may notice that there is a textbox in the URL on this page. Type the event name we used when we created the applet, `Motion-Detected-by-Gazer`, into it. By doing this, you will get a full URL—the endpoint of the webhook. It looks like `https://maker.ifttt.com/trigger/Motion-Detected-by-Gazer/with/key/-YOUR _KEY`. Please remember this endpoint, as we will be making a web request to it soon.

Now that we've created our account on IFTTT, we need to install the IFTTT app on our mobile phone. We can search on the Apple App Store or Google Play with the `IFTTT` keyword to find the app. Once the app has been installed, we should log in with the account we just created and enable its notifications on our phone so that we can receive them.

Now, let's go back to our application so that we can learn how we can make a request to that endpoint. We will do this in our `Utilities` class. In the `utilities.h` header file, we add a new static method:

```
static void notifyMobile(int cameraID);
```

Then, we will implement it in the `utilities.cpp` source file, as follows:

```
void Utilities::notifyMobile(int cameraID)
{
    // CHANGE endpoint TO YOURS HERE:
    QString endpoint = "https://maker.ifttt.com/trigger/...";
    QNetworkRequest request = QNetworkRequest(QUrl(endpoint));
    request.setHeader(QNetworkRequest::ContentTypeHeader,
"application/json");
    QJsonObject json;
    json.insert("value1", QString("%1").arg(cameraID));
    json.insert("value2", QHostInfo::localHostName());
    QNetworkAccessManager nam;
    QNetworkReply *rep = nam.post(request,
QJsonDocument(json).toJson());
    while(!rep->isFinished()) {
        QApplication::processEvents();
    }
    rep->deleteLater();
}
```

In this method, we create a QNetworkRequest object and set its content type header as "application/json" as IFTTT requires. Then, we construct the JSON that we will post to the webhook. Remember the message we typed in *step 7* while creating the applet? In that message, the {{Value1}} and {{Value2}} strings are placeholders, and they will be replaced by the value1 and value2 fields in the JSON that we post. Here, we use the camera index as the value of value1 and the hostname as the value of value2. Then, we create a network access manager and fire the POST request by calling its post method with the request object and the JSON object. The last thing we need to do is wait for the request to complete. When it's done, we tell Qt to delete the reply object in the next round of the event loop by calling its deleteLater method.

Let's call this method when motion is detected. Firing a web request and waiting for it to complete is a very slow process, so we can't do it in the capturing thread. If we do, it will block the video frames from being processed. Fortunately, Qt provides a way to run a function is another thread:

```
if(!motion_detected && has_motion) {
    motion_detected = true;
    setVideoSavingStatus(STARTING);
    qDebug() << "new motion detected, should send a
notification.";
    QtConcurrent::run(Utilities::notifyMobile, cameraID);
} else if (motion_detected && !has_motion) {
    // ...
```

As you can see, by using the QtConcurrent::run function, we can easily run a function in a thread that is picked up from the thread pool that is provided by the Qt library.

For this feature, we import two new Qt modules into our project: the network module and the concurrent module. Before we compile our project, we must tell the build system about that in our project file:

```
QT += core gui multimedia network concurrent
```

Now, we will compile our project and run the application, and then install the IFTTT app on our mobile phone. When a motion is detected, a notification will be received on our mobile phone. Mine looks like this:

 Don't forget to install the IFTTT app on your mobile phone and enable the notifications for it, and then log in with your IFTTT account. Otherwise, the notification won't be received.

Summary

In this chapter, we created a new desktop application, the Gazer, for capturing, playing, and saving videos from our cameras. For home security purposes, we also added a feature for motion detection. We built the UI with Qt and developed the video processing features with OpenCV. These two parts were integrated into our application organically. In the development of this application, we learned about how to use the Qt layout system to arrange the widgets on the UI, how to use multithreading technology to do slow work in a thread that differs from the main UI thread, how to detect motion using OpenCV, and how to send notifications to our mobile phone via IFTTT by firing a HTTP request.

In the next chapter, we will learn how to recognize faces in images or videos in real time, and we will build an interesting application so that we can put funny masks on the detected faces.

Questions

Try these questions to test your knowledge of this chapter:

1. Can we detect motions from a video file instead of a camera? How can we do that?
2. Can we do the motion detecting work in a thread that differs from the video capturing thread? Why or why not?
3. IFTTT allows you to include images in the notifications it sends—How could we send an image with the motion we detected while sending notifications to your mobile phone via this feature of IFTTT?

4
Fun with Faces

In Chapter 3, *Home Security Applications*, we created a new application named **Gazer**, with which we can capture video and detect motion from the webcams attached to our computers. In this chapter, we will continue playing with our webcams—instead of detecting motion, we will create a new application that is able to detect faces using our camera. First, we will detect the faces in our webcams. Then, we will detect the facial landmarks on the detected faces. With these facial landmarks, we can know where the eyes, the nose, the mouth, and the cheeks are on each detected face so that we can apply some funny masks onto the faces.

The following topics will be covered in this chapter:

- Taking photos from webcams
- Detecting faces using OpenCV
- Detecting facial landmarks using OpenCV
- The resource system of the Qt library
- Applying masks on faces

Technical requirements

As we saw in the previous chapters, users are required to have at least Qt version 5 installed and have basic knowledge of C++ and Qt programming. Also, the latest version of OpenCV, 4.0, should be correctly installed. Additionally, besides the core and imgproc modules, the video and videoio modules of OpenCV will also be used in this chapter. If you have been through the previous chapters, then these requirements will have already been met.

We will use some pretrained machine learning models provided by OpenCV to detect faces and facial landmarks, so it is better if you have some basic knowledge of machine learning technology. Some of these machine learning models are from the extra modules of the OpenCV library, so the extra modules of OpenCV must also be installed along with the core modules. If you are not sure about this, don't worry, we will install the extra OpenCV modules step by step before we use them in this chapter.

All the code of this chapter can be found in our code repository at `https://github.com/PacktPublishing/Qt-5-and-OpenCV-4-Computer-Vision-Projects/tree/master/Chapter-04`.

Check out the following video to see the code in action: `http://bit.ly/2FfQOmr`

The Facetious application

Since the application we are going to create in this chapter will give us a lot of fun by applying funny masks onto detected faces in real time, I name the application **Facetious**. The first thing that the Facetious application could do is open a webcam and play the video feed from it. That is the work we had done in our Gazer application, which was built by us in the preceding chapter. So here, I will borrow the skeleton of the Gazer application as the basis of our new application. The plan is, first, we make a copy of Gazer, rename it to `Facetious`, delete the features about motion detecting and change the video recording feature into a new feature of photo taking. By doing so, we will get a simple and clean application onto which we can add our new features of faces and facial landmark detecting.

From Gazer to Facetious

Let's start by copying the source of the Gazer application:

```
$ mkdir Chapter-04
$ cp -r Chapter-03/Gazer Chapter-04/Facetious
$ ls Chapter-04
Facetious
$ cd Chapter-04/Facetious
$ make clean
$ rm -f Gazer
$ rm -f Makefile
```

With these commands, we copy the `Gazer` directory under the `Chapter-03` directory to `Chapter-04/Facetious`. Then, we enter that directory, run `make clean` to clean all the intermediate files generated in the compiling process, and remove the old target executable file using `rm -f Gazer`.

Now, let's rename and clean the project file by file.

First is the `Gazer.pro` project file. We rename it to `Facetious.pro`, and then open it with an editor to edit its content. In the editor, we change the value of the `TARGET` key from `Gazer` to `Facetious`, remove the Qt modules, network and concurrent, which we won't use in this new application, from the value of the `QT` key, and then delete the relevant `GAZER_USE_QT_CAMERA` lines at the end of the files. The changed lines in `Facetious.pro` are listed as follows:

```
TARGET = Facetious
# ...
QT += core gui multimedia
# ...
# the below lines are deleted in this update:
# Using OpenCV or QCamera
# DEFINES += GAZER_USE_QT_CAMERA=1
# QT += multimediawidgets
```

Next is the `main.cpp` file. This file is simple since we just change the window title from `Gazer` to `Facetious`:

```
window.setWindowTitle("Facetious");
```

Next is the `capture_thread.h` file. In this file, we delete many fields and methods from the `CaptureThread` class. The fields that will be deleted include the following:

```
// FPS calculating
bool fps_calculating;
int fps;

// video saving
// int frame_width, frame_height; // notice: we keep this line
VideoSavingStatus video_saving_status;
QString saved_video_name;
cv::VideoWriter *video_writer;

// motion analysis
bool motion_detecting_status;
bool motion_detected;
cv::Ptr<cv::BackgroundSubtractorMOG2> segmentor;
```

The methods in this class that will be deleted are as follows:

```
    void startCalcFPS() {...};
    void setVideoSavingStatus(VideoSavingStatus status) {...};
    void setMotionDetectingStatus(bool status) {...};
// ...
signals:
    // ...
    void fpsChanged(int fps);
    void videoSaved(QString name);

private:
    void calculateFPS(cv::VideoCapture &cap);
    void startSavingVideo(cv::Mat &firstFrame);
    void stopSavingVideo();
    void motionDetect(cv::Mat &frame);
```

The `enum VideoSavingStatus` type is not needed anymore either, so we will delete it as well.

OK, the `capture_thread.h` file is cleaned, so let's move on to
the `capture_thread.cpp` file. According to the changes in the header file, we should do
the following first:

- In the constructors, delete the initialization of the fields that we have deleted in the header file.
- Delete the implementations of the methods (including slots) that we deleted in the header file.
- In the implementation of the `run` method, delete all the code about video saving, motion detecting, and **frames per second** (**FPS**) calculating.

OK, all code about video saving, motion detecting, and FPS calculating is removed from the capturing thread. Now let's see the next file, `mainwindow.h`. In this chapter, we will still use OpenCV to do the video capturing work, so first, let's remove the code between the `#ifdef GAZER_USE_QT_CAMERA` and `#endif` lines. There are two blocks of this kind of code and we remove both of them. Then, we delete many methods and fields, most of which are also about video saving, motion detecting, and FPS calculating. These fields and methods are as follows:

```
    void calculateFPS();
    void updateFPS(int);
    void recordingStartStop();
    void appendSavedVideo(QString name);
    void updateMonitorStatus(int status);
```

```
private:
    // ...
    QAction *calcFPSAction;
    // ...
    QCheckBox *monitorCheckBox;
    QPushButton *recordButton;
```

Please notice that the `appendSavedVideo` method and the `QPushButton *recordButton` field are not really deleted. We rename them `appendSavedPhoto` and `QPushButton *shutterButton`, respectively:

```
void appendSavedPhoto(QString name);
// ...
QPushButton *shutterButton;
```

This is the preparation for taking photos in our new application—as we have said, in Facetious, we don't record video, but only take photos.

Then, in the `mainwindow.cpp` file, similar to what we do with its header file, first, we remove the code between the `#ifdef GAZER_USE_QT_CAMERA` and `#else` lines. There are also two blocks of this kind to be removed; don't forget to remove the `#endif` line for each of these blocks. After that, we remove the implementations of the five deleted methods:

- `void calculateFPS();`
- `void updateFPS(int);`
- `void recordingStartStop();`
- `void appendSavedVideo(QString name);`
- `void updateMonitorStatus(int status);`

Most of the deletion is done, but there is still much work to do for the `MainWindow` class. Let's start with the user interface. In the `MainWindow::initUI` method, we remove the code about the monitor status checkbox, the record button, and the placeholder beside the record button and then create the new shutter button:

```
shutterButton = new QPushButton(this);
shutterButton->setText("Take a Photo");
tools_layout->addWidget(shutterButton, 0, 0, Qt::AlignHCenter);
```

With the previous code, we make the shutter button the only child widget of `tools_layout` and ensure that the button is centrally aligned.

Then, after creating the status bar, we change the startup message on the status bar to
`Facetious is Ready`:

```
mainStatusLabel->setText("Facetious is Ready");
```

Next is the `MainWindow::createActions` method. In this method, the changes we should
implement are to delete the code about the `calcFPSAction` action, including the creation
and the signal slot connection.

Then, in the `MainWindow::openCamera` method, we delete all the code about the FPS
calculating and the video saving, most of which are signal slot connecting and
disconnecting. The code about the checkbox and push button at the end of this method
should also be deleted.

The last things we should do about this file are to give the newly
added `appendSavedPhoto` method an empty implementation and to empty the body of
the `populateSavedList` method. We will give them their new implementations in the
following subsection:

```
void MainWindow::populateSavedList()
{
    // TODO
}

void MainWindow::appendSavedPhoto(QString name)
{
    // TODO
}
```

It's the turn of the `utilities.h` and `utilities.cpp` files now. In the header file, we
remove the `notifyMobile` method and rename the `newSavedVideoName` and
`getSavedVideoPath` methods to `newPhotoName` and `getPhotoPath`, respectively:

```
public:
    static QString getDataPath();
    static QString newPhotoName();
    static QString getPhotoPath(QString name, QString postfix);
```

In the `utilities.cpp` file, besides renaming and deleting according to the changes in the
header file, we also change the implementation of the `getDataPath` method:

```
QString Utilities::getDataPath()
{
    QString user_pictures_path =
QStandardPaths::standardLocations(QStandardPaths::PicturesLocation)[0];
    QDir pictures_dir(user_pictures_path);
```

```
        pictures_dir.mkpath("Facetious");
        return pictures_dir.absoluteFilePath("Facetious");
    }
```

The most important change of it is that now we use
`QStandardPaths::PicturesLocation` instead
of `QStandardPaths::MoviesLocation` to obtain the standard directory for photos rather
than for videos.

Now, by abridging the Gazer application, we have successfully got the basis of our new
Facetious application. Let's try to compile and run it:

```
$ qmake -makefile
$ make
g++ -c #...
# output truncated
$ export LD_LIBRARY_PATH=/home/kdr2/programs/opencv/lib
$ ./Facetious
```

If all goes well, you will see a blank window that is very similar to Gazer's main window.
All the code changes of this subsection can be found in a single Git commit at https://
github.com/PacktPublishing/Qt-5-and-OpenCV-4-Computer-Vision-Projects/commit/
0587c55e4e8e175b70f8046ddd4d67039b431b54. If you have trouble finishing this
subsection, feel free to refer to that commit.

Taking photos

In the preceding subsection, we set up the basis of our new application, Facetious, by
removing the video saving and motion detecting features from the Gazer application. We
also placed some stubs of photo taking in a new application. In this subsection, we will
complete the photo taking feature.

Compared to the video recording feature, photo taking is much simpler. First, in
the `capture_thread.h` header file, we add a field and many methods to
the `CaptureThread` class:

```
    public:
        // ...
        void takePhoto() {taking_photo = true; }
        // ...
    signals:
        // ...
        void photoTaken(QString name);
```

```
private:
    void takePhoto(cv::Mat &frame);

private:
    // ...
    // take photos
    bool taking_photo;
```

The `bool taking_photo` field is the flag that indicates whether the capturing thread should save the current frame as a photo on the hard disk, and the `void takePhoto()` public inline method is for setting this flag to true. We will call this method in the main thread when the user clicks the shutter button on the main window. The `void photoTaken(QString name)` signal will be emitted after each time a photo is taken and the Qt meta-object system will take care of its implementation. The `void takePhoto(cv::Mat &frame)` private method is the one that is in charge of saving a frame as a photo on the disk, and it is the only method to which we need give an implementation in the `capture_thread.cpp` source file. Let's see its implementation:

```cpp
void CaptureThread::takePhoto(cv::Mat &frame)
{
    QString photo_name = Utilities::newPhotoName();
    QString photo_path = Utilities::getPhotoPath(photo_name, "jpg");
    cv::imwrite(photo_path.toStdString(), frame);
    emit photoTaken(photo_name);
    taking_photo = false;
}
```

In the body of the method, we use the functions we had written in the `Utilities` class to generate a new name and obtain a path for the photo we are going to save with the generated name and `jpg` as the extension name. Then, we use the `imwrite` function from the OpenCV's `imgcodecs` module to write the frame as a JPEG image file onto the disk with the specified path. After the photo is saved, we emit the `photoTaken` signal with the photo name. If someone is interested in this signal, they must connect a slot to it and the slot will be called at the moment when the signal is emitted. At the end of the method body, we set the `taking_photo` flag back to `false`.

With the `CaptureThread::takePhoto(cv::Mat &frame)` method being implemented, let's call it in the capturing infinite loop in the `CaptureThread::run()` method:

```cpp
if(taking_photo) {
    takePhoto(tmp_frame);
}
```

In this piece of code, we check the `taking_photo` flag to see whether we should take a photo. If it's true, we call the `takePhoto(cv::Mat &frame)` method to save the current frame as a photo. This piece of code must be placed after `tmp_frame` passes the non-empty check and before the color order of that frame is converted from BGR to RGB, to ensure that it is a proper frame in proper color order, which can be passed to the `imwrite` function.

The last thing to do with the `CaptureThread` class is to initialize the `taking_photo` flag to `false` in its constructors.

Now, let's move on to the user interface. First, we add a new private slot to the `MainWindow` class in `mainwindow.h`:

```
private slots:
    // ...
    void takePhoto();
```

This slot will be connected to a signal of the shutter button. Let's see its implementation in the `mainwindow.cpp` source file:

```
void MainWindow::takePhoto()
{
    if(capturer != nullptr) {
        capturer->takePhoto();
    }
}
```

It's simple. In this method, we call the `void takePhoto()` method of the `CaptureThread` instance, `capturer`, to tell it to take a photo if it is not null. Then, in the `MainWindow::initUI()` method, after the creation of the shutter button, we connect this slot to the `clicked` signal of `shutterButton`:

```
connect(shutterButton, SIGNAL(clicked(bool)), this,
SLOT(takePhoto()));
```

With the work we have previously done, we can now tell the capturing thread to take a photo. But when the photo is taken, how does the main window know that? It's done by the connection between the `CaptureThread::photoTaken` signal and the `MainWindow::appendSavedPhoto` slot. We make this connection after the capturing thread instance is created in the `MainWindow::openCamera()` method:

```
connect(capturer, &CaptureThread::photoTaken, this,
&MainWindow::appendSavedPhoto);
```

Also, don't forget to disconnect them before the capturing thread instance that has been closed in the same method:

```
            disconnect(capturer, &CaptureThread::photoTaken, this,
    &MainWindow::appendSavedPhoto);
```

Now, let's see what the `MainWindow::appendSavedPhoto(QString name)` slot does. In the preceding subsection, we just gave it an empty body. Now it has to take its responsibility:

```
    void MainWindow::appendSavedPhoto(QString name)
    {
        QString photo_path = Utilities::getPhotoPath(name, "jpg");
        QStandardItem *item = new QStandardItem();
        list_model->appendRow(item);
        QModelIndex index = list_model->indexFromItem(item);
        list_model->setData(index,
    QPixmap(photo_path).scaledToHeight(145), Qt::DecorationRole);
        list_model->setData(index, name, Qt::DisplayRole);
        saved_list->scrollTo(index);
    }
```

What it does is very similar to what we did when we appended the cover image of a newly recorded video to the saved video list in the Gazer application in Chapter 3, *Home Security Applications*. Thus, I will not explain this piece of code line by line here.

There is another method, `MainWindow::populateSavedList()`, which is used to populate all the photos we had taken in the saved photos list while the application is starting up, to be implemented. This method is also very similar to the one we used to populate the saved videos in the Gazer application, so I leave it up to you to implement it. If you have any trouble, you can refer to the accompanying code repository of this book on GitHub. All the changes in this subsection can be found in this commit: https://github.com/PacktPublishing/Qt-5-and-OpenCV-4-Computer-Vision-Projects/commit/744d445ad4c834cd52660a85a224e48279ac2cf4.

Now, let's compile and run our application again. After the application reveals its main window, we can click the **Open Camera** action under the **File** menu to open the camera, and then click the shutter button to take some photos. After these actions, my main window looks like the following screenshot:

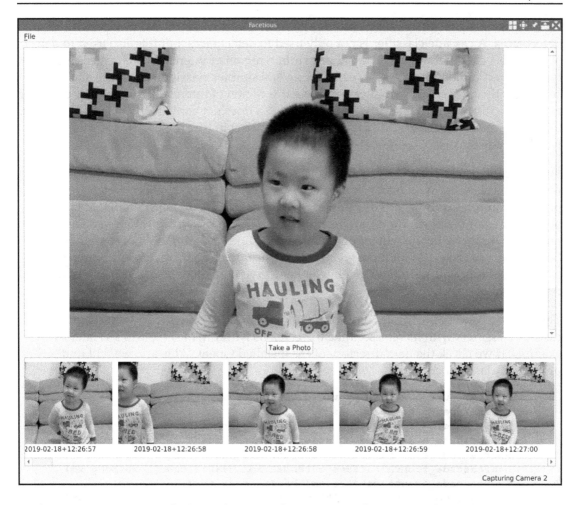

In this section, we set up the basic features of our new application. In the next section, we will use OpenCV to detect faces in the captured frames in real time.

Detecting faces using cascade classifiers

In the preceding section, we created our new application, Facetious, with which we can play the video feed from our camera and take photos. In this section, we will add a new feature to it—detecting faces in videos in real time by using the OpenCV library.

We will use some facilities called **cascade classifiers**, which are offered by OpenCV, to detect faces. A cascade classifier is not only used to detect faces, but it is also used to detect objects. As a classifier, it tells us whether a certain region of interest in an image is a certain type of object or not. The classifier contains several simpler classifiers or stages and subsequently applies these simpler classifiers to a region of interest. If any simpler classifier gives a negative result, we say the region of interest does not contain any objects of interest. Otherwise, if all stages pass, we say we found the object in that region. This is what the word cascade means.

Before a cascade classifier is ready for use, it must be trained first. In the training process, we feed the classifier with many sample views of a certain kind of object, which are called positive examples, and negative examples, many images that do not contain that kind of object. For example, if we want the cascade classifier to help us to detect human faces, we must prepare many images containing human faces and many images not containing human faces to train it. With these given positive examples and negative examples, the cascade classifier will learn how to tell whether a given region of an image contains a certain kind of object.

The training process is complex, but fortunately, OpenCV delivers many pretrained cascade classifiers with its release. Take the **Haar classifier**, which we will use later as an example. If we check the data directory of the installed OpenCV library, we will find lots of pretrained classifier data in it:

```
# if you use a system provided OpenCV, the path is
/usr/share/opencv/haarcascades
$ ls /home/kdr2/programs/opencv/share/opencv4/haarcascades/
haarcascade_eye_tree_eyeglasses.xml haarcascade_lefteye_2splits.xml
haarcascade_eye.xml haarcascade_licence_plate_rus_16stages.xml
haarcascade_frontalcatface_extended.xml haarcascade_lowerbody.xml
haarcascade_frontalcatface.xml haarcascade_profileface.xml
haarcascade_frontalface_alt2.xml haarcascade_righteye_2splits.xml
haarcascade_frontalface_alt_tree.xml
haarcascade_russian_plate_number.xml
haarcascade_frontalface_alt.xml haarcascade_smile.xml
haarcascade_frontalface_default.xml haarcascade_upperbody.xml
haarcascade_fullbody.xml
```

We can easily distinguish the pretrained data files by their names. The filenames containing `frontalface` are what we need for face detection.

With this knowledge about object detection, especially about face detection, let's now go back to our application to detect the faces from our video feed.

First, we should update our `Facetious.pro` project file:

```
# ...
unix: !mac {
    INCLUDEPATH += /home/kdr2/programs/opencv/include/opencv4
    LIBS += -L/home/kdr2/programs/opencv/lib -lopencv_core -
lopencv_imgproc -lopencv_imgcodecs -lopencv_video -lopencv_videoio -
lopencv_objdetect
}

# ...
DEFINES +=
OPENCV_DATA_DIR=\\\"/home/kdr2/programs/opencv/share/opencv4/\\\"
#...
```

In the configuration for the `LIBS` key, we append the `opencv_objdetect` OpenCV module to its value because the feature of object detection, including face detection, which we are going to use, is offered by this OpenCV core module. The second part of the changes is a macro definition that defines the data directory of our OpenCV installation. We will use this macro to load the pretrained classifier data in our code.

Then, let's go to the `capture_thread.h` header file. We add a private method and a private member field to the `CaptureThread` class in this file:

```
#include "opencv2/objdetect.hpp"
//...

private:
    // ...
    void detectFaces(cv::Mat &frame);

private:
    // ...

    // face detection
    cv::CascadeClassifier *classifier;
```

Obviously, the member field is the cascade classifier that we will use to detect faces, and the work of face detecting will be done in the newly added `detectFaces` method.

Now, let's go to the `capture_thread.cpp` source file to see how we would use the cascade classifier there. First, we update the body of the `CaptureThread::run` method:

```
        classifier = new cv::CascadeClassifier(OPENCV_DATA_DIR
    "haarcascades/haarcascade_frontalface_default.xml");

        while(running) {
            cap >> tmp_frame;
            if (tmp_frame.empty()) {
                break;
            }

            detectFaces(tmp_frame);
            // ...
        }
        cap.release();
        delete classifier;
        classifier = nullptr;
```

After entering this method and opening the webcam, we create a `cv::CascadeClassifier` instance and assign it to the `classifier` member field. While creating the instance, we pass the pretrained classifier data path to the constructor. The path is constructed with the `OPENCV_DATA_DIR` macro, which is defined in the project file by us. Also, we use the `haarcascades/haarcascade_frontalface_default.xml` file under the OpenCV data directory to create the classifier for face detecting.

In the infinite loop in the `run` method, we call the newly added `detectFaces` method with the frame that we just captured from the opened webcam.

After the infinite loop ends, before the capturing threads exit, we do the cleaning work, release the opened camera, delete the classifier, and set it to null.

At last, let's see the implementation of the `detectFaces` method:

```
void CaptureThread::detectFaces(cv::Mat &frame)
{
    vector<cv::Rect> faces;
    cv::Mat gray_frame;
    cv::cvtColor(frame, gray_frame, cv::COLOR_BGR2GRAY);
    classifier->detectMultiScale(gray_frame, faces, 1.3, 5);

    cv::Scalar color = cv::Scalar(0, 0, 255); // red
    for(size_t i = 0; i < faces.size(); i++) {
        cv::rectangle(frame, faces[i], color, 1);
    }
}
```

In the body of this method, we first declare a `cv::Rect` vector for saving the circumscribed rectangles of the faces that will be detected. Next, we convert the input frame to a grayscale image because the face detecting process has nothing to do with the features of RGB colors. Then, we call the `detectMultiScale` method of classifier. The first argument of this method is the gray scaled input frame in which we want to detect faces. The second argument is the reference to the rectangle vector, which is used to save the circumscribed rectangles of the detected faces we just defined. The third argument is for specifying how much the image size is reduced at each image scale, which is made to compensate for a false perception of the size that occurs when one face appears to be bigger than the other simply because it is closer to the camera. This detection algorithm uses a moving window to detect objects; the fourth argument is for defining how many objects are found near the current one before it can declare the face to be found.

After the `detectMultiScale` method returns, we will get all the regions of the detected faces in our `faces` vector, and then we draw these rectangles on the captured frame with one-pixel red borders.

OK, the feature for face detecting is done now, so let's compile and run our project. When someone enters the eyeshot of the opened webcam, you will see a red rectangle around their face:

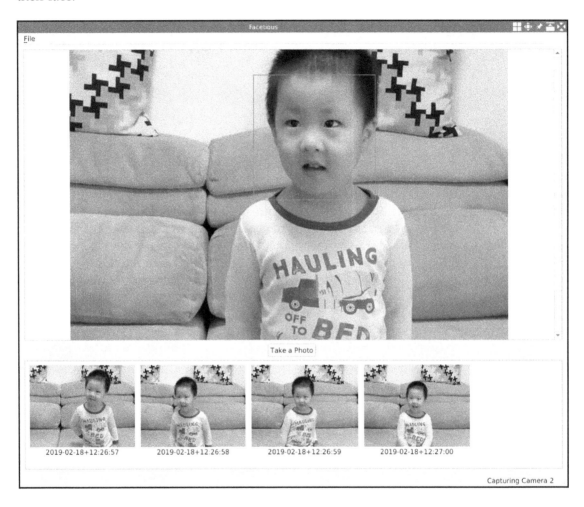

In our code, when we created the cascade classifier, we used the `haarcascade_frontalface_default.xml` file. But you may notice that when we list the data directory of the OpenCV installation, there is more than one file whose name indicates it is for front face detection, such as `haarcascade_frontalface_alt.xml`, `haarcascade_frontalface_alt2.xml`, or `haarcascade_frontalface_alt_tree.xml`. Why do we choose `haarcascade_frontalface.xml` but not others? This pretrained model data is trained on different datasets or with a different configuration. The details are documented in these XML files as comments at the beginning of each file, so you can refer to the document there if you want. Another straightforward way to choose the model file is to try all of them, test them on your dataset, calculate the precision and the recall rate, and then choose the best one for your case.

Except for the Haar cascade classifier, there is also another cascade classifier named the **local binary pattern** (**LBP**) cascade classifier, which is shipped with the OpenCV release by default. You can find its trained model data under the `lbpcascades` directory in the data path of the OpenCV installation. The LBP cascade classifier is faster then Haar, but also has less precision. We can compare them with the following table:

Algorithm	Advantages	Disadvantages
HAAR	High detection accuracy; Low false positive rate;	Computationally complex and slow; Longer training time; Less accurate on black faces; Limitations in difficult lightening conditions; Less robust to occlusion;
LBP	Computationally simple and fast; Shorter training time; Robust to local illumination changes; Robust to occlusion;	Less accurate; High false positive rate;

Please feel free to try these algorithms and the pretrained model data in order to find the best one to suit your case.

Detecting facial landmarks

In the preceding section, by detecting faces with a cascade classifier provided by OpenCV we know which regions are faces in an image. But with only rectangular regions, we don't know many details about the faces: where are the eyes, eyebrows, and nose on the faces? In face recognition technology, we call these details **facial landmarks**. In this section, we will try to find a way to detect these facial landmarks.

Unfortunately, the OpenCV core modules don't provide an algorithm to detect facial landmarks, so we should resort to the face module, which is an extra OpenCV module.

Before using the face extra module, we must ensure that the module is installed on our computer. In Chapter 2, *Editing Images Like a Pro*, in the *Building and installing OpenCV from the source* section, we built and installed OpenCV v4.0.0 from a source without the extra modules. Now, let's rebuild and reinstall it with the extra modules included.

We downloaded and unzipped the source of OpenCV and placed it to a certain directory the last time we built it. Now, let's download the source of OpenCV extra modules from its release page, https://github.com/opencv/opencv_contrib/releases. Since the version of the core modules we downloaded and used is v4.0.0, we download the same version of the extra module from https://github.com/opencv/opencv_contrib/archive/4.0.0.zip. After the source is downloaded, we unzip it, place it in the same directory where the unzipped core modules source lies, and build them in our Terminal:

```
$ ls ~
opencv-4.0.0 opencv_contrib-4.0.0 # ... other files
$ cd ~/opencv-4.0.0 # path to the unzipped source of core modules
$ mkdir release # create the separate dir
$ cd release
$ cmake -D OPENCV_EXTRA_MODULES_PATH=../../opencv_contrib-4.0.0/modules \
    -D CMAKE_BUILD_TYPE=RELEASE \
    -D CMAKE_INSTALL_PREFIX=$HOME/programs/opencv ..
# ... output of cmake ...
# rm ../CMakeCache.txt if it tells you are not in a separate dir
$ make
# ... output of make ...
$ make install
```

As you can see, in contrast to the last installation, we add the -D OPENCV_EXTRA_MODULES_PATH=../../opencv_contrib-4.0.0/modules option to the cmake command to tell it where the source of the extra modules resides. After these commands finish, we can check whether the face module is correctly installed:

```
$ ls ~/programs/opencv/include/opencv4/opencv2/face
bif.hpp facemark.hpp facerec.hpp
face_alignment.hpp facemarkLBF.hpp mace.hpp
facemarkAAM.hpp facemark_train.hpp predict_collector.hpp
$ ls ~/programs/opencv/lib/libopencv_face*
/home/kdr2/programs/opencv/lib/libopencv_face.so
/home/kdr2/programs/opencv/lib/libopencv_face.so.4.0
/home/kdr2/programs/opencv/lib/libopencv_face.so.4.0.0
$
```

If the header files and the shared objects are in the path of the OpenCV installation, as the previous shell commands show, you have successfully installed the OpenCV extra modules.

After the face module is installed, let's open its document by opening `https://docs.opencv.org/4.0.0/d4/d48/namespacecv_1_1face.html` in the web browser to see what facilities it provides.

The `FacemarkKazemi`, `FacemarkAAM`, and `FacemarkLBF` classes are the algorithms utilized for detecting facial landmarks. These algorithms are all machine learning-based approaches, so there are also many facilities for dataset manipulating and model training. Training a machine learning model is beyond the scope of this chapter, so in this section, we will still use a pretrained model.

In our application, we will use the algorithm implemented by the `FacemarkLBF` class. A pretrained model data file can be downloaded from `https://raw.githubusercontent.com/kurnianggoro/GSOC2017/master/data/lbfmodel.yaml`. Let's download it and place it into a subdirectory named `data` in our project's root directory:

```
$ mkdir -p data
$ cd data/
$ pwd
/home/kdr2/Work/Books/Qt-5-and-OpenCV-4-Computer-Vision-
Projects/Chapter-04/Facetious/data
$ curl -O
https://raw.githubusercontent.com/kurnianggoro/GSOC2017/master/data/lbfmode
l.yaml
  % Total % Received % Xferd Average Speed Time Time Time Current
                                 Dload Upload Total Spent Left Speed
  0 53.7M 0 53.7k 0 0 15893 0 0:59:07 0:59:07 0:00:00 0
$ ls
lbfmodel.yaml
```

All the preparation work is done now, so let's go back to the code sources of our project in order to finish the development of the facial landmarks detection feature. In the `capture_thread.h` file, we add a new `include` directive and a new private member field for the `CaptureThread` class:

```
// ...
#include "opencv2/face/facemark.hpp"
// ...
class CaptureThread : public QThread
{
    // ...
private:
```

```
        // ...
        cv::Ptr<cv::face::Facemark> mark_detector;
};
```

The `mark_detector` member field, which is of
the `cv::Ptr<cv::face::Facemark>` type, is the exact detector we will use to detect facial
landmarks. Let's instantiate it in the `CaptureThread::run` method in
the `capture_thread.cpp` source file:

```
        classifier = new cv::CascadeClassifier(OPENCV_DATA_DIR
    "haarcascades/haarcascade_frontalface_default.xml");
        mark_detector = cv::face::createFacemarkLBF();
        QString model_data = QApplication::instance()->applicationDirPath()
    + "/data/lbfmodel.yaml";
        mark_detector->loadModel(model_data.toStdString());
```

As you can see in the following code, in the `run` method, after creating the classifier that is
used for face detecting, we create an instance of `FacemarkLBF` by calling
`cv::face::createFacemarkLBF()` and assign it to the `mark_detector` member field.
Then, we construct a string to hold the path to the pretrained model data file we had
downloaded. At last, we call the `loadModel` method with the path of the model data file to
load the data into `mark_detector`. At this point, the detector is ready to use. Let's see how
we use it in the `CaptureThread::detectFaces` method:

```
        vector< vector<cv::Point2f> > shapes;
        if (mark_detector->fit(frame, faces, shapes)) {
            // draw facial land marks
            for (unsigned long i=0; i<faces.size(); i++) {
                for(unsigned long k=0; k<shapes[i].size(); k++) {
                    cv::circle(frame, shapes[i][k], 2, color, cv::FILLED);
                }
            }
        }
```

At the end of the `CaptureThread::detectFaces` method, we declare a variable with the type of a vector whose element type is a vector of `cv::Point2f`. The facial landmarks of one single face are a series of points that are represented by the `vector<cv::Point2f>` type, and more than one face may be detected in a single frame, so we should use such a complex data type to represent them. Then, the crucial part appears—we call the `fit` method of the `mark_detector` member field to detect the facial landmarks. In this call, we pass the input frame, the rectangles of the faces we have detected with the cascade classifier, and the variable for saving the output landmarks to that method. If the `fit` method returns a non zero value, we get the landmarks successfully. After we get the facial landmarks, we iterate over the detected faces and then iterate over the points of the landmarks of each face in order to draw a 2-pixel circle for each point to show the landmarks.

 As we mentioned, if you are using macOS, the compiled application is actually a directory named `Facetious.app`, and the value of the `QApplication::instance()->applicationDirPath()` express will be `Facetious.app/Contents/MacOS`. So, on macOS, you should place the `lbfmodel.yaml` model data under the `Facetious.app/Contents/MacOS/data` directory.

Almost everything is done, except for the project file. Let's add the extra face module we used for the `LIBS` configuration in that file:

```
unix: !mac {
    INCLUDEPATH += /home/kdr2/programs/opencv/include/opencv4
    LIBS += -L/home/kdr2/programs/opencv/lib -lopencv_core -
lopencv_imgproc -lopencv_imgcodecs -lopencv_video -lopencv_videoio -
lopencv_objdetect -lopencv_face
}
```

OK, it's time to compile and run our application. Here is what these landmarks look like while the application is running:

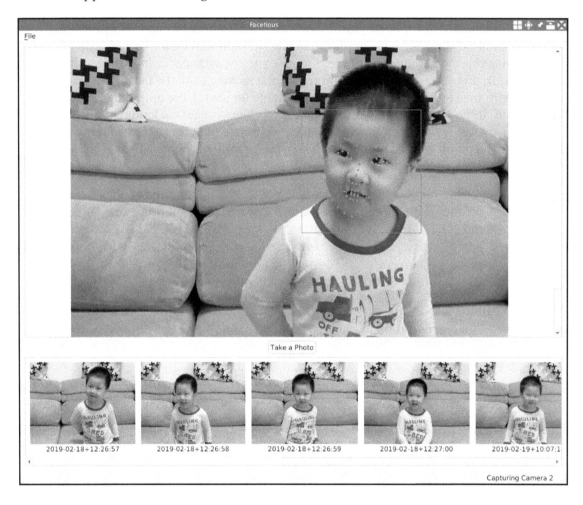

As you can see, we get many landmarks on the eyes, eyebrows, nose, mouth, and jaw. But we still can't tell which points are for which facial features. Considering the order of points in the landmarks of each face is fixed, we can use the indices of the points to determine whether a point is for a certain facial feature. To make this clear, we draw the index number of each point instead of the 2-pixel circle to see their distribution:

```
// cv::circle(frame, shapes[i][k], 2, color, cv::FILLED);
QString index = QString("%1").arg(k);
cv::putText(frame, index.toStdString(), shapes[i][k],
cv::FONT_HERSHEY_SIMPLEX, 0.4, color, 2);
```

Then, when we detect and draw the facial landmarks on a human face, it looks like this:

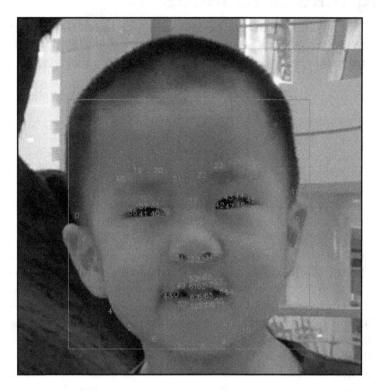

As we can see, the points represented by their index numbers have fixed positions on the face, so we can access these facial features by the following indices of the points:

- The mouth can be accessed through points [48, 68].
- The right eyebrow through points [17, 22].
- The left eyebrow through points [22, 27].
- The right eye using [36, 42].
- The left eye with [42, 48].
- The nose using [27, 35].
- The jaw via [0, 17].

In the next section, we will use this position information to apply masks on the detected faces.

Applying masks to faces

In the previous sections of this chapter, we successfully detected the faces and the facial landmarks in our video feed. In this section, we will do something more interesting—I have three masks or **ornaments** here. Let's try to apply them onto the detected faces in real time:

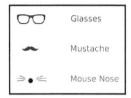

These ornaments are images on the disk. Different to the data from the users, for example the images we viewed in `Chapter 1`, *Building an Image Viewer*, the images we edited in `Chapter 2`, *Editing Images Like a Pro*, and the videos we recorded in `Chapter 3`, *Home Security Applications*, these ornaments are not data from the users; they are a part of our application, just like our code source files. We must somehow bind them to our application, especially when we ship the application to the users. You can simply pack up these resources along the compiled binary, let the users unpack it, then place these resources onto a certain path. But this can cause difficulty for the users, especially when the users run the application on different platforms. Fortunately, the Qt library provides a resource system to cope with this situation. That resource system is a platform-independent mechanism. It can store the resource files we used in the executable of the application. If your application uses a certain set of static files (for instance, icons, images, translation files, cascade style sheets, and so on) and you don't want trouble with shipping the application or run the risk of losing the files, then the Qt resource system is for you.

Let's see how we use this resource system to manage and load our ornament's images.

Loading images with the Qt resource system

The Qt resource system requires that the resource files we are using in the application must be part of the application's source tree. So, first, we save each ornament we mention as a JPEG image and place it into a subdirectory of our project's root directory named `images`:

```
$ pwd
/home/kdr2/Work/Books/Qt-5-and-OpenCV-4-Computer-Vision-
Projects/Chapter-04/Facetious
$ ls images
glasses.jpg mouse-nose.jpg mustache.jpg
```

We are going to superimpose these ornaments onto the frames of our video feed. In order to make this superimposition simple, these ornament images are saved as 3-channels JPEG images whose foreground color is black, the background color is white, and the shape is square. We will explain why doing so can make the ornaments application simple later.

After the images are ready, we create a Qt resource collection file to describe them. A Qt resource file is an XML-based file format whose extension name is .qrc, the abbreviation for Qt resource collection. We name our resource file as images.qrc and place it in the root directory of our project. Let's see its content:

```
<!DOCTYPE RCC>
<RCC version="1.0">
  <qresource>
    <file>images/glasses.jpg</file>
    <file>images/mustache.jpg</file>
    <file>images/mouse-nose.jpg</file>
  </qresource>
</RCC>
```

It's very straightforward. We list all the paths of the resource images as file nodes in the Qt resources collection file. The specified paths are relative to the directory containing the .qrc file, which is the root directory of the project here. Note that the listed resource files must be located in the same directory as the .qrc file or one of its subdirectories, and here we use a subdirectory.

Then, we add this resource collection file to the Facetious.pro project file to tell qmake to handle it:

```
RESOURCES = images.qrc
```

With this, when we compile our project with qmake -makefile and make, a command which invokes rcc will be placed in Makefile and then executed. As a result, a C++ source file named qrc_images.cpp will be generated. That file is generated by rcc, which is the Qt resource compiler. Also, all the images listed in the .qrc file are embedded into this generated C++ source file as byte arrays and will be compiled into the executable of our application when we compile the project.

OK, we successfully embedded the ornament images into our application's executable. But how do we access them? It's easy; these resources can be accessed in our code under the same filename that they have in the source tree with a :/ prefix, or by a URL with a qrc scheme. For example, the :/images/glasses.jpg file path or the qrc:///images/glasses.jpg URL would give access to the glasses.jpg file, whose location in the application's source tree is images/glasses.jpg.

With this knowledge about the Qt resource system, let's load our ornaments to our application as instances of `cv::Mat`. First is the change of the `capture_thread.h` header file:

```
// ...
private:
    // ...
    void loadOrnaments();
// ...
private:
    // ...
    // mask ornaments
    cv::Mat glasses;
    cv::Mat mustache;
    cv::Mat mouse_nose;
    // ...
```

As you can see, we add three private member fields with the `cv::Mat` type to hold the loaded ornaments and a private method to load them. The implementation of the newly added method is in the `capture_thread.cpp` source file:

```
void CaptureThread::loadOrnaments()
{
    QImage image;
    image.load(":/images/glasses.jpg");
    image = image.convertToFormat(QImage::Format_RGB888);
    glasses = cv::Mat(
        image.height(), image.width(), CV_8UC3,
        image.bits(), image.bytesPerLine()).clone();

    image.load(":/images/mustache.jpg");
    image = image.convertToFormat(QImage::Format_RGB888);
    mustache = cv::Mat(
        image.height(), image.width(), CV_8UC3,
        image.bits(), image.bytesPerLine()).clone();

    image.load(":/images/mouse-nose.jpg");
    image = image.convertToFormat(QImage::Format_RGB888);
    mouse_nose = cv::Mat(
        image.height(), image.width(), CV_8UC3,
        image.bits(), image.bytesPerLine()).clone();
}
```

In this method, we first define an object with `QImage` as its type, and then call its `load` method to load an image. While calling the `load` method, we use the `:/images/glasses.jpg` string as its argument. This is a string that starts with `:/` and, as we mentioned, it's the way to load a resource from the Qt resource system. Here, using the `qrc:///images/glasses.jpg` string is also fine.

After the image is loaded, we convert it to the format of 3-channel and 8-depth so that we can construct a `cv::Mat` instance with `CV_8UC3` as its data type. After the conversion, we construct a `cv::Mat` object from `QImage`, as we have done in our previous projects. It's worth noting that we called the `clone` method to make a deep copy of the just constructed `Mat` instance, and then assigned it to the class member field. It's because of this that the just constructed `Mat` object shares the underlying data buffer with the `QImage` object. When we reload that `QImage`, or when the method returns and that `QImage` destructs, that data buffer will be deleted.

In the same way, we then load the ornaments of the mustache and mouse nose. Then, we call this newly added `loadOrnaments` method in the constructors of the `CaptureThread` class.

At this point, thanks to the Qt resource system, we can compile all the three ornament images into the application executable and load them in our code conveniently. Actually, the Qt resource system can do more than what we are using in this chapter. For example, it can select different resource files to use according to the environment where the application is running. It can also compile all the resource files into a single `rcc` binary file instead of embedding them into the application executable, and then use the `QResource` API to register and load them. For these details, you can refer to the official document of the Qt resource system at `https://doc.qt.io/qt-5/resources.html`.

Drawing masks on the faces

In the preceding subsection, we loaded our prepared ornaments as instances of `cv::Mat` into our application. Now, let's draw them onto the faces we detected from the camera in this subsection.

Now, let's see the glasses ornament. There are many things to do before we put the glasses on a face. First, our glasses in the ornament image have a fixed width, but the faces we detected in the video may be any width, so we should resize the glasses to match the faces according to width. Then, our glasses are placed horizontally, but the faces in the video may be tilted, or even rotated 90 degrees, so we must rotate our glasses to fit the slant of the faces. At last, we should find a proper position to draw the glasses.

Let's see how we do these things in our code. In the `capture_thread.h` header file, we add new a method declaration in the class:

```
private:
    // ...
    void drawGlasses(cv::Mat &frame, vector<cv::Point2f> &marks);
```

The first argument of this method is the frame on which we want to draw the glasses, and the second one is the facial landmarks of a certain face we have detected in this frame. Then, we give its implementation in the `capture_thread.cpp` source file:

```
    void CaptureThread::drawGlasses(cv::Mat &frame, vector<cv::Point2f>
&marks)
    {
        // resize
        cv::Mat ornament;
        double distance = cv::norm(marks[45] - marks[36]) * 1.5;
        cv::resize(glasses, ornament, cv::Size(0, 0), distance /
glasses.cols, distance / glasses.cols, cv::INTER_NEAREST);

        // rotate
        double angle = -atan((marks[45].y - marks[36].y) / (marks[45].x -
marks[36].x));
        cv::Point2f center = cv::Point(ornament.cols/2, ornament.rows/2);
        cv::Mat rotateMatrix = cv::getRotationMatrix2D(center, angle * 180
/ 3.14, 1.0);

        cv::Mat rotated;
        cv::warpAffine(
            ornament, rotated, rotateMatrix, ornament.size(),
            cv::INTER_LINEAR, cv::BORDER_CONSTANT, cv::Scalar(255, 255,
255));

        // paint
        center = cv::Point((marks[45].x + marks[36].x) / 2, (marks[45].y +
marks[36].y) / 2);
        cv::Rect rec(center.x - rotated.cols / 2, center.y - rotated.rows
/ 2, rotated.cols, rotated.rows);
        frame(rec) &= rotated;
    }
```

As you can see in the previous code, the first part of this method is to resize the glasses. We calculate the distance between the points, `marks[45]` and `marks[36]`, by calling the `cv::norm` function. What are these two points and why choose them? Remember in the *Detecting facial landmarks* section of this chapter, we used a picture to demonstrate the positions of all the 69 facial landmarks on a face? In that picture, we found `marks[45]` is the outermost point of the left eye while `marks[36]` is the outermost point of the right eye. Usually, the width of the glasses is a little larger than the distance between these two points, so we multiply the distance by 1.5 as the proper width of the glasses, and then resize the glasses ornament image to the proper size. Note that the width and the height are scaled in the same ratio when the image is resized.

The second part is to rotate the ornament. We divide the vertical distance by the horizontal distance of the two chosen points and then pass the result to the `atan` function to calculate the angle of how the face tilts. Please note that the resulting angle is expressed in radians, and we should convert it into degrees when we rotate it using OpenCV. Then, we use the `cv::warpAffine` function that we used in `Chapter 2`, *Editing Images Like a Pro*, in the *Rotating images* section about using `RotatePlugin` to rotate the ornament. When an image is rotated, it might be cropped unless we calculate the proper size for the rotated image instead of using the size of the input image. But when the input image is a square and the maximum width and height of the objects in it are both less than the side length of the square, we can use the size of the input image as the output size to rotate it safely without it being cropped. That's why we prepared our ornament images as squares in the preceding subsection; it really makes our rotation here simple and easy.

The last part is to draw the resized and rotated glasses onto the face. We use the central point of the chosen two points as the central point of our glasses image to calculate a rectangle to which the glasses image should be placed. Then, we draw the ornament with the `frame(rec) &= rotated;` statement. This statement may need some explanation. The `frame` variable is of the `cv::Mat` type and `frame(rec)` calls its `Mat` `cv::Mat::operator()(const Rect &roi) const` operator method. This method returns a new `cv::Mat` type, which is determined by the `Rect` argument and shares the data buffer with the original `cv::Mat` type. So, any operation on this matrix will actually be applied to the corresponding region of the original matrix. Since our ornament image has white as its background color and black as its foreground color, we can simply use a **Bitwise AND** operation to draw it.

Now the implementation of the method is done, let's call it in `detectFaces` in order to draw it on each face we detected after we got the facial landmarks from them:

```
// ...
for (unsigned long i=0; i<faces.size(); i++) {
    for(unsigned long k=0; k<shapes[i].size(); k++) {
```

```
                    // cv::circle(frame, shapes[i][k], 2, color,
    cv::FILLED);
                }
                drawGlasses(frame, shapes[i]);
            }
            // ...
```

To make the video clear, we also comment out the statement that is used to draw the facial landmarks. Now, let's compile and run the application to see how it's doing:

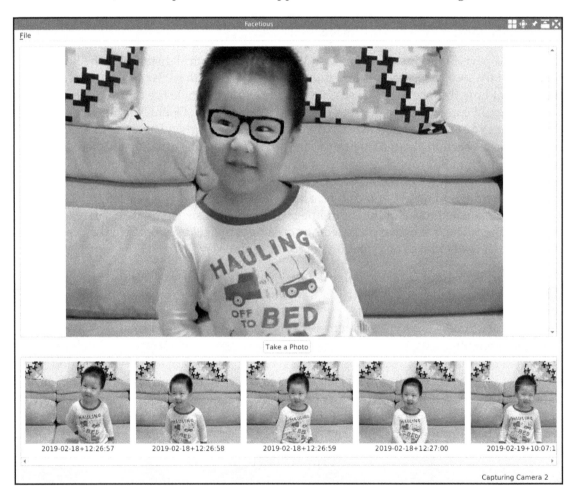

Ha, not bad! Let's move on. We still have two ornaments to draw, but that can be done in almost the same way that we drew the glasses:

- For the mustache, we use marks[54], which is the left corner of the mouth, and marks[48], which is the right corner of the mouth, to calculate the width and the slant. Use marks[33] and marks[51] to determine the central point.
- For the mouse nose, we use marks[13] and marks[3] to determine the width, marks[16] and marks[0] to calculate the slant, and marks[30] and the nasal tip as the central point.

With the previous information, you can implement the drawMustache and drawMouseNose methods yourself, or refer the code in our code repository. The following photographs show how our application does all these ornaments:

My boy is so cute, isn't he?

Selecting masks on the UI

In the previous sections of this chapter, we have done much work to detect faces and facial landmarks in the video feed from a webcam in real time. In that process, we drew circumscribe rectangles around the faces, drew facial landmarks as 2-pixel circles on the faces, and applied 3 different masks to the faces. That way teaches us a lot about face recognition using OpenCV, but from the perspective of the users, that's too much to draw on the faces. So, in this section, we will give our users a chance to select which marks or masks to draw on the detected faces through the checkboxes on the user interface—we will add five checkboxes on the main window under the shutter button for that.

Before changing the user interface, we must make our `CaptureThread` class have the ability to choose which marks or masks to draw first. So, let's open the `capture_thread.h` file to add something into the class:

```
public:
    // ...
    enum MASK_TYPE{
                RECTANGLE = 0,
                LANDMARKS,
                GLASSES,
                MUSTACHE,
                MOUSE_NOSE,
                MASK_COUNT,
    };

    void updateMasksFlag(MASK_TYPE type, bool on_or_off) {
        uint8_t bit = 1 << type;
        if(on_or_off) {
            masks_flag |= bit;
        } else {
            masks_flag &= ~bit;
        }
    };

// ...
private:
    // ...
    bool isMaskOn(MASK_TYPE type) {return (masks_flag & (1 << type))
!= 0; };
private:
    // ...
    uint8_t masks_flag;
    // ...
```

First, we add an enumerate `MASK_TYPE` type to indicate the type of the marks or masks:

- `RECTANGLE`, whose value, 0, is for the circumscribed rectangle around the faces.
- `LANDMARKS`, whose value, 1, is for the facial landmarks on the faces.
- `GLASSES`, whose value, 2, is for the glasses ornament (or mask).
- `MUSTACHE` is for the mustache ornament and has the value 3.
- `MOUSE_NOSE` is for the mouse nose ornament and has the value 4.
- `MASK_COUNT` is not for any mark or mask, it has the value 5 (the preceding value plus one), and is used for the total count of the marks and masks for convenience.

Then, we add a new `uint8_t masks_flag` private field to save the states of whether these marks and masks are turned on or off. This field is used as a bitmap—if a kind of mark or mask is turned on, the corresponding bit will be set to 1, otherwise, the bit will be set to 0. This is done by the newly added `updateMasksFlag` public inline method. We also provide the `isMaskOn` private inline method to test whether a certain mark or mask is turned on or not. Now, let's put these facilities to use in the `capture_thread.cpp` source file.

First, in the `CaptureThread::run` method, in the place we call the `detectFaces` method, we add a condition check:

```
// detectFaces(tmp_frame);
if(masks_flag > 0)
    detectFaces(tmp_frame);
```

If the `masks_flag` bitmap is zero, we know that no mark or mask is turned on, so we have no need to call the `detectFaces` method. But if that bitmap is greater than zero, we must call and enter that method to detect faces. Let's see how we do the condition check here:

```
// ...
    if (isMaskOn(RECTANGLE)) {
        for(size_t i = 0; i < faces.size(); i++) {
            cv::rectangle(frame, faces[i], color, 1);
        }
    }
// ...

                if (isMaskOn(LANDMARKS)) {
                    for(unsigned long k=0; k<shapes[i].size(); k++) {
                        cv::circle(frame, shapes[i][k], 2, color,
cv::FILLED);
                    }
                }
        // ...
                if (isMaskOn(GLASSES))
```

```
                    drawGlasses(frame, shapes[i]);
            if (isMaskOn(MUSTACHE))
                    drawMustache(frame, shapes[i]);
            if (isMaskOn(MOUSE_NOSE))
                    drawMouseNose(frame, shapes[i]);
    // ...
```

They're simple and straightforward. We check the flag of each mask type with the isMaskOn method and then determine whether we are going to draw that type of mark or mask.

The last thing for the CaptureThread class is to not forget to initialize masks_flag to zero in the constructors. After all these things about the CaptureThread class are finished, let's move on to the main window for the user interface changes.

In the mainwindow.h header file, we add a new private slot and an array of checkboxes:

```
private slots:
    // ...
    void updateMasks(int status);

// ...
private:
    // ...
    QCheckBox *mask_checkboxes[CaptureThread::MASK_COUNT];
```

The preceding array has CaptureThread::MASK_COUNT elements, which is 5, as we mentioned. The updateMasks slot is for these checkboxes. Let's create and arrange these checkboxes in the initUI method in the mainwindow.cpp source file:

```
    // masks
    QGridLayout *masks_layout = new QGridLayout();
    main_layout->addLayout(masks_layout, 13, 0, 1, 1);
    masks_layout->addWidget(new QLabel("Select Masks:", this));
    for (int i = 0; i < CaptureThread::MASK_COUNT; i++){
        mask_checkboxes[i] = new QCheckBox(this);
        masks_layout->addWidget(mask_checkboxes[i], 0, i + 1);
        connect(mask_checkboxes[i], SIGNAL(stateChanged(int)), this,
SLOT(updateMasks(int)));
    }
    mask_checkboxes[0]->setText("Rectangle");
    mask_checkboxes[1]->setText("Landmarks");
    mask_checkboxes[2]->setText("Glasses");
    mask_checkboxes[3]->setText("Mustache");
    mask_checkboxes[4]->setText("Mouse Nose");
```

In the `initUI` method, we add the previous code into the following lines of creating the shutter button in order to create a new grid layout for the checkboxes. That grid layout occupies one row of the main layout, the 14th row. Then, we add a new label into the newly created grid layout and set its text to `Select Masks:`, to introduce the functionality of this area. After that, in a `for` loop, we create a checkbox for each type of mask, add them to the grid layout, and then connect their `stateChanged(int)` signal to the newly added `updateMasks(int)` slot. After the `for` loop, we set a proper text for each checkbox we just created.

Considering the newly added area occupies the 14th row of the main layout, we must move the area of the list for saved photos a row down in the same method:

```
// main_layout->addWidget(saved_list, 13, 0, 4, 1);
main_layout->addWidget(saved_list, 14, 0, 4, 1);
```

The following is the implementation of the `updateMasks` slot, let's take a look at it now:

```
void MainWindow::updateMasks(int status)
{
    if(capturer == nullptr) {
        return;
    }

    QCheckBox *box = qobject_cast<QCheckBox*>(sender());
    for (int i = 0; i < CaptureThread::MASK_COUNT; i++){
        if (mask_checkboxes[i] == box) {
            capturer->updateMasksFlag(static_cast<CaptureThread::MASK_TYPE>(i), status != 0);
        }
    }
}
```

In the slot, we first check whether the capturing thread is null. If it isn't null, we find the signal sender, that is, which checkbox is clicked so that this slot is called by calling the `sender` function from the Qt library. Then, we find the index of the sender in the `mask_checkboxes` checkbox array. The index we just found is rightly the value of the type of the corresponding mask in the `MASK_TYPE` enum, so next, we call the `updateMasksFlag` method of the capturing thread instance to turn the mask on or off, according to the status of the sender checkbox.

The last thing about the user interface change is that we set all `checkboxes` unchecked after a new instance of the capturing thread is created and started in the `MainWindow::openCamera` method:

```
for (int i = 0; i < CaptureThread::MASK_COUNT; i++){
    mask_checkboxes[i]->setCheckState(Qt::Unchecked);
}
```

OK, finally, all the work on our new application, Facetious, is done! Let's compile and run it to see how it looks:

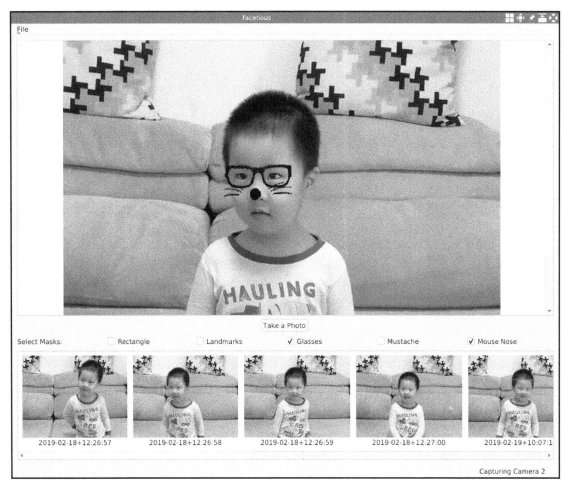

Now the users can select which mark or mask to show by utilizing the checkboxes under the shutter button.

Summary

In this chapter, we created a new application named Facetious by abridging the Gazer application, which was built in the preceding chapter. In the abridging process, the features of video saving and motion detecting were removed and a new feature of photo taking was added. As a result, we got a clean application that allows us to focus on face recognition. Then, in the application, we developed the feature of face detecting using a pretrained cascade classifier and the feature of facial landmarks detecting using another pretrained machine learning model. At last, which is the funny part, we applied many ornaments on the detected faces with the help of the detected landmarks.

In the next chapter, we will talk about **Optical Character Recognition (OCR)** technology and use that technology to extract text from images or scanned documents.

Questions

Try out these questions to test your knowledge of this chapter:

1. Try the LBP cascade classifier to detect faces by yourself.
2. There are some other algorithms that can be used to detect facial landmarks in the OpenCV library and most of them can be found at `https://docs.opencv.org/4.0.0/db/dd8/classcv_1_1face_1_1Facemark.html`. Please try them by yourself.
3. How do you apply a colored ornament to a face?

Optical Character Recognition 5

In the previous chapters, we did a lot of work with videos and cameras. We created applications (**Gazer** and **Facetious**) with which we can play video from webcams attached to our computers. We can also record videos, take photos, detect motion and faces, and apply masks to faces detected in the video feed in real time with these apps.

Now we will move our focus to the text in images. There are many situations in which we want to extract the text or characters from an image. In the area of computer vision, there is a technology called **Optical Character Recognition** (**OCR**) to do this kind of work automatically instead of transcribing the text manually. In this chapter, we will build a new application to extract text from images and scanned documents with Qt and a number of OCR libraries.

We will cover the following topics in this chapter:

- Extracting text from images
- Detecting text regions in images
- Accessing screen content
- Drawing on widgets and cropping portions of the screen

Technical requirements

As we saw from the previous chapters, users are required to have at least Qt version 5 installed and some basic knowledge of C++ and Qt programming. Also, the latest version of Tesseract, version 4.0, should be correctly installed, as we will use this library as the OCR facility in this chapter. For Windows, a prebuilt binary package of Tesseract can be found at `https://github.com/UB-Mannheim/tesseract/wiki`. For UNIX-like systems, we will build Tesseract from the source step by step before we use it.

Some knowledge of deep learning will also be a big help in understanding the content of this chapter.

All the code for this chapter can be found in our code repository at `https://github.com/PacktPublishing/Qt-5-and-OpenCV-4-Computer-Vision-Projects/tree/master/Chapter-05`.

Check out the following video to see the code in action: `http://bit.ly/2FhuTvq`

Creating Literacy

As we said, we will create a new application to extract text from images or scanned documents, hence, its name of Literacy. The first thing is to clarify what the application aims to do. The main feature is extracting text from images, but, for the convenience of users, we should provide more than one way to specify the image:

- The image may be from the local hard disk.
- The image may be captured from the screen.

With this requirement clarified, let's now design the UI.

Designing the UI

The following wireframe is drawn as the design of the UI of our application:

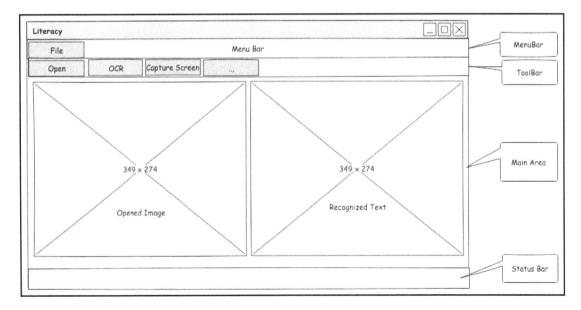

As you can see, we split the main area vertically into two parts—the left-hand part is used to display the opened, or captured, image, while the right-hand part is for the extracted text. Other parts of the window, such as the menu bar, toolbar, and status bar, are all aspects with which we are very familiar.

You can find the source file for this design from our code repository on GitHub: `https://github.com/PacktPublishing/Qt-5-and-OpenCV-4-Computer-Vision-Projects`. The file resides in the root directory of the repository, named `WireFrames.epgz`, and the wireframe for this chapter is located on the third page. Don't forget that it should be opened using the Pencil application.

Setting up the UI

In the previous subsection, we designed the UI of our new application, Literacy. Now, let's create the Qt project for it and set up its full UI in a Qt main window.

First, let's create the project in the Terminal:

```
$ mkdir Literacy/
$ cd Literacy/
$ touch main.cpp
$ ls
main.cpp
$ qmake -project
$ ls
Literacy.pro main.cpp
$
```

Then, we open the project file, `Literacy.pro`, and fill it with the following content:

```
TEMPLATE = app
TARGET = Literacy

QT += core gui
greaterThan(QT_MAJOR_VERSION, 4): QT += widgets

INCLUDEPATH += .

# Input
HEADERS += mainwindow.h
SOURCES += main.cpp mainwindow.cpp
```

This is straightforward, as we have done this many times. However, it is still worth noting that we specify one header file and two source files in this project file while, at this point, we only have one empty source file, `main.cpp`. Don't worry about this. We will complete all these source files mentioned before we compile the project.

The `main.cpp` file is also very straightforward:

```
#include <QApplication>
#include "mainwindow.h"

int main(int argc, char *argv[])
{
    QApplication app(argc, argv);
    MainWindow window;
    window.setWindowTitle("Literacy");
    window.show();
    return app.exec();
}
```

Similar to what we did in other projects, we create an instance of `QApplication` and an instance of `MainWindow`, and then call the `show` method of the window and the `exec` method of the application to start the application. However, the `MainWindow` class doesn't yet exist, so let's create this now.

In the root directory of the project, we create a new file named `mainwindow.h` to accommodate the `MainWindow` class. Omitting the `ifndef`/`define` idiom and the `include` directives, this class appears as follows:

```
class MainWindow : public QMainWindow
{
    Q_OBJECT

public:
    explicit MainWindow(QWidget *parent=nullptr);
    ~MainWindow();

private:
    void initUI();
    void createActions();
    void setupShortcuts();

private:
    QMenu *fileMenu;

    QToolBar *fileToolBar;
```

```
          QGraphicsScene *imageScene;
          QGraphicsView *imageView;

          QTextEdit *editor;

          QStatusBar *mainStatusBar;
          QLabel *mainStatusLabel;

          QAction *openAction;
          QAction *saveImageAsAction;
          QAction *saveTextAsAction;
          QAction *exitAction;
    };
```

It is obviously a subclass of QMainWindow and, hence, it has the Q_OBJECT macro at the beginning of its body. The most important aspects are the widgets we declare in the private section, including the file menu, fileMenu; a toolbar, fileToolBar; QGraphicsScene and QGraphicsView to show the target image; QTextEditor to place the recognized text, a status bar, and a label on it; and then, finally, four QAction pointers.

Apart from these widget declarations, we also have three private methods to instantiate these widgets and arrange them in the main windows as we designed:

- initUI: To instantiate all the widgets except the actions.
- createActions: To create all the actions; this is called by the initUI method.
- setupShortcuts: To set up a few hotkeys to make our application more convenient to use. This is called by the createActions method.

Now it's time to implement these methods. We create a new source file named mainwindow.cpp in the root directory of the project to accommodate these implementations. First, let's look at the initUI method:

```
    void MainWindow::initUI()
    {
        this->resize(800, 600);
        // setup menubar
        fileMenu = menuBar()->addMenu("&File");

        // setup toolbar
        fileToolBar = addToolBar("File");

        // main area
        QSplitter *splitter = new QSplitter(Qt::Horizontal, this);

        imageScene = new QGraphicsScene(this);
```

```
        imageView = new QGraphicsView(imageScene);
        splitter->addWidget(imageView);

        editor = new QTextEdit(this);
        splitter->addWidget(editor);

        QList<int> sizes = {400, 400};
        splitter->setSizes(sizes);

        setCentralWidget(splitter);

        // setup status bar
        mainStatusBar = statusBar();
        mainStatusLabel = new QLabel(mainStatusBar);
        mainStatusBar->addPermanentWidget(mainStatusLabel);
        mainStatusLabel->setText("Application Information will be here!");

        createActions();
    }
```

In this method, we first set the window size, create the file menu, and add it to the menu bar, create the file toolbar, and, finally, we create the status bar and then place a label on it. All this work is the same as we have done in our previous projects. The salient part that differs from the previous projects is the creation of the main area, which is the middle part of the method body. In this part, we create a QSplitter object with horizontal orientation, instead of a QGridLayout instance to accommodate the graphics view and the editor.

Using QSplitter gives us the ability to change the widths of its children widgets freely by dragging its splitter bar, something that is not possible with QGridLayout. After that, we create the graphics scene, along with the graphics view, and the editor then adds them to the splitter in an orderly manner. The widths of the children of the splitter are set by calling the setSizes method with a list of int; we make each child occupy an equal width of 400 pixels. Finally, we set the splitter as the central widget of the main window.

The following code relates to the createActions method:

```
    void MainWindow::createActions()
    {
        // create actions, add them to menus
        openAction = new QAction("&Open", this);
        fileMenu->addAction(openAction);
        saveImageAsAction = new QAction("Save &Image as", this);
        fileMenu->addAction(saveImageAsAction);
        saveTextAsAction = new QAction("Save &Text as", this);
        fileMenu->addAction(saveTextAsAction);
        exitAction = new QAction("E&xit", this);
```

```
    fileMenu->addAction(exitAction);

    // add actions to toolbars
    fileToolBar->addAction(openAction);

    setupShortcuts();
}
```

Here, we create all the actions we declared and add them to the file menu and toolbar. At the end of this method, we call `setupShortcuts`. Now, let's see what shortcuts we set up in it:

```
void MainWindow::setupShortcuts()
{
    QList<QKeySequence> shortcuts;
    shortcuts << (Qt::CTRL + Qt::Key_O);
    openAction->setShortcuts(shortcuts);

    shortcuts.clear();
    shortcuts << (Qt::CTRL + Qt::Key_Q);
    exitAction->setShortcuts(shortcuts);
}
```

As you can see, we use `Ctrl-O` to trigger `openAction`, and `Ctrl-Q` to trigger `exitAction`.

Finally, there is the constructor and the destructor:

```
MainWindow::MainWindow(QWidget *parent) :
    QMainWindow(parent)
{
    initUI();
}

MainWindow::~MainWindow()
{
}
```

These are both fairly straightforward, so we won't go into too much detail here. Now, we can compile and run the Literacy application:

```
$ qmake -makefile
$ make
g++ -c -pipe -O2 -Wall -W # ...
# output trucated
$ ./Literacy
```

After we run the application, a window that looks like the following will appear on our desktop:

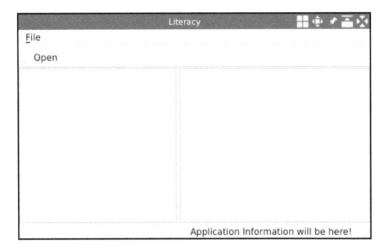

So, we have set up the full UI without any interactive features. Next, we will add a number of interactive features to our application, including the following:

- Opening an image from the local disk
- Saving the current image as a file onto the local disk
- Saving the text in the editor widget as a text file onto the local disk

In order to achieve these goals, we should add some methods, slots, and member fields to the `MainWindow` class in the `mainwindow.h` header file:

```
private:
    // ...
    void showImage(QString);
    // ...
private slots:
    void openImage();
    void saveImageAs();
    void saveTextAs();

private:
    // ...
    QString currentImagePath;
    QGraphicsPixmapItem *currentImage;
```

The `showImage` method and the `openImage` slot have the same implementations as those of the `MainWindow::showImage` and `MainWindow::openImage` methods we had written in the ImageViewer application (see `Chapter 1`, *Building an Image Viewer*). Also, the `saveImageAs` slot has exactly the same implementation as the `MainWindow::saveAs` method in that ImageViewer application. We just use a different name here on account of the fact that we should save images as well as text in our new application, and this method is just for saving images. So, we just copy these implementations into our new project. We won't go into too much detail about them here in order to keep the chapter brief.

The only method we haven't yet covered is the `saveTextAs` slot. So, let's now look at its implementation:

```cpp
void MainWindow::saveTextAs()
{
    QFileDialog dialog(this);
    dialog.setWindowTitle("Save Text As ...");
    dialog.setFileMode(QFileDialog::AnyFile);
    dialog.setAcceptMode(QFileDialog::AcceptSave);
    dialog.setNameFilter(tr("Text files (*.txt)"));
    QStringList fileNames;
    if (dialog.exec()) {
        fileNames = dialog.selectedFiles();
        if(QRegExp(".+\\.(txt)").exactMatch(fileNames.at(0))) {
            QFile file(fileNames.at(0));
            if (!file.open(QIODevice::WriteOnly | QIODevice::Text)) {
                QMessageBox::information(this, "Error", "Can't save
text.");
                return;
            }
            QTextStream out(&file);
            out << editor->toPlainText() << "\n";
        } else {
            QMessageBox::information(this, "Error", "Save error: bad
format or filename.");
        }
    }
}
```

It is very similar to the `saveImageAs` method. The differences are as follows:

- In the file dialog, we set a name filter with the extension name `txt` to ensure that only text files can be chosen.
- While saving the text, we create a `QFile` instance with the chosen filename and then create a `QTextStream` instance with that `QFile` instance that can be written to. Finally, we get the content of the text editor by calling its `toPlainText()` method and write it to the stream we just created.

Now, all the methods and slots are finished, so let's connect the signals and these slots in the `createActions` method:

```
// connect the signals and slots
connect(exitAction, SIGNAL(triggered(bool)),
QApplication::instance(), SLOT(quit()));
connect(openAction, SIGNAL(triggered(bool)), this,
SLOT(openImage()));
connect(saveImageAsAction, SIGNAL(triggered(bool)), this,
SLOT(saveImageAs()));
connect(saveTextAsAction, SIGNAL(triggered(bool)), this,
SLOT(saveTextAs()));
```

Finally, we initialize the `currentImage` member field to `nullptr` in the constructor:

```
MainWindow::MainWindow(QWidget *parent) :
    QMainWindow(parent), currentImage(nullptr)
{
    initUI();
}
```

Now, we compile and run our application again to test these newly added interactive features. Click on the actions, open an image, type some words in the editor, drag the splitter bar to adjust the width of the columns, and save the image or text as files. The main window with which we are interacting looks like this:

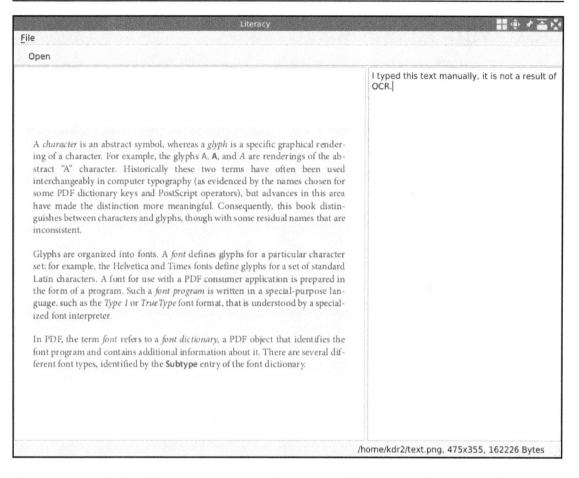

As you can see in the diagram, we open an image containing many characters and type some text in the editor on the right-hand side. In the next section, we will extract the text from the image and fill the editor with the extracted text automatically by clicking a button on the toolbar.

All the changes in the code in this section can be found in this commit: `https://github.com/PacktPublishing/Qt-5-and-OpenCV-4-Computer-Vision-Projects/commit/bc1548b97cf79ddae5184f8009badb278c2750b2`.

OCR with Tesseract

In this section, we are going to extract the text from images with Tesseract. As we mentioned, to install Tesseract on Windows, we can use a prebuilt binary package. On a UNIX-like system, we can use the system package manager to install, for example, `apt-get` on Debian, or `brew` on macOS. Take Debian as an example—we can install the `libtesseract-dev` and `tesseract-ocr-all` packages to install all the library and data files we need. No matter how you install it, please ensure that you have the correct version, 4.0.0, installed.

Although there are prebuilt packages, for the pedagogical purpose, we will build it from the source on a Linux system to see what components it contains and how to use its command-line tool.

Building Tesseract from the source

We will build version 4.0.0 from the source, so first, we select the zip file under the **4.0.0 Release** on its release page at `https://github.com/tesseract-ocr/tesseract/releases` to download it. After the `.zip` file is downloaded, we unzip it and enter the directory to build it:

```
$ curl -L https://github.com/tesseract-ocr/tesseract/archive/4.0.0.zip -o
tesseract-4.0.0.zip
  % Total % Received % Xferd Average Speed Time Time Time Current
                                   Dload Upload Total Spent Left Speed
100 127 0 127 0 0 159 0 --:--:-- --:--:-- --:--:-- 159
100 2487k 0 2487k 0 0 407k 0 --:--:-- 0:00:06 --:--:-- 571k
$ unzip tesseract-4.0.0.zip
# output omitted
$ cd tesseract-4.0.0/
$ ./configure --prefix=/home/kdr2/programs/tesseract
# output omitted
$ make && make install
# output omitted
```

Tesseract uses `autotools` to construct its building system, so its build process is quite easy. We first run the `configure` script, and then `make && make install`. We give an argument, `--prefix=/home/kdr2/programs/tesseract`, to specify the install prefix when we run the `configure` script, so, if everything goes according to plan, the Tesseract library, including the header files, static library, dynamic library, and many other files besides, will be installed under that specified directory.

A new OCR engine based on the **Long Short-Term Memory (LSTM)** neural network, which is focused on line recognition, was introduced in Tesseract 4, while the legacy Tesseract OCR engine of Tesseract 3, which works by recognizing character patterns, was also retained. Hence, we can choose which engine to use freely in Tesseract 4. To use the new OCR engine, we must download the pretrained data for the LSTM AI model in that engine. This pretrained data can be found in the GitHub repository at `https://github.com/tesseract-ocr/tessdata`. We download the content of this repository and place it under our Tesseract installation directory:

```
$ curl -O -L https://github.com/tesseract-ocr/tessdata/archive/master.zip
# output omitted
$ unzip master.zip
Archive: master.zip
590567f20dc044f6948a8e2c61afc714c360ad0e
   creating: tessdata-master/
  inflating: tessdata-master/COPYING
  inflating: tessdata-master/README.md
  inflating: tessdata-master/afr.traineddata
  . . .
$ mv tessdata-master/* /home/kdr2/programs/tesseract/share/tessdata/
$ ls /home/kdr2/programs/tesseract/share/tessdata/ -l |head
total 1041388
-rw-r--r-- 1 kdr2 kdr2 7851157 May 10 2018 afr.traineddata
-rw-r--r-- 1 kdr2 kdr2 8423467 May 10 2018 amh.traineddata
-rw-r--r-- 1 kdr2 kdr2 2494806 May 10 2018 ara.traineddata
-rw-r--r-- 1 kdr2 kdr2 2045457 May 10 2018 asm.traineddata
-rw-r--r-- 1 kdr2 kdr2 4726411 May 10 2018 aze_cyrl.traineddata
-rw-r--r-- 1 kdr2 kdr2 10139884 May 10 2018 aze.traineddata
-rw-r--r-- 1 kdr2 kdr2 11185811 May 10 2018 bel.traineddata
-rw-r--r-- 1 kdr2 kdr2 1789439 May 10 2018 ben.traineddata
-rw-r--r-- 1 kdr2 kdr2 1966470 May 10 2018 bod.traineddata
```

As you can see, in this step, we get lots of files whose extension name is `traineddata`. These files are the pretrained data files for different languages; the language names are used as the base filenames. For example, `eng.traineddata` is for recognizing English characters.

Actually, you do not have to place this trained data under the Tesseract installation data directory. You can place these files anywhere you like, and then set the environment variable, `TESSDATA_PREFIX`, to that directory. Tesseract will find them by following this environment variable.

Tesseract provides a command-line tool to extract text from an image. Let's use this tool to check whether the Tesseract library is installed correctly:

```
$ ~/programs/tesseract/bin/tesseract -v
tesseract 4.0.0
 leptonica-1.76.0
  libgif 5.1.4 : libjpeg 6b (libjpeg-turbo 1.5.2) : libpng 1.6.36 : libtiff
4.0.9 : zlib 1.2.11 : libwebp 0.6.1 : libopenjp2 2.3.0
 Found AVX
 Found SSE
```

The -v option tells the tesseract tool to do nothing but print the version information. We can see that Tesseract 4.0.0 is installed. The word leptonica in this message is another image process library that is used as the default image process library by Tesseract. In our project, we already have Qt and OpenCV to manipulate images, so we can just ignore this information.

Now, let's try to extract text from an image with this command-line tool. The following diagram is prepared as the input:

A *character* is an abstract symbol, whereas a *glyph* is a specific graphical rendering of a character. For example, the glyphs A, **A**, and *A* are renderings of the abstract "A" character. Historically these two terms have often been used interchangeably in computer typography (as evidenced by the names chosen for some PDF dictionary keys and PostScript operators), but advances in this area have made the distinction more meaningful. Consequently, this book distinguishes between characters and glyphs, though with some residual names that are inconsistent.

Glyphs are organized into fonts. A *font* defines glyphs for a particular character set; for example, the Helvetica and Times fonts define glyphs for a set of standard Latin characters. A font for use with a PDF consumer application is prepared in the form of a program. Such a *font program* is written in a special-purpose language, such as the *Type 1* or *TrueType* font format, that is understood by a specialized font interpreter.

In PDF, the term *font* refers to a *font dictionary*, a PDF object that identifies the font program and contains additional information about it. There are several different font types, identified by the **Subtype** entry of the font dictionary.

And this is the result of the performance of the command-line tool on the diagram:

```
[000]kdr2@Debian-X230:~$ ~/programs/tesseract/bin/tesseract  text.png stdout -l eng
A character is an abstract symbol, whereas a glyph is a specific graphical render-
ing of a character. For example, the glyphs A, A, and A are renderings of the ab-
stract A" character. Historically these two terms have often been used
interchangeably in computer typography (as evidenced by the names chosen for
some PDF dictionary keys and PostScript operators), but advances in this area
have made the distinction more meaningful. Consequently, this book distin-
guishes between characters and glyphs, though with some residual names that are
inconsistent.

Glyphs are organized into fonts. A font defines glyphs for a particular character
set; for example, the Helvetica and Times fonts define glyphs for a set of standard
Latin characters. A font for use with a PDF consumer application is prepared in
the form of a program. Such a font program is written in a special-purpose lan-
guage, such as the Type 1 or TrueType font format, that is understood by a special-
ized font interpreter.

In PDE, the term font refers to a font dictionary, a PDE object that identifies the
font program and contains additional information about it. There are several dif-
ferent font types, identified by the Subtype entry of the font dictionary.

[000]kdr2@Debian-X230:~$ █
```

As you can see, we give many arguments to the command-line tool on this occasion:

- The first one is the input image.
- The second one is the output. We use `stdout` to tell the command-line tool to write the result to the standard output of the Terminal. We can specify a base filename here; for example, using `text-out` will tell the tool to write the result to the text file, `text-out.txt`.
- The rest arguments are the options. We use `-l eng` to tell it that the text we want to extract is written in English.

You can see that Tesseract recognizes the text very well in our diagram.

Besides the `-l` option, there are two more important options for the Tesseract command-line tool: `--oem` and `--psm`.

The `--oem` option, as we can guess from its name, is for selecting the OCR engine mode. We can list all the OCR engine modes that Tesseract supports by running the following command:

```
$ ~/programs/tesseract/bin/tesseract --help-oem
OCR Engine modes:
  0 Legacy engine only.
  1 Neural nets LSTM engine only.
  2 Legacy + LSTM engines.
  3 Default, based on what is available.
```

The LSTM mode is used by default in Tesseract 4.0 and, in most situations, it performs very well. You can try the legacy engine by appending `--oem 0` to the end of the command we ran to extract the text and you will see that the legacy engine doesn't perform very well on our diagram.

The `--psm` option is for specifying a page segmentation mode. If we run `tesseract --help-psm`, we will find that there are many modes for page segmentation in Tesseract:

```
$ ~/programs/tesseract/bin/tesseract --help-psm
Page segmentation modes:
   0 Orientation and script detection (OSD) only.
   1 Automatic page segmentation with OSD.
   2 Automatic page segmentation, but no OSD, or OCR.
   3 Fully automatic page segmentation, but no OSD. (Default)
   4 Assume a single column of text of variable sizes.
   5 Assume a single uniform block of vertically aligned text.
   6 Assume a single uniform block of text.
   7 Treat the image as a single text line.
   8 Treat the image as a single word.
   9 Treat the image as a single word in a circle.
  10 Treat the image as a single character.
  11 Sparse text. Find as much text as possible in no particular order.
  12 Sparse text with OSD.
  13 Raw line. Treat the image as a single text line,
        bypassing hacks that are Tesseract-specific.
```

If you are dealing with scanned documents that have complex typesetting, perhaps you should select a page segmentation mode for it. But since we are now handling a simple image, we just ignore this option.

Hitherto, we have successfully installed the Tesseract library and learned how to use its command-line tool to extract text from images. In the next subsection, we will integrate this library in our application, Literacy, to facilitate the text recognition feature.

Recognizing characters in Literacy

Our Tesseract library is ready, so let's use it to recognize characters in our Literacy application.

The first thing we should do is update the project file to incorporate the information relating to the Tesseract library:

```
# use your own path in the following config
unix: {
    INCLUDEPATH += /home/kdr2/programs/tesseract/include
```

```
    LIBS += -L/home/kdr2/programs/tesseract/lib -ltesseract
}

win32 {
    INCLUDEPATH += c:/path/to/tesseract/include
    LIBS += -lc:/path/to/opencv/lib/tesseract
}

DEFINES +=
TESSDATA_PREFIX=\\\"/home/kdr2/programs/tesseract/share/tessdata/\\\"
```

In the preceding changeset, we add the include path and the library path of the Tesseract library for different platforms, and then define a macro, TESSDATA_PREFIX, whose value is the path to the data path of the Tesseract library. We will use this macro to load the pretrained data in our code later.

Then, we open the mainwindow.h header file to add some new lines:

```
#include "tesseract/baseapi.h"

class MainWindow : public QMainWindow
{
    // ...
private slots:
    // ...
    void extractText();

private:
    // ...
    QAction *ocrAction;
    // ...
    tesseract::TessBaseAPI *tesseractAPI;
};
```

In this changeset, we first add an include directive to include the base API header file of the Tesseract library and then add one slot and two members to the MainWindow class.

The QAction *ocrAction member will appear on the toolbar of the main window. When this action is triggered, the newly added slot, extractText, will be called, and that slot will use the tesseract::TessBaseAPI *tesseractAPI member to recognize the characters in the image that has been opened.

Now, let's see how these things happen in the source file, mainwindow.cpp.

In the constructor of the `MainWindow` class, we initialize the member field, `tesseractAPI`, to `nullptr`:

```
MainWindow::MainWindow(QWidget *parent) :
    QMainWindow(parent)
    , currentImage(nullptr)
    , tesseractAPI(nullptr)
{
    initUI();
}
```

In the `createActions` method, we create the `ocrAction` action, add it to the toolbar, and then connect its `triggered` signal to the newly added `extractText` slot:

```
void MainWindow::createActions()
{
    // ...
    ocrAction = new QAction("OCR", this);
    fileToolBar->addAction(ocrAction);

    // ...
    connect(ocrAction, SIGNAL(triggered(bool)), this,
SLOT(extractText()));
    // ...
}
```

Now, the only thing left is the most complex and important part; the implementation of the `extractText` slot:

```
void MainWindow::extractText()
{
    if (currentImage == nullptr) {
        QMessageBox::information(this, "Information", "No opened
image.");
        return;
    }

    char *old_ctype = strdup(setlocale(LC_ALL, NULL));
    setlocale(LC_ALL, "C");
    tesseractAPI = new tesseract::TessBaseAPI();
    // Initialize tesseract-ocr with English, with specifying tessdata
path
    if (tesseractAPI->Init(TESSDATA_PREFIX, "eng")) {
        QMessageBox::information(this, "Error", "Could not initialize
tesseract.");
        return;
    }
```

```
            QPixmap pixmap = currentImage->pixmap();
            QImage image = pixmap.toImage();
            image = image.convertToFormat(QImage::Format_RGB888);

            tesseractAPI->SetImage(image.bits(), image.width(),
    image.height(),
                3, image.bytesPerLine());
            char *outText = tesseractAPI->GetUTF8Text();
            editor->setPlainText(outText);
            // Destroy used object and release memory
            tesseractAPI->End();
            delete tesseractAPI;
            tesseractAPI = nullptr;
            delete [] outText;
            setlocale(LC_ALL, old_ctype);
            free(old_ctype);
        }
```

At the beginning of the method body, we check whether the `currentImage` member field is null. If it is null, there's no image opened in our application, so we immediately return after showing a message box.

If it is not null, then we are going to create the Tesseract API instance. Tesseract requires that we must have our locale set to C, so first, we call the `setlocale` function with the `LC_ALL` category and null value to get and save the current locale setting, and then call this function again with the same category and the value, C, to set the locale as required by Tesseract. Once the OCR work is complete, we will recover the locale setting using the saved `LC_ALL` value.

After setting the locale to C, now, we can create the Tesseract API instance. We create it by using the expression, `new tesseract::TessBaseAPI()`. The newly created API instance must be initialized before it is used. Initialization is executed by calling the `Init` method. There are many versions (overloads) of the `Init` method:

```
// 1
int Init(const char* datapath, const char* language, OcrEngineMode mode,
        char **configs, int configs_size,
        const GenericVector<STRING> *vars_vec,
        const GenericVector<STRING> *vars_values,
        bool set_only_non_debug_params);
// 2
int Init(const char* datapath, const char* language, OcrEngineMode oem) {
  return Init(datapath, language, oem, nullptr, 0, nullptr, nullptr,
false);
}
// 3
```

```
int Init(const char* datapath, const char* language) {
   return Init(datapath, language, OEM_DEFAULT, nullptr, 0, nullptr,
nullptr, false);
}
// 4
int Init(const char* data, int data_size, const char* language,
         OcrEngineMode mode, char** configs, int configs_size,
         const GenericVector<STRING>* vars_vec,
         const GenericVector<STRING>* vars_values,
         bool set_only_non_debug_params, FileReader reader);
```

In some of these versions, we can specify the pretrained data path, the language name, the OCR engine mode, the page segmentation mode, and a number of other configurations. To simplify the code, we use the simplest version, the third version, of this method to initialize the API instance. In this call, we just pass the data path and language name. It is worth noting that the data path is represented by the macro we defined in the project file. The initialization process may fail, so we check its result and return immediately after showing a brief message if the initialization fails.

After the Tesseract API instance is ready, we get the currently opened image and convert it to an image of the QImage::Format_RGB888 format, as we had done in our previous projects.

Once we have the image with the RGB888 format, we can feed it to the Tesseract API instance by calling its SetImage method. The SetImage method also has a number of different overload versions:

```
// 1
void SetImage(const unsigned char* imagedata, int width, int height,
              int bytes_per_pixel, int bytes_per_line);
// 2
void SetImage(Pix* pix);
```

The first one can be called with the information of the data format of a given image. It is not restricted to any library-defined class, such as QImage in Qt, or Mat in OpenCV. The second version accepts a Pix pointer as the input image. The Pix class is defined by the image processing library, Leptonica. Obviously, it is the first version that is best suited in this instance. All the information it requires can be retrieved from the QImage instance, which has 3 channels and a depth of 8 bits; hence, it uses 3 bytes for each pixel:

```
        tesseractAPI->SetImage(image.bits(), image.width(),
image.height(),
            3, image.bytesPerLine());
```

Once the Tesseract API instance gets the image, we can call its `GetUTF8Text()` method to obtain the text it recognizes from the image. It's worth noting here that it is the caller's responsibility to free the resulting data buffer of this method.

The remaining tasks are to set the extracted text to the editor widget, destroy the Tesseract API instance, delete the resulting data buffer of the `GetUTF8Text` call, and recover the locale setting.

OK. Let's compile and restart our application. After the application starts, we open an image with text in it and click the **OCR** action on the toolbar. Then, the application will fill the editor with the text extracted from the image on the left-hand side:

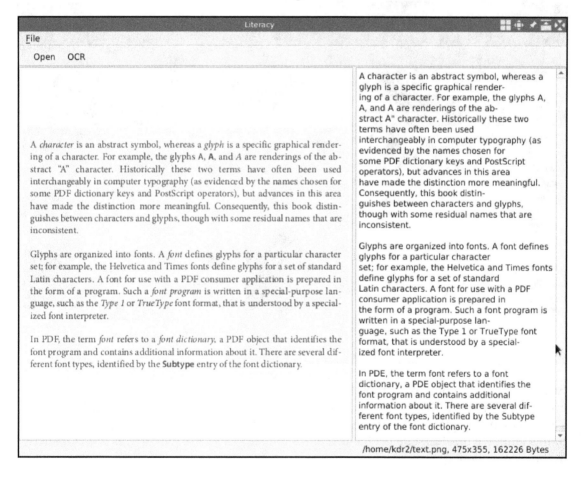

If you are satisfied with the result, you can save the text as a file by clicking the **Save Text as** item under the file menu.

So far, our application has the ability to recognize and extract text from the images that are photos of books or scanned documents. For these images, they have only text with good typesetting in them. If we give the application a photo that contains many different elements, and the text only occupies a small portion of it, such as a photo of a shop front, or a traffic sign on the road, it will, in all probability, fail to recognize the characters. We can test this with the following photo:

Just as we guessed, our application fails to extract the text in it. To handle these kinds of images, we shouldn't just simply pass the whole image to Tesseract. We also have to tell Tesseract which region of the image contains text. So, before we extract text from an image of this kind, we must first detect the text areas in that image. We will do this with OpenCV in the next section.

Detecting text areas with OpenCV

In the preceding section, we succeeded in extracting text from images with well-typeset text; for example, scanned documents. However, for text in photos of common scenes, our application doesn't work well. In this section, we are going to fix this issue of our application.

In this section, we will resort to the EAST text detector with OpenCV to detect the presence of text in an image. **EAST** is short for an **Efficient and Accurate Scene Text** detector, a description of which can be found at `https://arxiv.org/abs/1704.03155`. It is a neural network-based algorithm, but the architecture of its neural network model and the training process are beyond the scope of this chapter. In this section, we will focus on how to use a pretrained model of OpenCV's EAST text detector.

Before starting with the code, let's get the pretrained model ready first. A pretrained model file for the EAST model can be downloaded from `http://depot.kdr2.com/books/Qt-5-and-OpenCV-4-Computer-Vision-Projects/trained-model/frozen_east_text_detection.pb`. Let's download it and place it in the root directory of our project:

```
$ curl -O
http://depot.kdr2.com/books/Qt-5-and-OpenCV-4-Computer-Vision-Projects/trai
ned-model/frozen_east_text_detection.pb
# output omitted
$ ls -l
total 95176
-rw-r--r-- 1 kdr2 kdr2 96662756 Mar 22 17:03 frozen_east_text_detection.pb
-rwxr-xr-x 1 kdr2 kdr2 131776 Mar 22 17:30 Literacy
-rw-r--r-- 1 kdr2 kdr2 988 Mar 23 21:13 Literacy.pro
-rw-r--r-- 1 kdr2 kdr2 224 Mar 7 15:32 main.cpp
-rw-r--r-- 1 kdr2 kdr2 11062 Mar 23 21:13 mainwindow.cpp
-rw-r--r-- 1 kdr2 kdr2 1538 Mar 23 21:13 mainwindow.h
# output truncated
```

This is fairly straightforward. The preparation for the neural network mode is done. Now, let's move on to the code.

The first file that needs to be updated is the project file, `Literacy.pro`. We need to incorporate the settings of the OpenCV library, just like we did in the previous chapters:

```
# opencv config
unix: !mac {
    INCLUDEPATH += /home/kdr2/programs/opencv/include/opencv4
    LIBS += -L/home/kdr2/programs/opencv/lib -lopencv_core -lopencv_imgproc
-lopencv_dnn
}
```

```
unix: mac {
    INCLUDEPATH += /path/to/opencv/include/opencv4
    LIBS += -L/path/to/opencv/lib -lopencv_world
}

win32 {
    INCLUDEPATH += c:/path/to/opencv/include/opencv4
    LIBS += -lc:/path/to/opencv/lib/opencv_world
}
```

It's worth noting that we add the `opencv_dnn` module to the `LIBS` setting. Because of that, the implementation of the EAST algorithm, which is actually a deep neural network, is in this module.

The next file we are going to update is the header file, `mainwindow.h`. We include two OpenCV header files in it and then add some fields and methods to the `MainWindow` class in this file:

```
// ...
#include <QCheckBox>
// ...
#include "opencv2/opencv.hpp"
#include "opencv2/dnn.hpp"

class MainWindow : public QMainWindow
{
    // ...
private:
    // ...
    void showImage(cv::Mat);
    // ...
    void decode(const cv::Mat& scores, const cv::Mat& geometry, float scoreThresh,
        std::vector<cv::RotatedRect>& detections, std::vector<float>& confidences);
    cv::Mat detectTextAreas(QImage &image, std::vector<cv::Rect>&);

    // ...
private:
    // ...
    QCheckBox *detectAreaCheckBox;
    // ...
    cv::dnn::Net net;
};
```

Let's examine the newly added private fields first. The member field, `cv::dnn::Net net`, is a deep neural network instance that will be used for detecting the text areas. The `detectAreaCheckBox` field is a checkbox that will appear on the toolbar, allowing users to give us an indicator to determine whether we should detect text areas before executing the OCR work with Tesseract.

The `detectTextAreas` method is for detecting areas with OpenCV, while the `decode` method constitutes an auxiliary method. After we detect the text area on an image, we will draw a rectangle for each text area on that image. All these steps are done with OpenCV. Hence, the image will be represented as an instance of `cv::Mat`, so we overload another version of the `showImage` method, which takes an instance of `cv::Mat` as its only argument to show the updated image on the UI.

Now, let's go to the `mainwindow.cpp` source file to see the changes.

First, let's see the most important method, `MainWindow::detectTextAreas`. As intended, this method takes a `QImage` object as the input image as its first argument. The second argument of it is a reference to a vector of `cv::Rect`, which is used to hold the detected text areas. The return value of this method is `cv::Mat`, which represents the input image with the detected rectangle drawn on it. Let's see its implementation in the following code snippet:

```
cv::Mat MainWindow::detectTextAreas(QImage &image,
std::vector<cv::Rect> &areas)
    {
        float confThreshold = 0.5;
        float nmsThreshold = 0.4;
        int inputWidth = 320;
        int inputHeight = 320;
        std::string model = "./frozen_east_text_detection.pb";
        // Load DNN network.
        if (net.empty()) {
            net = cv::dnn::readNet(model);
        }

        // more ...
    }
```

The code is the first part of the method body. In this part, we define many variables and create a deep neural network. The first two thresholds are for confidence and non-maximum suppression. We will use them to filter the detection result of the AI model. The EAST model requires that the width and the height of the image must be multiples of 32, so we define two int variables, whose values are both 320. Before we send the input image to the DNN model, we will resize it to the dimensions described by these two variables, that is, 320 x 320 in this instance.

Then, we define a string with the path to the pretrained model data file we have downloaded and load it by calling the cv::dnn::readNet function on condition that the class member, net, is empty. The DNN of OpenCV supports many kinds of pretrained model data files:

- *.caffemodel (Caffe, http://caffe.berkeleyvision.org/)
- *.pb (TensorFlow, https://www.tensorflow.org/)
- *.t7 or *.net (Torch, http://torch.ch/)
- *.weights (Darknet, https://pjreddie.com/darknet/)
- *.bin (DLDT, https://software.intel.com/openvino-toolkit)

From the previous list, you can ascertain that the pretrained model we use is constructed and trained using the TensorFlow framework.

So, the DNN model is loaded. Now, let's send our input image to the model to perform text detection:

```
std::vector<cv::Mat> outs;
std::vector<std::string> layerNames(2);
layerNames[0] = "feature_fusion/Conv_7/Sigmoid";
layerNames[1] = "feature_fusion/concat_3";

cv::Mat frame = cv::Mat(
    image.height(),
    image.width(),
    CV_8UC3,
    image.bits(),
    image.bytesPerLine()).clone();
cv::Mat blob;

cv::dnn::blobFromImage(
    frame, blob,
    1.0, cv::Size(inputWidth, inputHeight),
    cv::Scalar(123.68, 116.78, 103.94), true, false
```

```
);
net.setInput(blob);
net.forward(outs, layerNames);
```

In this piece of code, we define a vector of `cv::Mat` to save the output layers of the model. Then, we put the names of the two layers we need to extract from the DNN model into a string vector, which is the `layerNames` variable. The two layers contain the information that we want:

1. The first layer, `feature_fusion/Conv_7/Sigmoid`, is the output layer of the Sigmoid activation. The data in this layer contains the probability of whether a given region contains text.
2. The second layer, `feature_fusion/concat_3`, is the output layer of the feature map. The data in this layer contains the geometry of the image. We will get many bounding boxes by decoding the data in this layer later.

After this, we convert the input image from `QImage` to `cv::Mat`, and then convert the matrix to another matrix, which is a 4-dimensional blob that can be used as the input of the DNN model, in other words, the input layer. The latter conversion is implemented by calling the `blobFromImage` function in the `cv::dnn` namespace of the OpenCV library. Many operations are executed in this conversion, such as resizing and cropping the image from the center, subtracting mean values, scaling values by a scale factor, and swapping R and B channels. In this call to the `blobFromImage` function, we have many arguments. Let's explain them now one by one:

1. The first argument is the input image.
2. The second argument is the output image.
3. The third argument is the scale factor of each pixel value. We use 1.0 because we don't need to scale the pixels here.
4. The fourth argument is the spatial size of the output image. We said that the width and the height of this size must be multiples of 32, and we use 320 x 320 here with the variables we defined.
5. The fifth argument is the mean that should be subtracted from each image since this was used while training the model. Here, the mean used is (`123.68`, `116.78, 103.94`).
6. The next argument is whether we want to swap the R and B channels. This is required since OpenCV uses the BGR format, and TensorFlow uses the RGB format.
7. The final argument is whether we want to crop the image and take the center crop. We specify `false` in this case.

After that call returns, we get the blob that can be used as the input of the DNN model. Then, we pass it to the neural network and perform a round of forwarding to get the output layers by calling the `setInput` method and the `forward` method of the model. Once forwarding is complete, the two output layers we want will be stored in the `outs` vector we defined. The next thing is to process these output layers to get the text areas:

```
cv::Mat scores = outs[0];
cv::Mat geometry = outs[1];

std::vector<cv::RotatedRect> boxes;
std::vector<float> confidences;
decode(scores, geometry, confThreshold, boxes, confidences);

std::vector<int> indices;
cv::dnn::NMSBoxes(boxes, confidences, confThreshold, nmsThreshold,
indices);
```

The first element of the `outs` vector is the score, while the second element is the geometry. Then, we call another method of the `MainWindow` class, `decode`, to decode the positions of the textboxes along with their orientation. With this decoding process, we will have the candidate text areas as `cv::RotatedRect` and store them in the `boxes` variable. The corresponding confidences of these boxes are stored in the `confidences` variable.

Since we may get many candidates for a textbox, we need to filter out the best looking textboxes. This is done using non-maximum suppression, that is, the call to the `NMSBoxes` method. In this call, we give the decoded boxes, the confidences, and the thresholds of the confidences and non-maximum suppression, and the indices of the boxes that are not eliminated will be stored in the last argument, `indices`.

The `decode` method is used to extract the confidences and box information from the output layers. Its implementation can be found at `https://github.com/opencv/opencv/blob/master/samples/dnn/text_detection.cpp#L119`. To understand it, you should understand the data structures in the DNN model, especially the ones in the output layers. However, that is beyond the scope of this book. If you are interested in it, you can refer to the paper pertaining to EAST at `https://arxiv.org/abs/1704.03155v2`, and one of its implementations using Tensorflow at `https://github.com/argman/EAST`.

For now, we get all the text areas as instances of cv::RotatedRect, and these are for the resized image, so we should map them onto the original input image:

```
        cv::Point2f ratio((float)frame.cols / inputWidth, (float)frame.rows
    / inputHeight);
        cv::Scalar green = cv::Scalar(0, 255, 0);

        for (size_t i = 0; i < indices.size(); ++i) {
            cv::RotatedRect& box = boxes[indices[i]];
            cv::Rect area = box.boundingRect();
            area.x *= ratio.x;
            area.width *= ratio.x;
            area.y *= ratio.y;
            area.height *= ratio.y;
            areas.push_back(area);
            cv::rectangle(frame, area, green, 1);
            QString index = QString("%1").arg(i);
            cv::putText(
                frame, index.toStdString(), cv::Point2f(area.x, area.y -
    2),
                cv::FONT_HERSHEY_SIMPLEX, 0.5, green, 1
            );
        }
        return frame;
```

In order to map the text areas to the original image, we should know how the image is resized before it is sent to the DNN model, and then reverse that resizing process on the text areas. So, we calculate the resizing ratios in terms of the width aspect and the height aspect and then save them to cv::Point2f ratio. Then, we iterate over the retained indices, and get each cv::RotatedRect object indicated by each index. To reduce the complexity of our code, instead of rotating cv::RotatedRect and its content to a regular rectangle, we simply get the bounding rectangle of it. Then, we do the reverse resizing on the rectangle and push it into the areas vector. In order to demonstrate how these areas appear, we also draw them onto the original image and insert a number in the top-right corner of each rectangle to indicate the order in which they will be processed.

At the end of the method, we return the updated original image.

Now that we have finished the text area detection method, let's integrate it into our application.

First, in the `initUI` method, we create the checkbox that is used to determine whether we should detect text areas before performing OCR, and add it to the file toolbar:

```
detectAreaCheckBox = new QCheckBox("Detect Text Areas", this);
fileToolBar->addWidget(detectAreaCheckBox);
```

Then, in the `MainWindow::extractText` method, we check the state of that checkbox after setting the entire image to the Tesseract API:

```
tesseractAPI->SetImage(image.bits(), image.width(), image.height(),
    3, image.bytesPerLine());

if (detectAreaCheckBox->checkState() == Qt::Checked) {
    std::vector<cv::Rect> areas;
    cv::Mat newImage = detectTextAreas(image, areas);
    showImage(newImage);
    editor->setPlainText("");
    for(cv::Rect &rect : areas) {
        tesseractAPI->SetRectangle(rect.x, rect.y, rect.width,
rect.height);
        char *outText = tesseractAPI->GetUTF8Text();
        editor->setPlainText(editor->toPlainText() + outText);
        delete [] outText;
    }
} else {
    char *outText = tesseractAPI->GetUTF8Text();
    editor->setPlainText(outText);
    delete [] outText;
}
```

As you can see, if the checkbox is checked, we call the `detextTextAreas` method to detect the text areas. The call returns the image as an instance of `cv::Mat`, with the text areas and indices drawn on it, and then we call the `showImage` method with this image to show it on the window. Then, we iterate over the text areas and send them to the Tesseract API by calling its `SetRectangle` method to tell it to only endeavor to recognize the characters inside this rectangle. Then, we obtain the recognized text, append it to the editor, and free the memory of the text.

If the checkbox is not checked, we apply long-established logic. Let Tesseract recognize the text in the entire image.

We also perform a small optimization of our code here. Since the Tesseract API instance can be reused, we only create and initialize it once:

```
if (tesseractAPI == nullptr) {
    tesseractAPI = new tesseract::TessBaseAPI();
    // Initialize tesseract-ocr with English, with specifying
tessdata path
    if (tesseractAPI->Init(TESSDATA_PREFIX, "eng")) {
        QMessageBox::information(this, "Error", "Could not
initialize tesseract.");
        return;
    }
}
```

And we destroy it in the destructor of the `MainWindow` class:

```
MainWindow::~MainWindow()
{
    // Destroy used object and release memory
    if(tesseractAPI != nullptr) {
        tesseractAPI->End();
        delete tesseractAPI;
    }
}
```

So, the final thing left to do is to implement the overloaded `showImage` method. Since we have already done lots of work in terms of image format conversions and displaying images with Qt, this really is a piece of cake to us:

```
void MainWindow::showImage(cv::Mat mat)
{
    QImage image(
        mat.data,
        mat.cols,
        mat.rows,
        mat.step,
        QImage::Format_RGB888);

    QPixmap pixmap = QPixmap::fromImage(image);
    imageScene->clear();
    imageView->resetMatrix();
    currentImage = imageScene->addPixmap(pixmap);
    imageScene->update();
    imageView->setSceneRect(pixmap.rect());
}
```

OK. Finally, we can compile and run our application to test it:

```
$ make
# output omitted
$ export
LD_LIBRARY_PATH=/home/kdr2/programs/opencv/lib:/home/kdr2/programs/tesseract/lib
$ ./Literacy
```

Let's open a photo containing text with our application, keep the **Detect Text Areas** checkbox unchecked, and then click on the **OCR** button. The following bad result will be visible:

Then, we check the checkbox and click the **OCR** button again, and see what happens:

Four text areas are correctly detected, and text in three of them is correctly recognized. Not bad!

Recognizing characters on the screen

In the previous sections, we finished discussing almost all of the features of our Literacy application. In this section, in order to improve the user experience of the application, we will add a feature to allow the user to grab a part of the screen as the input image of the application. With this feature, the user can click the mouse button and then drag it to select a rectangular region of the screen as an image. Then, they can either save the image as a file or perform OCR on it.

We will create a new class to implement this feature. The new class is called ScreenCapturer, and is defined in the header file, screencapturer.h:

```
class ScreenCapturer : public QWidget {
    Q_OBJECT

public:
    explicit ScreenCapturer(MainWindow *w);
    ~ScreenCapturer();

protected:
    void paintEvent(QPaintEvent *event) override;
    void mouseMoveEvent(QMouseEvent *event) override;
    void mousePressEvent(QMouseEvent *event) override;
    void mouseReleaseEvent(QMouseEvent *event) override;

private slots:
    void closeMe();
    void confirmCapture();

private:
    void initShortcuts();
    QPixmap captureDesktop();

private:
    MainWindow *window;
    QPixmap screen;
    QPoint p1, p2;
    bool mouseDown;
};
```

After omitting the include directives, the class definition is very clear. It is a subclass of QWidget, and has the Q_OBJECT macro at the beginning of the class body. We define many member fields in this class:

- MainWindow *window is a pointer that points to the main window object of our application. When an image is grabbed, we will call its showImage method to show the grabbed image.
- QPixmap screen is for storing the image of the whole screen or screens.
- QPoint p1, p2 are the top-right and bottom-left points of the selected rectangle.
- bool mouseDown is a flag that is used to indicate whether a mouse button is pressed; that is, if the user is dragging or moving the mouse.

There are also many methods in the class. Let's first look at its constructor and destructor. Its constructor takes a pointer to the main window object as its argument:

```
ScreenCapturer::ScreenCapturer(MainWindow *w):
    QWidget(nullptr), window(w)
{
    setWindowFlags(
        Qt::BypassWindowManagerHint
        | Qt::WindowStaysOnTopHint
        | Qt::FramelessWindowHint
        | Qt::Tool
    );

    setAttribute(Qt::WA_DeleteOnClose);

    screen = captureDesktop();
    resize(screen.size());
    initShortcuts();
}
```

In the implementation of the constructor, we call its parent class constructor with a null pointer and initialize the `window` member with the only argument. In the method body, we set many flags for our widget:

- `Qt::BypassWindowManagerHint` tells it to ignore the arrangement of the window manager.
- `Qt::WindowStaysOnTopHint` tells it to stay on the topmost layer of the desktop if possible.
- `Qt::FramelessWindowHint` makes the widget have no title bar or window border.
- `Qt::Tool` indicates that the widget is a tool window.

With these flags, our widget will be a borderless tool window that always stays on the top layer of our desktop.

The `Qt::WA_DeleteOnClose` attribute ensures that the widget instance will be deleted after it is closed.

After all flags and attributes are set, we call the `captureDesktop()` method to grab the entire desktop as one big image and assign it to the `screen` member field. Then, we resize the widget to the size of the big image and call `initShortcuts` to set up some hotkeys.

We omit the destructor here since it has nothing to do. Thus, it only has an empty method body. Now, let's go to the `captureDesktop` method to see how we grab the entire desktop as one big image:

```
QPixmap ScreenCapturer::captureDesktop() {
    QRect geometry;
    for (QScreen *const screen : QGuiApplication::screens()) {
        geometry = geometry.united(screen->geometry());
    }

    QPixmap pixmap(QApplication::primaryScreen()->grabWindow(
                    QApplication::desktop()->winId(),
                    geometry.x(),
                    geometry.y(),
                    geometry.width(),
                    geometry.height()
            ));
    pixmap.setDevicePixelRatio(QApplication::desktop()->devicePixelRatio());
    return pixmap;
}
```

A desktop might have multiple screens, so we get all these screens by means of `QGuiApplication::screens()` and combine their geometries in a big rectangle. Then, we get the ID of the desktop widget (also called the root window) by means of `QApplication::desktop()->winId()` and grab the desktop root window as an instance of `QPixmap`. Since we pass the position and the size of the combined rectangle to the `grabWIndow` function, the entire desktop, including all the screens, is grabbed. Finally, we set the device pixel ratio of the image to a proper one that fits the local device and then return it.

Now that we know how the widget is constructed and how the desktop is grabbed in the construction process, the next thing is to show the grabbed image on the widget. This is done by overriding its `paintEvent` method:

```
void ScreenCapturer::paintEvent(QPaintEvent*) {
    QPainter painter(this);
    painter.drawPixmap(0, 0, screen);

    QRegion grey(rect());
    painter.setClipRegion(grey);
    QColor overlayColor(20, 20, 20, 50);
    painter.fillRect(rect(), overlayColor);
    painter.setClipRect(rect());
}
```

This method, `paintEvent`, will be called every time a widget needs to update itself; for instance, when it is opened, resized, or moved. In this method, we define a `QPainter` method, and then draw the grabbed image on the widget with it. Since the grabbed image looks exactly the same as the desktop, the user may not realize that we are showing a grabbed image. In order to tell users that what they are facing is a grabbed image but not the desktop, we draw a translucent gray overlay on the top of the grabbed image.

Then, we should figure out a way to allow the user to select a region of the grabbed image. This is done by overriding three mouse event handlers:

- `mousePressEvent`, which is called when a button of the mouse is pressed
- `mouseMoveEvent`, which is called when the mouse is moved
- `mouseReleaseEvent`, which is called when the pressed mouse button is released

When a mouse button is pressed, we save the position where it is pressed to the members p1 and p2, mark the `mouseDown` flag as true, and call `update` to tell the widget to repaint itself:

```
void ScreenCapturer::mousePressEvent(QMouseEvent *event)
{
    mouseDown = true;
    p1 = event->pos();
    p2 = event->pos();
    update();
}
```

When the mouse is moved, we check the `mouseDown` flag. If it is true, the user is dragging the mouse, so we update the current position of the mouse to the member field, p2, and then call `update` to repaint the widget:

```
void ScreenCapturer::mouseMoveEvent(QMouseEvent *event)
{
    if(!mouseDown) return;
    p2 = event->pos();
    update();
}
```

When the pressed mouse button is released, things are straightforward:

```
void ScreenCapturer::mouseReleaseEvent(QMouseEvent *event)
{
    mouseDown = false;
    p2 = event->pos();
    update();
}
```

We mark the `mouseDown` flag as `false`, save the event position to `p2`, and update the widget.

With these three event handlers, while the user is dragging the mouse, we can get a rectangle determined by the continuously updated points, `p1` and `p2`. That rectangle is the selection area. Now, let's draw this rectangle to the widget in the `paintEvent` method:

```
void ScreenCapturer::paintEvent(QPaintEvent*) {
    QPainter painter(this);
    painter.drawPixmap(0, 0, screen);

    QRegion grey(rect());
    if(p1.x() != p2.x() && p1.y() != p2.y()) {
        painter.setPen(QColor(200, 100, 50, 255));
        painter.drawRect(QRect(p1, p2));
        grey = grey.subtracted(QRect(p1, p2));
    }
    painter.setClipRegion(grey);
    QColor overlayColor(20, 20, 20, 50);
    painter.fillRect(rect(), overlayColor);
    painter.setClipRect(rect());
}
```

As you can see, in the method body, we add four lines of code. We check whether `p1` and `p2` are the same points; if not, we draw the border of the rectangle determined by `p1` and `p2` and subtract the rectangle from the region in which the translucent gray overlay is drawn. Now, if the user drags their mouse, they will see the rectangle selected.

Now, the user can open the fullscreen widget and select a region of the image grabbed from the entire desktop. After that, the user will want to use the selection or give up the operation. These are implemented by the slots, `confirmCapture` and `closeMe`:

```
void ScreenCapturer::confirmCapture()
{
    QPixmap image = screen.copy(QRect(p1, p2));
    window->showImage(image);
    closeMe();
}
```

```
void ScreenCapturer::closeMe()
{
    this->close();
    window->showNormal();
    window->activateWindow();
}
```

In the `confirmCapture` slot, we copy the selected rectangle on the grabbed image of the entire desktop as a new image, and then call the `showImage` method of the main window with it to show it and use it. Finally, we call `closeMe` to close the widget window.

In the `closeMe` slot, we do nothing apart from closing the current widget window and recovering the state of the main window.

Then, we connect these slots to some hotkeys in the `initShortcuts` method:

```
void ScreenCapturer::initShortcuts() {
    new QShortcut(Qt::Key_Escape, this, SLOT(closeMe()));
    new QShortcut(Qt::Key_Return, this, SLOT(confirmCapture()));
}
```

As you can see, if the user presses the *Esc* key on the keyboard, we close the widget, and, if the user presses the *Enter* key, we use the user's selection as the input image of our application and close the capturing widget.

For now, the screen capturing widget is done, so let's integrate it into the main window. Let's see the change in the header file, `mainwindow.h`:

```
class MainWindow : public QMainWindow
{
    // ...
public:
    // ...
    void showImage(QPixmap);
    // ...
private slots:
    // ...
    void captureScreen();
    void startCapture();

private:
    // ..
    QAction *captureAction;
    // ...
};
```

First, we add another version of the `showImage` method that takes a `QPixmap` object. This is used by the screen capturing widget. Since we already have many versions of this method, this is left to the reader to implement. You can refer to the accompanying code repository if necessary.

Then, we add two slots and one action. We create the action and add it to the toolbar in the `createActions` method:

```
captureAction = new QAction("Capture Screen", this);
fileToolBar->addAction(captureAction);
// ...
connect(captureAction, SIGNAL(triggered(bool)), this,
SLOT(captureScreen()));
```

In the preceding code, we connect the newly added action to the `captureScreen` slot, so let's see the implementation of this slot:

```
void MainWindow::captureScreen()
{
    this->setWindowState(this->windowState() | Qt::WindowMinimized);
    QTimer::singleShot(500, this, SLOT(startCapture()));
}
```

In this slot, we minimize the main window and then schedule a call to the `startCapture` slot after 0.5 seconds. In the `startCapture` slot, we will create a screen capturing widget instance, open it, and then activate it:

```
void MainWindow::startCapture()
{
    ScreenCapturer *cap = new ScreenCapturer(this);
    cap->show();
    cap->activateWindow();
}
```

Here, we use another slot and schedule it a short time later because, if we were to do this immediately, the minimization of the main window would not be finished when the screen is captured.

Now, there's only one thing left to do before we can compile and run our project; update the project file and incorporate the new source files:

```
HEADERS += mainwindow.h screencapturer.h
SOURCES += main.cpp mainwindow.cpp screencapturer.cpp
```

Now, let's compile and start our application. Click on the **Capture Screen** button on the toolbar, and then drag the mouse to select a region like this:

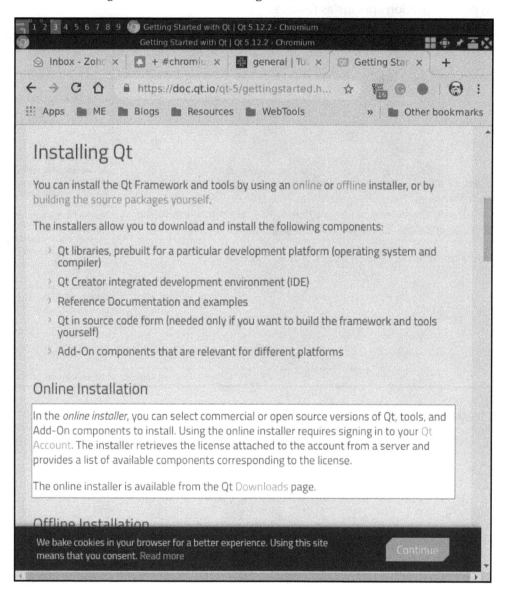

At this point, you can press the *Esc* key to cancel the selection, or press the *Enter* key to confirm the selection. If you press the *Enter* key and then click the **OCR** button on the toolbar, our application appears as follows:

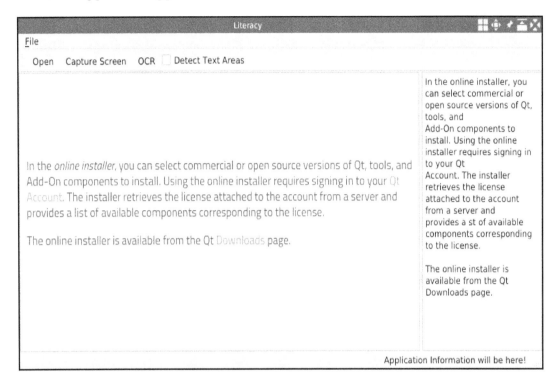

OK! It works exactly as per our expectations and our application is finally finished.

Summary

In this chapter, we created a new application named Literacy. In this application, we recognized characters on images using the Tesseract library. For images that have well-typeset characters, Tesseract worked well; but for the characters in photos of ordinary everyday life, it failed to recognize them. To fix this issue, we resorted to the EAST model with OpenCV. With a pretrained EAST model, we first detected the text areas in photos and then instructed the Tesseract library to only recognize the characters in the detected regions. At this point, Tesseract performed well again. In the last section, we learned how to grab the desktop as an image and how to select a region on it by dragging the mouse.

We used several pretrained neural network models in this and previous chapters. In the next chapter, we will learn more about them; for instance, how to use pretrained classifiers or models to detect objects and how to train a model.

Questions

Try these questions to test your knowledge from this chapter:

1. How can characters in non-English languages be recognized with Tesseract?
2. When we used the EAST model to detect text areas, the detected areas were actually rotated rectangles, and we simply used their bounding rectangles instead. Is this always correct? If not, how can this be fixed?
3. Is it possible to figure out a way to allow users to adjust the selected region after dragging the mouse while capturing images from the screen?

Object Detection in Real Time

6

In the preceding chapter, we learned about **Optical Character Recognition** (**OCR**) technology. We recognized text in scanned documents and photos with the help of the Tesseract library and a pretrained deep learning model (the EAST model), which is loaded with OpenCV. In this chapter, we will move on to the topic of object detection. We will discuss several approaches to object detection provided by OpenCV and other libraries and frameworks.

The following topics will be covered in this chapter:

- Training and using cascade classifiers to detect objects
- Object detection using deep learning models

Technical requirements

As with the previous chapters, readers are required to have Qt of at least version 5 and OpenCV 4.0.0 installed. Having some basic knowledge about C++ and Qt programming is also a basic requirement.

Though we are focusing on OpenCV 4.0.0, OpenCV 3.4.x is also required in this chapter. You should have multiple versions (4.0.0 and 3.4.5) of OpenCV installed to follow along with this chapter. I will explain why later.

Since we will use deep learning models to detect objects, having knowledge of deep learning will also be a big help in understanding the contents of this chapter.

All the code for this chapter can be found in our code repository at `https://github.com/PacktPublishing/Qt-5-and-OpenCV-4-Computer-Vision-Projects/tree/master/Chapter-06`.

Check out the following video to see the code in action: `http://bit.ly/2Fjx5SS`

Detecting objects using OpenCV

There are many approaches to object detection in OpenCV. These approaches can be categorized as follows:

- Color-based algorithms such as meanshift and **Continuously Adaptive Meanshift** (**CAMshift**)
- Template matching
- Feature extracting and matching
- **Artificial Neural Networks** (**ANNs**)
- Cascade classifier
- Pretrained deep learning models

The first three are the traditional approaches to object detection, while the last three are approaches of machine learning.

The color-based algorithms, such as meanshift and CAMshift, use histograms and back-projection images to locate an object in an image with incredible speed. The template matching approach uses the object of interest as a template and tries to find the object by scanning the image of a given scene. Feature extracting and matching approaches first extract all features, usually edge features and corner features, from both of the objects of interest and the scene image, then use these features to do the matching to find the object. All these approaches work well on simple and static scenes, and they are very easy to use. But they usually don't work well in complex and dynamic situations.

The ANN, cascade classifier, and deep learning approaches are categorized as machine learning approaches. All of them need to train a model before they are used. With the facilities provided by OpenCV, we can train an ANN model or a cascade classifier model, but we can't train a deep learning model with OpenCV for now. The following table shows whether these approaches can be trained or used with the OpenCV library, as well as their performance (on recall rate and accuracy) levels:

Approach	Can be trained by OpenCV	Can be loaded by OpenCV	Performance
ANN	Yes	Yes	Medium
Cascade classifier	Yes	Yes	Medium
Deep learning model	No	Yes (many kinds of format)	High

Actually, both ANN, and deep learning are neural networks. The difference between them is that an ANN model has a simple architecture and only a few hidden layers, while a deep learning model may have a complex architecture (such as LSTM, RNN, CNN, and so on) and a large number of hidden layers. In the last century, people used ANNs because they didn't have enough computing power, so it was not possible to train a complex neural network. Now, training a complex neural network is possible thanks to the development of heterogeneous computing over the past ten years. Nowadays, we use deep learning models because they have much higher performance (both in terms of recall rate and accuracy) than simple ANN models.

In this chapter, we will focus on the cascade classifier and deep learning approaches. Though training a deep learning model with the OpenCV library of the current version is not possible, it will probably become possible in the future.

Detecting objects using a cascade classifier

First, let's see how we can use a cascade classifier to detect objects. Actually, we have already used cascade classifiers in this book. In Chapter 4, *Fun with Faces*, we used a pretrained cascade classifier to detect faces in real time. The pretrained cascade classifier we used was one of the OpenCV built-in cascade classifiers and can be found in the data directory of the OpenCV installation:

```
$ ls ~/programs/opencv/share/opencv4/haarcascades/
haarcascade_eye_tree_eyeglasses.xml haarcascade_lefteye_2splits.xml
haarcascade_eye.xml haarcascade_licence_plate_rus_16stages.xml
haarcascade_frontalcatface_extended.xml haarcascade_lowerbody.xml
haarcascade_frontalcatface.xml haarcascade_profileface.xml
haarcascade_frontalface_alt2.xml haarcascade_righteye_2splits.xml
haarcascade_frontalface_alt_tree.xml haarcascade_russian_plate_number.xml
haarcascade_frontalface_alt.xml haarcascade_smile.xml
haarcascade_frontalface_default.xml haarcascade_upperbody.xml
haarcascade_fullbody.xml
```

As you can see, the `haarcascade_frontalface_default.xml` file is the one we used in Chapter 4, *Fun with Faces*.

In this chapter, we will try to train cascade classifiers by ourselves. Before we do that, we will first build an application to test the cascade classifiers. I am going to call this application **Detective**.

The application is very similar to the ones we built in Chapter 3, *Home Security Applications* (the Gazer application), and Chapter 4, *Fun with Faces* (the Facetious application), so we will build it quickly by coping one of these applications.

Do you remember what we did at the beginning of Chapter 4, *Fun with Faces*? We copied the Gazer application from Chapter 3, *Home Security Applications*, and then abridged it to a basic application with which we could play a video feed from our webcam and take photos. We can find that basic application at this commit at https://github.com/ PacktPublishing/Qt-5-and-OpenCV-4-Computer-Vision-Projects/tree/ 744d445ad4c834cd52660a85a224e48279ac2cf4. Let's copy it into a Terminal:

```
$ pwd
/home/kdr2/Work/Books/Qt-5-and-OpenCV-4-Computer-Vision-Projects
$ git checkout 744d445
Note: checking out '744d445'.

You are in 'detached HEAD' state. You can look around, make experimental
changes and commit them, and you can discard any commits you make in this
state without impacting any branches by performing another checkout.

If you want to create a new branch to retain commits you create, you may
do so (now or later) by using -b with the checkout command again. Example:

  git checkout -b <new-branch-name>

HEAD is now at 744d445 Facetious: take photos

$ mkdir Chapter-06
# !!! you should copy it to a different dir
$ cp -r Chapter-04/Facetious Chapter-06/Detective
$ ls Chapter-06
Detective
$git checkout master
$ cd Chapter-06/Detective/
```

In our code repository, we check out to the 744d445 commit, create a new directory for this chapter, then copy the source tree of the Facetious project at that revision to a new directory named Detective under the Chapter-06 directory. Then we switch back to the master branch.

I copied the basic application to the Chapter-06/Detective directory while writing this book, hence that directory already exists while you are reading the book. If you are coding by following the instructions, you can copy the basic application to a different new directory and work under that directory.

After getting the basic application, we make some minor changes to it:

- Rename the Facetious.pro project file to Detective.pro.
- Change the word Facetious to Detective in the following files:
    - Detective.pro
    - main.cpp
    - mainwindow.cpp
    - utilities.cpp

OK, now we have a basic Detective application. All the changes in this stage can be found in the commit at https://github.com/PacktPublishing/Qt-5-and-OpenCV-4-Computer-Vision-Projects/commit/0df07d6b452e69bd216599797057ee3e8a6ebf6e.

The next thing is to detect a certain kind of object with a pretrained cascade classifier. This time, we will use the haarcascade_frontalcatface_extended.xml file, which is included in the OpenCV library, to detect the faces of cats.

First, we open the capture_thread.h file to add some lines:

```
class CaptureThread : public QThread
{
    // ...
private:
    // ...
    void detectObjects(cv::Mat &frame);

private:
    // ...
    // object detection
    cv::CascadeClassifier *classifier;
};
```

Then, in the capture_thread.cpp file, we implement the detectObjects method as follows:

```
void CaptureThread::detectObjects(cv::Mat &frame)
{
    vector<cv::Rect> objects;
```

```
        classifier->detectMultiScale(frame, objects, 1.3, 5);

        cv::Scalar color = cv::Scalar(0, 0, 255); // red

        // draw the circumscribe rectangles
        for(size_t i = 0; i < objects.size(); i++) {
            cv::rectangle(frame, objects[i], color, 2);
        }
    }
}
```

In this method, we detect objects by calling the detectMultiScale method of the cascade classifier, then draw the detected rectangles on the image, just like what we did when we detected faces in Chapter 4, *Fun with Faces*.

Next, we instantiate the cascade classifier in the run method and call the detectObjects method in the video-capturing infinite loop:

```
    void CaptureThread::run() {
        // ...
        classifier = new cv::CascadeClassifier(OPENCV_DATA_DIR \
    "haarcascades/haarcascade_frontalcatface_extended.xml");
        // ...
        while(running) {
            // ...
            detectObjects(tmp_frame);
            // ...
        }
        // ...
        delete classifier;
        classifier = nullptr;
        running = false;
    }
```

As you see, we also destroy the cascade classifier after the infinite loop ends.

We update the Detective.pro project file, add the opencv_objdetect module to the link options, and define the OPENCV_DATA_DIR macro:

```
    # ...
    unix: !mac {
        INCLUDEPATH += /home/kdr2/programs/opencv/include/opencv4
        LIBS += -L/home/kdr2/programs/opencv/lib -lopencv_core -lopencv_imgproc
    -lopencv_imgcodecs -lopencv_video -lopencv_videoio -lopencv_objdetect
    }

    # ...
    DEFINES +=
```

```
OPENCV_DATA_DIR=\\\"/home/kdr2/programs/opencv/share/opencv4/\\\"
# ...
```

Now we compile and run the application, open the camera, then put a cat into the sight of the camera:

Maybe you don't have a cat; don't worry about that. The `cv::VideoCapture` class provides many other ways that we can test our app.

You can find a video of a cat and place it on your local disk, then pass its path to the construct of `cv::VideoCapture` instead of passing a camera ID, for example, `cv::VideoCapture cap("/home/kdr2/Videos/cats.mp4")`. The constructor also accepts URIs of video streams, for instance, `http://some.site.com/some-video.mp4` or `rtsp://user:password@192.168.1.100:554/camera/0?channel=1`.

If you have many pictures of cats, that's also OK. The constructor of the `cv::VideoCapture` class also accepts an image sequence represented by a string. For example, if you pass the `"image_%02d.jpg"` string to the constructor, the `cv::VideoCapture` instance will read images whose names are similar to `image_00.jpg`, `image_01.jpg`, `image_02.jpg`, and so on, then show them one by one as video frames.

OK, we have set up the Detective application to detect objects using a pretrained cascade classifier. In the next section, we will try to train a cascade classifier by ourselves. When we get the self-trained cascade classifier file, we can pass its path to the constructor of the `cv::CascadeClassifier` class to load it, and change the input of `cv::VideoCapture` to test it.

Training a cascade classifier

OpenCV provided several tools to train cascade classifiers, but they were removed from version 4.0.0. That removal was mainly because of the rise of the deep learning approach, as we mentioned. The deep learning approach became the modern one, while the others, including cascade classifiers, became legacy. But many cascade classifiers are still in use in the world, and in many situations, they are still a good choice. These tools may be added back in some day. You can find and participate in the discussion about this topic at `https://github.com/opencv/opencv/issues/13231`.

Fortunately, we can use OpenCV v3.4.x, which provides these tools to train the cascade classifiers. The resulting cascade classifier files trained by v3.4 are compatible with v4.0.x. In other words, we can train cascade classifiers with OpenCV v3.4.x and use them with OpenCV v4.0.x.

First, we should have OpenCV v3.4.x installed. We can install it using a system package manager, such as `yum` or `apt-get`. We can also download it from `https://github.com/opencv/opencv/archive/3.4.5.tar.gz` and build it from the source. If you decide to build it from source, remember to pass the `-D BUILD_opencv_apps=yes` option to the `cmake` command. Otherwise, the training tools will not be built. Once it is installed, we can find many executable files under its binary directory:

```
$ ls ~/programs/opencv-3.4.5/bin/
opencv_annotation opencv_createsamples
opencv_interactive-calibration opencv_traincascade
opencv_version opencv_visualisation
setup_vars_opencv3.sh
```

The tools we will use to train the cascade classifiers are `opencv_createsamples`, `opencv_traincascade`, and sometimes `opencv_annotation`.

The `opencv_createsamples` and `opencv_annotation` tools are used to create samples, and the `opencv_traincascade` tool is used to train the cascade classifier with the created samples.

Before training a cascade classifier, we must prepare two kinds of samples: the positive samples and the negative samples. The positive samples should contain the objects we want to detect, while the negative samples should contain everything but the objects we want to detect. The positive samples can be generated by the OpenCV-provided tool, `opencv_createsamples`. There's no tool for generating the negative samples because the negative samples can be any arbitrary images that don't contain the objects we want to detect.

How do we prepare or generate positive samples? Let's look at some examples.

The no-entry traffic sign

In this example, we are going to train a cascade classifier that will be used to detect a traffic sign, namely, the no-entry sign:

The first thing to do is to prepare the negative samples—the background images. As we mentioned, the negative samples can be arbitrary images that don't contain the objects of interest, so we can collect some images for that purpose easily. When these images are collected, we put their paths in a text file. In that file, the paths are listed in **one path per line** format, and the path can be either absolute or relative.

> We will use the phrases **negative sample images** and **background images** interchangeably in this chapter because they are the same thing in this context.

You could download many traffic photos from `http://benchmark.ini.rub.de/?section=gtsdbsubsection=dataset`, and pick some of them that don't contain any no-entry signs to use as background images:

We put them in a folder named `background` and save their relative paths to a file named
`bg.txt`:

```
$ ls background/
traffic-sign-bg-0.png traffic-sign-bg-1.png traffic-sign-bg-2.png traffic-
sign-bg-3.png
$ ls background/* > bg.txt
$ cat bg.txt
background/traffic-sign-bg-0.png
background/traffic-sign-bg-1.png
background/traffic-sign-bg-2.png
background/traffic-sign-bg-3.png
```

These images can be of different sizes. But none of them should be smaller than the training
window's size. Commonly, the training window size is the average size of our object of
interest, that is, the image of the no-entry sign. That is because the negative samples, which
have the training window size as their dimensions, will be taken from these background
images. If the background images are smaller than the sample images, this can't be done.

OK, the negative images are ready. Let's move on to the preparation of the positive
samples.

As we mentioned, we will use the `opencv_createsamples` tool to generate positive
samples. The positive samples will be used in the training process to tell the cascade
classifier what the object of interest actually looks like.

To create the positive samples, we save our object of interest, the no-entry sign, as a file
named `no-entry.png`, in the same directory where the `background` folder and the
`bg.txt` file lie. Then we call the `opencv_createsamples` tool as follows:

```
opencv_createsamples -vec samples.vec -img no-entry.png -bg bg.txt \
                -num 200 -bgcolor 0 -bgthresh 20 -maxidev 30 \
                -maxxangle 0.3 -maxyangle 0.3 -maxzangle 0.3 \
                -w 32 -h 32
```

As you see, we provide many arguments while running the tool, which may seem scary.
But don't worry about it. We will explain them one by one:

- The `-vec` argument is used to specify the positive samples file we are going to
  create. We use `samples.vec` as the file name in our case.
- The `-img` argument is for specifying the image of the object we want to detect.
  The tool will use it to generate positive samples. In our case, it's `no-entry.png`,
  as we mentioned.

- The −bg argument is used to specify the description file of the background images. Ours is bg.txt and contains the relative paths of the four chosen backgrounds.
- The −num argument is the number of positive samples to be generated.
- The −bgcolor argument is for specifying the background color of the image of the object of interest. The background color denotes the transparent color, it will be treated as transparent when generating samples. The background of our image of interest we are using here is black, so we use zero here. In some situations, the background color of the given images has a variety of colors rather than a single color value, for instance, when you get compression artifacts on the images. In order to cope with this situation, there is another argument named −bgthresh to specify an amount of color tolerance of the background. When this argument is given, the pixels whose color is between bgcolor − bgthresh and bgcolor + bgthresh will be interpreted as transparent.
- The −bgthresh argument specifies the threshold of the bgcolor, as we mentioned.
- The −maxidev argument is used to set the maximum intensity deviation of the foreground pixel values while generating the samples. A value of 30 means the intensity of the foreground pixels can vary between their original values + 30 and their original values - 30.
- The −maxxangle, −maxyangle, and −maxzangle arguments correspond to the maximum possible rotation allowed in the x, y, and z directions when creating new samples. These values are in radians. Here, we use 0.3, 0.3, and 0.3, since a traffic sign is usually not heavily rotated in photos.
- The −w and −h arguments define the width and height of the samples. We have used 32 for both of them, since the object we're looking to train a classifier for fits into a square shape. These same values will be used later on when training the classifier. Also, note that this will be the minimum detectable size in your trained classifier later on.

Once the command returns, the sample file is generated. We can use the same tool to view the samples:

```
opencv_createsamples −vec samples.vec −show
```

If you run this command, a window of size 32 x 32 will appear with a single sample image in it. You can press *N* to see the next one, or press the *Esc* key to quit. These positive samples look like follows on my computer:

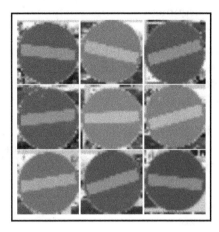

OK, the positive samples are ready now. Let's train the cascade classifier:

```
mkdir -p classifier
opencv_traincascade -data classifier -numStages 10 -featureType HAAR \
                    -vec samples.vec -bg bg.txt \
                    -numPos 200 -numNeg 200 -h 32 -w 32
```

We first create a new directory for the output files, then invoke the `opencv_traincascade` tool with many arguments:

- The `-data` argument specifies the output directory. The trained classifier and many intermediate files will be placed in this directory. The tool won't create the directory for us, so we should create it by ourselves before running the command just as what we did by the `mkdir` command.
- The `-vec` argument specifies the positive samples file, which is created by the `opencv_createsamples` tool.
- The `-bg` argument is used to specify the background description file, in our case, the `bg.txt` file.
- The `-numPos` argument specifies how many positive samples will be used in the training process for each classifier stage.

- The `-numNeg` argument specifies how many negative samples will be used in the training for each classifier stage.
- The `-numStages` argument specifies how many cascade stages will be trained.
- The `-featureType` argument specifies the type of features. Its value could be HAAR or LBP.
- The `-w` and `-h` arguments specify the width and height of the samples used in the training process in pixels. The values must be exactly the same as the width and height of the positive samples we generated using the `opencv_createsamples` tool.

The running of this command will take a while, from minutes to hours. Once it returns, we will find many output files in the directory we used as the value of the `-data` argument, that is, the `classifier` directory:

```
$ ls classifier/
cascade.xml stage10.xml stage5.xml stage9.xml
params.xml stage2.xml stage6.xml
stage0.xml stage3.xml stage7.xml
stage1.xml stage4.xml stage8.xml
```

Let's see what are these files for:

- The `params.xml` file contains the parameters used for training the classifier.
- The `stage<NN>.xml` files are checkpoints that are created after each training stage is completed. They can be used to resume the training later on if the training process was terminated unexpectedly.
- The `cascade.xml` file is the trained classifier and the last file that will be created by the training tool.

Let's test our newly trained cascade classifier now. Open the `capture_thread.cpp` file, find the line of the classifier creation in the `run` method, and pass the path of our newly trained classifier file to it:

```
classifier = new cv::CascadeClassifier("../no-
entry/classifier/cascade.xml");
```

In the `detectObjects` method, while calling the `detectMultiScale` method of the classifier, we change the fourth argument, the `minNeighbors`, to 3.

OK, everything is done. Let's compile and run the application. Open the camera; you will see a window like this:

If it's not convenient for you to capture a video that contains a no-entry sign with the webcam on your computer, you can search and download such a video or some pictures from the internet and pass them to the `cv::VideoCapture` instance to do the test.

I wrapped up all the commands that we need for training this cascade classifier into a shell script and put it into the `Chapter-06/no-entry` directory in the accompanying code repository of the book. There's also a cascade classifier file named `cascade.xml`, trained on my computer in that directory. Please note that the result of your training may be very different from mine. We will even get different results if we rerun the training in the same environment. You can fiddle with the object image, background images, and training parameters to find an acceptable output by yourself.

In this subsection, we train a classifier for a traffic sign, and we use a certain image of the traffic sign to generate positive samples. This approach of generating samples works nicely for stable objects, such as a fixed logo or a fixed traffic sign. But we will find it's a failure once we give it some less rigid objects, such as human or animal faces. In that case, we should use another approach to generate positive samples. In this alternative approach, we should collect many real object images, and annotate them using the `opencv_annotation` tool. Then we can use the `opencv_createsamples` tool to create positive samples from the annotated images. We will try this approach in the next subsection.

The faces of Boston Bulls

In this subsection, we will train a cascade classifier for a less rigid object: dog faces.

We will use the dataset from `http://vision.stanford.edu/aditya86/ImageNetDogs/`. This dataset contains 20,580 images of dogs, divided into 120 categories, and each category is a dog breed. Let's download and unpack the tarball of the images:

```
$ curl -O http://vision.stanford.edu/aditya86/ImageNetDogs/images.tar
$ tar xvf images.tar
# output omitted
$ ls Images/
n02085620-Chihuahua n02091635-otterhound
n02097298-Scotch_terrier n02104365-schipperke
n02109525-Saint_Bernard n02085782-Japanese_spaniel
# output truncated
```

We will set the faces of the Boston Bull breed as our target. There are 182 images of Boston Bulls in the `Images/n02096585-Boston_bull` directory. Unlike fixed objects, for example, the traffic sign, we won't find a standard image for the faces of Boston Bulls. We should annotate the dog faces on the 182 images we just selected. The annotation is done with the `opencv_annotation` tool provided by OpenCV v3.4.x:

```
rm positive -fr
cp -r Images/n02096585-Boston_bull positive
opencv_annotation --annotations=info.txt --images=positive
```

We copy the directory containing the Boston bull images into a new, `positive` directory, to use them as the positive image obviously and conveniently. Then we invoke the `opencv_annotation` tool with two arguments:

- The `--annotations` argument specifies the output file of the annotation.
- The `--images` argument specifies a folder that contains the images we want to annotate.

The invocation to the `opencv_annotation` tool will open a window showing the images that need to be annotated. We can do the annotation on the images with our mouse and keyboard:

1. Left-click the mouse to mark the starting point of the annotation.
2. Move the mouse. You will see a rectangle; adjust this rectangle to fit a dog face by moving the mouse.
3. When you get a proper rectangle, stop moving the mouse and left-click it again. You will get a fixed red rectangle.
4. Now you can press the *D* key on the keyboard to delete the rectangle, or press the *C* key to confirm the rectangle. If a rectangle is confirmed, it will turn green.
5. You can repeat these steps to mark multiple rectangles on an image.
6. When you've finished the annotation of the current image, press the *N* key on the keyboard to go to the next image.
7. You can press *Esc* to quit the tool.

This is a screenshot of the tool while I am annotating the dog faces:

We should mark all the dog faces on all of the 182 images carefully. This will be a tedious process, so I've provided the resulting file of my annotating process, the info.txt file in the Chapter-06/boston-bull directory, in our code repository. The data format of this file is very straightforward:

```
positive/n02096585_10380.jpg 1 7 4 342 326
positive/n02096585_11731.jpg 1 158 218 93 83
positive/n02096585_11776.jpg 2 47 196 104 120 377 76 93 98
positive/n02096585_1179.jpg 1 259 26 170 165
positive/n02096585_12825.jpg 0
positive/n02096585_11808.jpg 1 301 93 142 174
```

The preceding list is some lines picked from the info.txt file. We can see each line of this file is the information of a single image, and the information is organized in the PATH NUMBER_OF_RECT RECT0.x RECT0.y RECT0.width RECT0.height RECT1.x RECT1.y RECT1.width RECT1.height ... format.

With this annotation information file, we can create positive samples:

```
opencv_createsamples -info info.txt -vec samples.vec -w 32 -h 32
```

As you see, it is simpler than the last time we used the `opencv_createsamples` tool. We don't need to give it the background images, the image of the object of interest, and the max angles for distorting the objects. Just giving it the annotation data as the `-info` argument is enough.

After the invocation returns, we get the positive samples in the `samples.vec` file. Again, we can use the `opencv_createsamples` tool to view it:

```
opencv_createsamples -vec samples.vec -show
```

You can see all the samples one by one in the prompted window by pressing *N* on the keyboard. The following is what these samples look like:

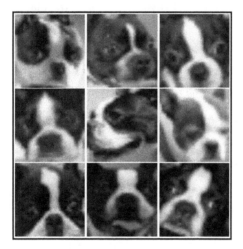

Now the positive samples are ready, it's time to prepare the background images. Dogs of the Briard breed are very different from Boston Bulls, so I decided to use these images as the background images:

```
rm negative -fr
cp -r Images/n02105251-briard negative
ls negative/* >bg.txt
```

We copy the directory `Images/n02105251-briard` to the `negative` directory and save the relative paths of all the images under that directory to the `bg.txt` file. The `bg.txt` file is just our background description file:

```
negative/n02105251_1201.jpg
negative/n02105251_1240.jpg
negative/n02105251_12.jpg
negative/n02105251_1382.jpg
negative/n02105251_1588.jpg
...
```

Both of the positive samples and background images are ready, so let's train the classifier:

```
mkdir -p classifier
opencv_traincascade -data classifier -vec samples.vec -bg bg.txt \
                    -numPos 180 -numNeg 180 -h 32 -w 32
```

This step is very similar to what we did when training the classifier for the no-entry traffic sign. It's worth noting that we use `-numPos 180` here because we only have 183 positive samples in the `samples.vec` file.

When the training process finishes, we will get the trained classifier as the `cascade.xml` file under the `classifier` directory. Let's try this newly trained classifier now.

First, we load it in the `CaptureThread::run()` method:

```
    classifier = new cv::CascadeClassifier("../boston-
bull/classifier/cascade.xml");
```

Then we change the `minNeighbors` argument of the `detectMultiScale` call to 5 in the `CaptureThread::detectObjects` method:

```
    int minNeighbors = 5; // 3 for no-entry-sign; 5-for others.
    classifier->detectMultiScale(frame, objects, 1.3, minNeighbors);
```

Let's compile and run the Detective application, and test our new classifier on some materials:

OK, not bad. We have trained two cascade classifiers. You may be curious as to how the HAAR or LBP features are selected in the training process, so let's go a little deeper.

OpenCV provides a tool named `opencv_visualisation` to help us visualize the trained cascade. With it, we can see which features the cascade classifier selected at each stage:

```
$ mkdir -p visualisation
$ opencv_visualisation --image=./test-visualisation.png \
                       --model=./classifier/cascade.xml \
                       --data=./visualisation/
```

We create a new directory and invoke the `opencv_visualisation` tool with many arguments:

- The `--image` argument is used to specify a path to an image. The image should be an object of interest image, with the dimensions we used while creating samples and training the classifier, that is, a 32 x 32 image of a Boston bulldog face.
- The `--model` argument is the path to the newly trained model.
- The `--data` is the output directory. It must end with a slash (/) and the directory must be created manually beforehand.

When this command returns, we will get many images and a video file in the output directory:

```
$ ls visualisation/
model_visualization.avi stage_14.png stage_1.png stage_7.png
stage_0.png stage_15.png stage_2.png stage_8.png
stage_10.png stage_16.png stage_3.png stage_9.png
stage_11.png stage_17.png stage_4.png
stage_12.png stage_18.png stage_5.png
stage_13.png stage_19.png stage_6.png
```

A video named `model_visualization.avi` is made for feature visualization in each stage; you can play it to see how the cascade classifier selects the features. Also, there is an image for each stage in the output directory. We can check these images to view the features selection as well.

All the materials we used to train this classifier, additionally with a worked `cascade.xml`, are in the `Chapter-06/boston-bull` directory in our code repository. Please feel free to fiddle with them.

Detecting objects using deep learning models

In the preceding section, we learned how to train and use cascade classifiers to detect objects. But that approach, compared to the increasingly expanding deep learning approach, provides worse performance, both in terms of the recall rate and accuracy. The OpenCV library has started to move on to the deep learning approach already. In version 3.x, it introduced the **Deep Neural Network** (**DNN**) module, and now in the latest version, v4.x, we can load many formats of neural network architecture, along with the pretrained weights for them. Also, as we mentioned, the tools for training cascade classifiers are deprecated in the latest version.

In this section, we will move on to the deep learning approach to see how to use OpenCV to detect objects the deep learning way. We used this approach once already. In Chapter 5, *Optical Character Recognition*, we used a pretrained EAST model to detect the regions of text on a photo. This is a deep learning model developed and trained with the TensorFlow framework. Besides the DNN models trained by the TensorFlow framework, OpenCV also supports models of many formats from many other frameworks:

- The *.caffemodel format from Caffe (http://caffe.berkeleyvision.org/, *not* Caffe2)
- The *.pb format from TensorFlow (https://www.tensorflow.org/)
- The *.t7 or *.net format from Torch (http://torch.ch/, *not* PyTorch)
- The *.weights format from Darknet (https://pjreddie.com/darknet/)
- The *.bin format from DLDT (https://software.intel.com/openvino-toolkit)

As you see, although OpenCV supports many kinds of DNN model, there are still several popular deep learning frameworks not in the preceding list, for instance; the PyTorch framework, the Caffe2 framework, the MXNet, and the Microsoft **Cognitive Toolkit** (**CNTK**). Fortunately, there is a format called **Open Neural Network Exchange** (**ONNX**), which is developed and supported by its community, and the OpenCV library now has the ability to load models of this format.

Most of the popular deep learning frameworks, including the ones I just mentioned, also support the ONNX format. So, if you developed a DNN model with a framework not in the OpenCV support list, you can save your model architecture and the trained weights in the ONNX format. Then it will be usable with the OpenCV library.

The OpenCV library itself doesn't have the ability to construct and train a DNN model, but since it can load and forward a DNN model and has fewer dependencies than the other deep learning frameworks, it is really a good solution to deploy a DNN model. The OpenCV team and Intel also create and maintain some other projects that focus on machine learning model deployment, for example, the DLDT and OpenVINO projects.

If we can't train a model using OpenCV, how do we get a model that can be used with OpenCV to detect objects? The easiest way is to find a pretrained model. Most popular deep learning frameworks have a `model zoo`, which collects many models constructed and pretrained with that framework. You can search the internet for the framework name plus the keywords `model zoo` to find them. These are a few I found:

- TensorFlow: `https://github.com/tensorflow/models/blob/master/research/object_detection/g3doc/detection_model_zoo.md`
- Caffe: `http://caffe.berkeleyvision.org/model_zoo.html`
- Caffe2: `https://caffe2.ai/docs/zoo.html`
- MXNet: `https://mxnet.apache.org/model_zoo/index.html`

Also, you can find many open source pretrained models at `https://modelzoo.co/`.

Now, let's go back to the topic of object detection. Generally, there are three kinds of deep learning-based object detectors:

- R-CNN-based detectors, including R-CNN, Fast R-CNN, and Faster R-CNN
- **Single Shot Detector (SSD)**
- **You Only Look Once (YOLO)**

In the **Regions with CNN features (R-CNN,** `https://arxiv.org/abs/1311.2524`) approach, we are required first to use some kind of algorithm to propose candidate bounding boxes that could contain objects, then send these candidate boxes to a **Convolutional Neural Network (CNN)** model to classify them. That's why this kind of detector is also called a two-stage detector. The problem with this approach is it is extremely slow and is not an end-to-end deep learning object detector (as we need to search the candidate boxes and do some other work before entering the CNN model). Although the R-CNN was improved twice (with Fast R-CNN, `https://arxiv.org/abs/1504.08083`, and Faster R-CNN, `https://arxiv.org/abs/1506.01497`), these approaches are still not speedy enough, even on a GPU.

While the R-CNN approaches use a two-stage strategy, the SSD and YOLO approaches use a one-stage strategy. The one-stage strategy treats object detection as a regression problem, taking a given input image and simultaneously learning bounding-box coordinates and corresponding class-label probabilities. Typically, one-stage detectors tend to be less accurate than two-stage detectors but are significantly faster. For instance, a well-known implementation of the one-stage strategy, YOLO, which is introduced by https://arxiv.org/abs/1506.02640, has a performance that soars to 45 FPS **on a GPU**, where two-stage detectors may only have a performance of 5-10 FPS.

In this section, we will use the pretrained YOLOv3 (https://arxiv.org/abs/1804.02767) detector to detect objects. This model is trained on the COCO dataset (http://cocodataset.org/); it can detect hundreds of classes of objects. To use this model in OpenCV, we should first download some files for it:

- The text file of the names of the object classes, at https://raw.githubusercontent.com/pjreddie/darknet/master/data/coco.names
- The configure file of the model, at https://raw.githubusercontent.com/pjreddie/darknet/master/cfg/yolov3.cfg
- The pretrained weights of the model, at https://pjreddie.com/media/files/yolov3.weights

Now, let's download them to the data sub-directory of our Detective application:

```
$ pwd
/home/kdr2/Work/Books/Qt-5-and-OpenCV-4-Computer-Vision-
Projects/Chapter-06/Detective
$ mkdir data
$ cd data/
$ curl -L -O
https://raw.githubusercontent.com/pjreddie/darknet/master/data/coco.names
# output omitted
$ curl -L -O
https://raw.githubusercontent.com/pjreddie/darknet/master/cfg/yolov3.cfg
# output omitted
$ curl -L -O https://pjreddie.com/media/files/yolov3.weights
# output omitted
$ ls -l
total 242216
-rw-r--r-- 1 kdr2 kdr2 625 Apr 9 15:23 coco.names
-rw-r--r-- 1 kdr2 kdr2 8342 Apr 9 15:24 yolov3.cfg
-rw-r--r-- 1 kdr2 kdr2 248007048 Apr 9 15:49 yolov3.weights
```

With these three files ready, we can load the model in our application. First, let's open our `capture_thread.h` header file to add some methods and fields:

```
// ...
#include "opencv2/dnn.hpp"
// ...

class CaptureThread : public QThread
{
    // ...
private:
    // ...
    void detectObjectsDNN(cv::Mat &frame);

private:
    // ...
    cv::dnn::Net net;
    vector<string> objectClasses;
};
```

First, we add an `include` directive to include the `opencv2/dnn.hpp` header file, since we will use the DNN module. These are the methods and fields:

- The method `detectObjectsDNN` is for detecting objects in a frame using the DNN model.
- The member field `cv::dnn::Net net` is the DNN model instance.
- The member field `vector<string> objectClasses` will hold the class names of objects in the COCO dataset.

Let's open the source `capture_thread.cpp` file to see the implementation of the `detectObjectsDNN` method:

```
void CaptureThread::detectObjectsDNN(cv::Mat &frame)
{
    int inputWidth = 416;
    int inputHeight = 416;

    if (net.empty()) {
        // give the configuration and weight files for the model
        string modelConfig = "data/yolov3.cfg";
        string modelWeights = "data/yolov3.weights";
        net = cv::dnn::readNetFromDarknet(modelConfig, modelWeights);

        objectClasses.clear();
        string name;
        string namesFile = "data/coco.names";
```

```
        ifstream ifs(namesFile.c_str());
        while(getline(ifs, name)) objectClasses.push_back(name);
    }
    // more code here ...
}
```

At the beginning of this method, we define the width and height of the input image for the YOLO model; there are three options: 320 x 320, 416 x 416, and 608 x 608. Here, we chose 416 x 416, and all of our input images will be resized to that dimension.

We check if the `net` field is empty. If it is empty, it means we didn't load in the model yet, so we call the `cv::dnn::readNetFromDarknet` function with the paths of the model configuration file and weights file to load the model.

After that, we open the `data/coco.names` file by creating an instance of `ifstream`. As we mentioned, this file contains all the class names of the objects in the COCO dataset:

```
$ wc -l data/coco.names
80 data/coco.names
$ head data/coco.names
person
bicycle
car
motorbike
aeroplane
bus
train
truck
boat
traffic light
```

In the shell commands and previous output, we can see there are 80 class names in total. We also get a rough impression of the names by looking at the first ten names using the `head` command. Let's move on to our C++ code. We read the opened file line by line, and push the name (that is, each line) we read to the member field `objectClasses`. When this is done, the `objectClasses` field will hold all the 80 names.

OK, the model and the class names are all loaded. Next, we should convert the input image and pass it to the DNN model to do a forward pass to get the output:

```
cv::Mat blob;
cv::dnn::blobFromImage(
    frame, blob, 1 / 255.0,
    cv::Size(inputWidth, inputHeight),
    cv::Scalar(0, 0, 0), true, false);
```

```
net.setInput(blob);

// forward
vector<cv::Mat> outs;
net.forward(outs, getOutputsNames(net));
```

The conversion is done by calling the `cv::dnn::blobFromImage` method. This call is a little complicated, so let's go through the arguments one by one:

- The first argument is the input image.
- The second argument is the output image.
- The third one is the scale factor of each pixel value. We use `1 / 255.0` here, because the model requires the pixel values be a float in the range of `0` to `1`.
- The fourth argument is the spatial size of the output image; we use 416 x 416 here, with the variables we defined.
- The fifth argument is the mean, which should be subtracted from each image, since this was used while training the model. YOLO doesn't do the mean subtraction, so we use zero here.
- The next argument is whether we want to swap the R and B channels. This is required for us since OpenCV uses BGR format and YOLO uses RGB format.
- The last argument is whether we want to crop the image and take the center crop. We specify `false` in this case.

The key arguments are the scale factor (the third one) and the mean (the fifth one). In the conversion, the mean is subtracted from each pixel of the input image first, then the pixels are multiplied by the scale factor, that is, the pixels of the output blob are calculated as `output_pixel = (input_pixel - mean) * scale_factor`.

But how do we know which values of these two arguments we should use for a model? Some models use both mean subtraction and pixel scaling, some models use only mean subtraction but no pixel scaling, and some models use only pixel scaling but no mean subsection. For a particular model, the only way to know the details of these values is to read the documentation.

After we get the input blob, we pass it to the DNN model by calling the `setInput` method of the model, then we perform forwarding on the model. But we must know which layers we want to get by forwarding while performing the forward pass. This is done via an auxiliary function named `getOutputsNames`, which we also implement in the `capture_thread.cpp` source file:

```
vector<string> getOutputsNames(const cv::dnn::Net& net)
{
```

```
        static vector<string> names;
        vector<int> outLayers = net.getUnconnectedOutLayers();
        vector<string> layersNames = net.getLayerNames();
        names.resize(outLayers.size());
        for (size_t i = 0; i < outLayers.size(); ++i)
            names[i] = layersNames[outLayers[i] - 1];

        return names;
    }
```

The indices of the output layers of a DNN model can be obtained by its getUnconnectedOutLayers method, while the names of all the layers can be obtained by the getLayerNames method. If we spy on the resulting vector of the getLayerNames method, we will find there are 254 layers in this YOLO model. In our function, we get all these 254 names and then pick the ones indicated by the indices of the unconnected output layers. In fact, this function is just another version of the cv::dnn::Net.getUnconnectedOutLayersNames() method. Here, we use our self-made version to learn more about the cv::dnn::Net class.

Let's go back to our detectObjectsDNN method. After the forwarding is done, we will get the data of the output layers in the vector<cv::Mat> outs variable. All the information—including objects in boxes we have detected, along with their confidences and class indices—is in this vector of matrices. We write another auxiliary function in the capture_thread.cpp source file to decode the vector to get all the information we need:

```
    void decodeOutLayers(
        cv::Mat &frame, const vector<cv::Mat> &outs,
        vector<int> &outClassIds,
        vector<float> &outConfidences,
        vector<cv::Rect> &outBoxes
    )
    {
        float confThreshold = 0.5; // confidence threshold
        float nmsThreshold = 0.4; // non-maximum suppression threshold

        vector<int> classIds;
        vector<float> confidences;
        vector<cv::Rect> boxes;

        // not finished, more code here ...
    }
```

This function takes the origin frame and the data of the output layers as its in-parameters and returns the detected boxes of objects along with their class indices and confidences through its out-parameters. At the beginning of the function body, we define several variables, such as the thresholds of confidence and non-maximum suppression, and the boxes information for all objects we detected before filtering.

Then we iterate over the matrices in the output layers:

```
for (size_t i = 0; i < outs.size(); ++i) {
    float* data = (float*)outs[i].data;
    for (int j = 0; j < outs[i].rows; ++j, data += outs[i].cols)
    {
        cv::Mat scores = outs[i].row(j).colRange(5, outs[i].cols);
        cv::Point classIdPoint;
        double confidence;
        // get the value and location of the maximum score
        cv::minMaxLoc(scores, 0, &confidence, 0, &classIdPoint);
        if (confidence > confThreshold)
        {
            int centerX = (int)(data[0] * frame.cols);
            int centerY = (int)(data[1] * frame.rows);
            int width = (int)(data[2] * frame.cols);
            int height = (int)(data[3] * frame.rows);
            int left = centerX - width / 2;
            int top = centerY - height / 2;

            classIds.push_back(classIdPoint.x);
            confidences.push_back((float)confidence);
            boxes.push_back(cv::Rect(left, top, width, height));
        }
    }
}
```

Let's take a single matrix in the output vector—that is, the outs[i] in the code—as an example. Each row in the matrix stands for a detected box. Each row contains (5 + x) elements, where x is the number of the class names in the coco.names file, which is 80, as we mentioned.

The first four elements represent the `center_x`, `center_y`, `width`, and `height` of the box. The fifth element represents the confidence that the bounding box encloses an object. The rest of the elements are the confidence associated with each class. The box is assigned to the class corresponding to the highest score for the box.

In other words, the value of `row[i + 5]` is the confidence of whether the box encloses an object of the `objectClasses[i]` class. So we use the `cv::minMaxLoc` function to get the maximum confidence and its location (index). Then we check if the confidence is greater then our defined confidence threshold. If true, we decode the box as a `cv::Rect`, then push the box along with its class index and confidence to the `boxes`, `classIds`, and `confidences` defined variables.

The next step is passing the decoded boxes and confidences to the non-maximum suppression to reduce the number of overlapping boxes. The indices of the boxes that are not eliminated will be stored in the last argument of the `cv::dnn::NMSBoxes` function, that is, the `indices` variable:

```
// non maximum suppression
vector<int> indices;
cv::dnn::NMSBoxes(boxes, confidences, confThreshold, nmsThreshold,
indices);
for (size_t i = 0; i < indices.size(); ++i) {
    int idx = indices[i];
    outClassIds.push_back(classIds[idx]);
    outBoxes.push_back(boxes[idx]);
    outConfidences.push_back(confidences[idx]);
}
```

At last, we iterate over the indices that we kept and push the corresponding boxes along with their class indices and confidences to the out-parameters.

After the `decodeOutLayers` function is finished, let's get back to the `detectObjectsDNN` method again. By calling the newly implemented `decodeOutLayers` function, we get all the information of the detected objects. Now let's draw them on the origin frame:

```
for(size_t i = 0; i < outClassIds.size(); i ++) {
    cv::rectangle(frame, outBoxes[i], cv::Scalar(0, 0, 255));

    // get the label for the class name and its confidence
    string label = objectClasses[outClassIds[i]];
    label += cv::format(":%.2f", outConfidences[i]);

    // display the label at the top of the bounding box
    int baseLine;
```

```
cv::Size labelSize = cv::getTextSize(label,
    cv::FONT_HERSHEY_SIMPLEX, 0.5, 1, &baseLine);
int left = outBoxes[i].x, top = outBoxes[i].y;
top = max(top, labelSize.height);
cv::putText(frame, label, cv::Point(left, top),
    cv::FONT_HERSHEY_SIMPLEX, 0.5, cv::Scalar(255,255,255));
}
```

With the preceding code, we draw the bounding boxes of the detected objects. And on the top-left corner of each box, we draw a string containing the class name and confidence of the corresponding detected object.

At this point, the work of detecting objects with YOLO is finished. But there are still a few things to do before we can compile and run the application.

First, in the `CaptureThread::run()` method, we change the call to the `detectObjects` method, which is using a cascade classifier to detect objects to the call to our newly added method `detectObjectsDNN`:

```
// detectObjects(tmp_frame);
detectObjectsDNN(tmp_frame);
```

Second, we add the `opencv_dnn` module to the end of the `LIBS` configuration in the `Detective.pro` project file:

```
unix: !mac {
    INCLUDEPATH += /home/kdr2/programs/opencv/include/opencv4
    LIBS += -L/home/kdr2/programs/opencv/lib -lopencv_core -lopencv_imgproc
-lopencv_imgcodecs -lopencv_video -lopencv_videoio -lopencv_objdetect -
lopencv_dnn
}
```

Now, let's compile and run our application to test it. Here is a screenshot of the Detective application while I am observing a desktop through the camera:

Here's a screenshot of an image of a sports scene:

As you see, YOLO really does well in object detection. But there are still some false predictions. In the first screenshot, YOLO recognizes my iPad as a laptop with a confidence of 0.67. In the second screenshot, it recognizes the football field as a TV monitor with a confidence of 0.62. To eliminate these false predictions, we can set our confidence threshold a little higher, for instance, 0.70. I will leave this to you to fiddle with the parameters.

It's worth noting that the YOLO model has its drawbacks. For example, it does not always handle small objects well, and it especially does not handle objects grouped close together. So, if you are handling video or images of small objects or objects grouped together, YOLO is not the best choice.

So far, we have talked about how to find a pretrained DNN model built with many deep learning frameworks, and how to use them with OpenCV. But what if there's not a pretrained model for your case, such as, for instance, detecting a kind of object not in the `coco` dataset? In this situation, you should build and train a DNN model by yourself. For each deep learning framework, there's a tutorial on how to build and train a model on the MNIST or CIFAR-10/100 dataset. Follow these tutorials. You will learn how to train a DNN model for your use case. There's also a framework called Keras (`https://keras.io/`), which provides a high-level API for building, training, and running a DNN model. It uses TensorFlow, CNTK, and Theano as its underlying framework. Using the friendly API provided by Keras is also a good choice for beginners. This book focuses on OpenCV and this knowledge is beyond its scope, so I will leave the task of learning to train a DNN model to you.

About real time

When we handle videos, either video files or real-time video feeds from cameras, we know that the frame rate of the videos is about 24-30 FPS in general. That means we have 33-40 milliseconds to process each frame. If we take more time than that, we will lose some frames from a real-time video feed, or get a slower playing speed from a video file.

Now, let's add some code to our application to measure how much time we spend on each frame while detecting objects. First, in the `Detective.pro` project file, we add a new macro definition:

```
DEFINES += TIME_MEASURE=1
```

We will use this macro to switch the time-measuring code on or off. If you want to turn off the time measuring, just comment this line out, then rebuild the application by running the `make clean && make` command.

Then, in the `CaptureThread::run` method, in the `capture_thread.cpp` file, we add some lines before and after the call to the `detectObjects` or `detectObjectsDNN` method:

```
#ifdef TIME_MEASURE
        int64 t0 = cv::getTickCount();
#endif
        detectObjects(tmp_frame);
        // detectObjectsDNN(tmp_frame);

#ifdef TIME_MEASURE
        int64 t1 = cv::getTickCount();
        double t = (t1 - t0) * 1000 /cv::getTickFrequency();
        qDebug() << "Detecting time on a single frame: " << t <<"ms";
#endif
```

In the preceding code, the `cv::getTickCount` function returns the number of the clock cycles from the beginning (the time when the system starts). We call it twice—before and after the detection. After that, use the `t1 - t0` expression to get the clock-cycle elapses while detecting objects. Since the `cv::getTickFrequency()` function returns how many clock cycles there are in one second, we can convert the number of elapsed clock cycles to milliseconds via `(t1 - t0) * 1000 /cv::getTickFrequency()`. Lastly, we output a message relating to time usage through `qDebug()`.

If you compile and run the Detective application using the cascade classifier approach, you will see messages like the following:

```
Detecting time on a single frame: 72.5715 ms
Detecting time on a single frame: 71.7724 ms
Detecting time on a single frame: 73.8066 ms
Detecting time on a single frame: 71.7509 ms
Detecting time on a single frame: 70.5172 ms
Detecting time on a single frame: 70.5597 ms
```

As you can see, I spent more than 70 milliseconds on each frame. That's greater than the value it should be (33-40). In my case, this is mainly because I have an old CPU in my computer, which I bought about ten years ago, and I didn't reduce the resolution of the input frames. To optimize this, we can use a more powerful CPU and resize our input frames to a smaller, more appropriate size.

Before we use the previous code to measure the time the YOLO approach used, let's add some lines of code to the `CaptureThread::detectObjectsDNN` method:

```
        // ...
        net.forward(outs, getOutputsNames(net));

#ifdef TIME_MEASURE
```

```
        vector<double> layersTimes;
        double freq = cv::getTickFrequency() / 1000;
        double t = net.getPerfProfile(layersTimes) / freq;
        qDebug() << "YOLO: Inference time on a single frame: " << t <<"ms";
    #endif
```

After we perform the forwarding on the DNN model, we call its
getPerfPerofile method to get the time spent in the forward pass. Then we convert it to
milliseconds and print it. With this piece of code, we will get two times: one is the total time
spent on the call to the detectObjectsDNN method; the other is the inference time, the
time spent on the forward pass. If we subtract the second one from the first one, we will get
the time spent on the blob preparation and result decoding.

Let's switch to the YOLO approach in the run method and run the application:

```
YOLO: Inference time on a single frame: 2197.44 ms
Detecting time on a single frame: 2209.63 ms
YOLO: Inference time on a single frame: 2203.69 ms
Detecting time on a single frame: 2217.69 ms
YOLO: Inference time on a single frame: 2303.73 ms
Detecting time on a single frame: 2316.1 ms
YOLO: Inference time on a single frame: 2203.01 ms
Detecting time on a single frame: 2215.23 ms
```

Oh no—it is painfully slow. But we said YOLO performance soars to 45 FPS, which means
it only spends 22 milliseconds on each frame. Why is our result 100 times slower? The
performance could soar to 45 FPS, but this is measured *on a GPU*, not a CPU. A deep neural
network requires a large scale of computation, which is not suitable for running on a CPU,
but is good to run on a GPU. Currently, the most mature solutions to put computation onto
a GPU are CUDA and OpenCL, and the DNN module of the OpenCV library only supports
the OpenCL approach right now.

The cv::dnn::Net class has two methods to set its backend and target device:

- setPreferableBackend()
- setPreferableTarget()

If you have a GPU and have the OpenCL along with GPU driver properly installed, you
can build OpenCV with the -DWITH_OPENCL=ON flag to enable OpenCL support. After that,
you can use net.setPreferableTarget(cv::dnn::DNN_TARGET_OPENCL) to use the
GPU and do the computation. This will bring about a big improvement in performance.

Summary

In this chapter, we created a new application named Detective to detect objects using different approaches. First, we used an OpenCV built-in cascade classifier to detect the faces of cats. Then we learned how to train cascade classifiers by ourselves. We trained a cascade classifier for a rigid object (a no-entry traffic sign) and a cascade classifier for a less rigid object (the faces of Boston Bulls), then tested this with our application.

We moved on to the deep learning approach. We talked about the increasingly expanding deep learning technology, introduced many frameworks, and learned about the different ways in which a DNN model may detect objects using two-stage detectors and one-stage detectors. We combined the DNN module of the OpenCV library and the pretrained YOLOv3 model to detect objects in our application.

At the end, we talked about real time and the performance of the detector briefly. We learned about moving the computation to a GPU to allow for a big improvement in performance.

In this chapter, we detected many kinds of objects. In the next chapter, we will discuss how to measure the distance between them with the help of computer vision technology.

Questions

Try these questions to test your knowledge from this chapter:

1. When we trained the cascade classifier for the faces of the Boston Bulls, we annotated the dog faces on each image by ourselves. The annotation process cost us much time. There is a tarball of annotation data for that dataset at this website: `http://vision.stanford.edu/aditya86/ImageNetDogs/annotation.tar`. Could we generate the `info.txt` file from this annotation data via a piece of code? How would we do that?
2. Try to find a pretrained (fast/faster) R-CNN model and a pretrained SSD model. Run them and compare their performance to YOLOv3.
3. Could we use YOLOv3 to detect a certain kind of object, but not all the 80 classes of objects?

7
Real-Time Car Detection and Distance Measurement

In the previous chapter, we learned how to detect objects using the OpenCV library, both via the cascade classifiers approach and the deep learning approach. In this chapter, we will discuss how to measure the distance between the detected objects or between the object of interest and our camera. We will detect cars in a new application and measure the distance between cars and the distance between a car and the camera.

The following topics will be covered in this chapter:

- Detecting cars using the YOLOv3 model with OpenCV
- Methods to measure distance in different view angles
- Measuring the distance between cars in the bird's eye view
- Measuring the distance between a car and the camera in the eye-level view

Technical requirements

Like the previous chapters, you need to have Qt version 5 at a minimum and OpenCV 4.0.0 installed. Having basic knowledge of C++ and Qt programming is also a requirement.

We will use a deep learning model, YOLOv3, to detect cars, so having knowledge of deep learning will also be a big help. Since we introduced deep learning models in Chapter 6, *Object Detection in Real Time*, reading that chapter prior to this chapter is recommended.

All of the code for this chapter can be found in this book's code repository at `https://github.com/PacktPublishing/Qt-5-and-OpenCV-4-Computer-Vision-Projects/tree/master/Chapter-07`.

Check out the following video to see the code in action: `http://bit.ly/2FdC0VF`

Car detection in real time

Before measuring the distance between objects, we must detect the objects of interest to find out where they are. In this chapter, we have decided to measure the distance between cars, so we should start by detecting cars. In the preceding chapter, `Chapter 6`, *Object Detection in Real Time*, we learned how to detect objects in many ways, we saw that the YOLOv3 model has good performance in terms of accuracy, and fortunately, the `car` object class is in the category list of the coco dataset (that is, the `coco.names` file). Therefore, we will follow that method and use the YOLOv3 model to detect cars.

As we did in the previous chapters, we will create the new project of this chapter by copying one of the projects we have already finished. This time, let's copy the Detective application that we completed in the previous chapter as the new project for this chapter. We will name the new project `DiGauge` to indicate that it is being used to gauge the distances between detected objects. Let's do the straightforward copying:

```
$ pwd
/home/kdr2/Work/Books/Qt-5-and-OpenCV-4-Computer-Vision-Projects
$ mkdir Chapter-07
# !!! you should copy it to a different dir
$ cp -r Chapter-06/Detective Chapter-07/DiGauge
$ ls Chapter-07
DiGauge
$ cd Chapter-07/DiGauge/
```

If you have been following along, you should have copied the project to another directory other than `Chapter-07` because the `DiGauge` directory already exists in that folder in our code repository.

Now that we've done the copying, let's do some renaming:

1. Rename the `Detective.pro` project file to `DiGauge.pro`.
2. Rename the target value from `Detective` to `DiGauge` in that project file.
3. Change the `Detective` window title to `DiGauge` in the call to `window.setWindowTitle` in the `main.cpp` source file.
4. Change the text on the status bar from `Detective is Ready` to `DiGauge is Ready` in the call to `mainStatusLabel->setText` in the `MainWindow::initUI` method, which resides in the `mainwindow.cpp` source file.
5. Change the `Detective` string to `DiGauge` in the call to `pictures_dir.mkpath` and `pictures_dir.absoluteFilePath` in the `Utilities::getDataPath` method, which lies in the `utilities.cpp` source file.

At this point, we have a new application which is the same as the Detective application, except for the word `Detective` in its name and relative paths. The text on the UI has also changed to `DiGauge`. To see this, we can compile and run it.

The changeset in the renaming can be found in the following commit: `https://github.com/PacktPublishing/Qt-5-and-OpenCV-4-Computer-Vision-Projects/commit/a0777b515129788bc93768ec813f2f1fe77796b6`. If you are confused about it at all, just refer to the commit.

Since we decided to use the YOLOv3 deep learning model to detect cars, we'd better remove all the code related to the cascade classifier approach to make the code of our project concise and clear. This step is also very straightforward:

1. In the `DiGauge.pro` project file we remove the `opencv_objdetect` module in the `LIBS` configuration, because this module will not be used after the code which uses the cascade classifier is removed. The macros which are defined in the `DEFINES` configuration can be removed as well, since we won't use them either.

2. In the `capture_thread.h` file, we remove the `void detectObjects(cv::Mat &frame)` private method and the `cv::CascadeClassifier *classifier;` field from the `CaptureThread` class.

3. Finally, we make some changes to the `capture_thread.cpp` source file:

- Remove the implementation of the `void CaptureThread::detectObjects(cv::Mat &frame)` method.
- In the `void CaptureThread::run()` method, remove all of the cascade classifier-related code, including the following:
  - The creation of the classifier
  - The call to the `detectObjects` method
  - The deletion of the classifier
- Remove the `vector<string> getOutputsNames(const cv::dnn::Net& net)` function.
- Change the call to the method we just removed, `getOutputsNames(net)`, to `net.getUnconnectedOutLayersNames()` to get the names of the output layers.

At this point, we have a clean project that only uses the YOLOv3 model to detect objects. This changeset can be found at `https://github.com/PacktPublishing/Qt-5-and-OpenCV-4-Computer-Vision-Projects/commit/d0f47d13979a1aae7a1a98f1f54c694383f107a9`.

Now, by using the YOLOv3 model, our application can detect all the 80 classes of objects in videos or images. But, for this application, we are not interested in all of these classes—we are only interested in cars. Let's find the `car` class in the `coco.names` file:

```
$ grep -Hn car data/coco.names
data/coco.names:3:car
data/coco.names:52:carrot
$
```

As we can see, the `car` class is the third line in the `coco.names` file, so the class ID of it is 2 (it has a 0-based index). Let's rewrite the `decodeOutLayers` function in the `capture_thread.cpp` source file to filter out all the classes except the one whose ID is 2:

```
void decodeOutLayers(
    cv::Mat &frame, const vector<cv::Mat> &outs,
    vector<cv::Rect> &outBoxes
)
{
    float confThreshold = 0.65; // confidence threshold
```

```
float nmsThreshold = 0.4; // non-maximum suppression threshold

// vector<int> classIds; // this line is removed!
// ...
}
```

Let's look at the changes we made in the preceding code:

- Changes to the function signature:
    - The `outClassIds` parameter will not be useful anymore since there is only one class of objects that we will detect, so we will remove it.
    - The `outConfidences` parameter is removed as well, because we don't care about the confidence of each detected car.

- Changes to the function body:
    - The `confThreshold` variable is changed from `0.5` to `0.65` to improve accuracy.
    - The `classIds` local variable, which is used to store the class IDs of the detected objects, is also removed for the same reason that we removed the `outClassIds` parameter.

Then, while we process the bounding box of the detected objects in the second level `for` loop after we get the class ID by calling the `cv::minMaxLoc` function, we check whether the class ID is `2`. If it isn't `2`, we ignore the current bounding box and go to the next one:

```
cv::minMaxLoc(scores, 0, &confidence, 0, &classIdPoint);
if (classIdPoint.x != 2) // not a car!
    continue;
```

Finally, we remove all of the lines that try to update the removed `classIds`, `outClassIds`, and `outConfidences` variables. For now, the changes to the `decodeOutLayers` function are finished, so let's move on to the function that calls `decodeOutLayers`, that is, the `CaptureThread::detectObjectsDNN` method.

For the `CaptureThread::detectObjectsDNN` method, we just need to update the end part of its body:

```
// remove the bounding boxes with low confidence

// vector<int> outClassIds; // removed!
// vector<float> outConfidences; // removed!

vector<cv::Rect> outBoxes;
// decodeOutLayers(frame, outs, outClassIds, outConfidences,
outBoxes); // changed!
decodeOutLayers(frame, outs, outBoxes);

for(size_t i = 0; i < outBoxes.size(); i ++) {
    cv::rectangle(frame, outBoxes[i], cv::Scalar(0, 0, 255));
}
```

As you can see, we removed the class ID and confidence-related variables and called the `decodeOutLayers` function with the `outBoxes` variable as its only out parameter. Then, we iterated over the detected bounding boxes and drew them in red.

Finally, we have finished rebuilding the Detective application so that it's a new one named DiGauge that detects cars using the YOLOv3 deep learning model. Let's compile and run it:

```
$ qmake
$ make
g++ -c -pipe -O2 -Wall #...
# output trucated
$ export LD_LIBRARY_PATH=/home/kdr2/programs/opencv/lib
$ ./DiGauge
```

Don't forget to copy the YOLOV3 model-related files (`coco.names`, `yolov3.cfg`, and `yolov3.weights`) to the `data` subdirectory of our project, or the model won't be loaded successfully. If you have doubts about how to get these files, you should read `Chapter 6`, *Object Detection in Real Time*.

After the application starts, if you test it on some scenes that have cars in it, you will find that there's a red bounding box for each detected car:

Now that we can detect cars, let's talk about how to measure the distance between them in the next section.

Distance measurement

There are many ways to measure or estimate the distance between the objects or between the object and the camera in different situations. For example, if our objects of interest or our camera are moving in a known and fixed velocity, with the motion detection and object detection technology, we can estimate the distance between the objects in the view of the camera easily. Alternatively, if we get our hands on a stereo camera, we can follow `https:/` `/www.ijert.org/research/distance-measurement-system-using-binocular-stereo-` `vision-approach-IJERTV2IS121134.pdf` to measure the distance.

However, for our situation, we only have a common webcam in a fixed position, so how could we measure the distance from it? Well, it's possible to do with some prerequisites.

Let's talk about measuring the distance between the objects first. The prerequisites in this situation are that we should install our camera to a fixed position where we can take a video of the objects in a bird's eye view, and there must be an object of a fixed known size, which will be used as a reference in the sight of the camera. Let's take a look at a photo that was taken with my camera:

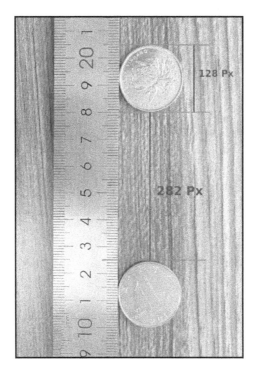

In the preceding photo, I have two coins on my desk. The diameter of the coins is 25 millimeters, and this length occupies 128 pixels in the photo. With this information, we can measure the distance of the two coins in pixels—it's a distance of 282 pixels in the photo. OK, a length of 128 pixels in the photo stands for 25 millimeters on my desk, so how long does a 282 pixels length stand for? It's very straightforward: `25 / 128 * 282 = 55.07` millimeters. So, in this situation, once we detect the reference object and the vertices of the distance we want to measure, we will get the distance by a simple calculation. We will measure the distance between cars with this succinct method in our application in the next section.

Now, let's move on to the topic of measuring the distance between the object of interest and the camera. In this situation, the prerequisites are that we should install our camera to a fixed position where we can take a video of the objects in the eye-level view, and we must have a reference too. However, the reference here is very different from the one of the bird's eyes-view situation. Let's see why:

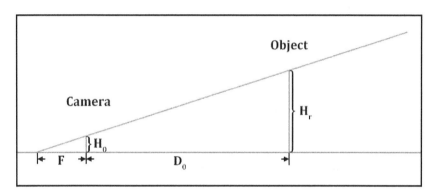

The preceding diagram demonstrates the positional relationship between the object and the camera while we are taking photos. Here, **F** is the focal length of the camera and **D0** is the distance between the camera and the object. **Hr** is the height of the object and **H0** is the height of the image of the object on the lens of the camera (measured in meters, not in pixels).

Since we have two obvious similar triangles in the pictures, we can get some equations:

$$\frac{H_0}{F} = \frac{H_r}{F + D_0} \tag{1}$$

$$F = \frac{H_0 \times D_0}{H_r - H_0} \tag{2}$$

$$F = \frac{H_1 \times D_1}{H_r - H_1} \tag{3}$$

$$\frac{H_0 \times D_0}{H_r - H_0} = \frac{H_1 \times D_1}{H_r - H_1} \tag{4}$$

$$D_1 = \frac{H_r - H_1}{H_r - H_0} \times \frac{H_0 \times D_0}{H_1} \tag{5}$$

$$\frac{H_r - H_1}{H_r - H_0} \approx 1 \tag{6}$$

$$D_1 = \frac{H_0}{H_1} \times D_0 \tag{7}$$

There are so many equations in the preceding diagram, so let's look at them one by one:

1. The first equation is from the triangle similarity.
2. From equation **(1)**, we know that the focal, **F**, can be calculated as equation **(2)**.
3. Then, if we move the object to another position and mark the distance as **D1** and the height of the image on the lens as **H1**, and considering the focal of the camera is a fixed value, we will get equation **(3)**.
4. If we combine equation **(2)** and equation **(3)**, we will get equation **(4)**.
5. From equation **(4)**, with a few transformations, we can get the distance, **D1**, which can be calculated as equation **(5)**.
6. Since we've compared to the height of the real object, **Hr**, the values of **H0** and **H1** are extremely small, so we can guess that the values of **Hr - H0** and **Hr - H1** are almost the same. This is what equation **(6)** says.
7. With equation **(6)**, we can reduce equation **(4)** to equation **(7)**.

Since that, regardless of measuring in meters on the lens or measuring in pixels on the photos, the value of **H0 / H1** is always the same, we can change **H0** and **H1** to the count of pixels they occupy, so that we can measure it in the digital photos.

Here, we will use **D0** (in meters) and **H0** (in pixels) as references, which means that, before we measure the distance between the camera and the object, we must put it somewhere before the camera, then measure the distance as **D0**, and take a photo of it. Then, we can write down the height of the object in the photo as **H0** and use these values as the reference values. Let's look at an example:

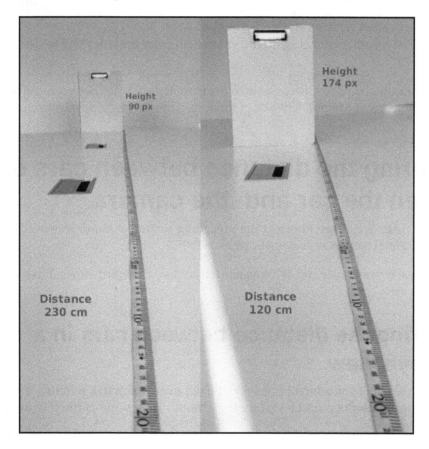

In the preceding photo, on the left-hand side, I put a folder standing on a desk 230 cm away from the camera and took a photo of it. Here, it occupies 90 pixels in a vertical direction. Then, I moved it a few centimeters closer to the camera and took a photo again. This time, its height is 174 pixels. We can use the values from the left-hand side as the reference values, that is:

- **D0** is 230 cm
- **H0** is 90 pixels
- **H1** is 174 pixels

According to equation **(7)**, we can calculate **D1** as `H0 / H1 * D0 = 90 / 174 * 230 = 118.96` `cm`. The result is very close to the value I get from the ruler on the desk, which is 120 cm.

Now that we know the principles of how to measure the distance between the objects or between the object and camera, let's adopt them into the DiGauge application.

Measuring the distance between cars or between the car and the camera

With the principles we talked about in the preceding section at hand, let's utilize them in order to measure distances in our application.

As we mentioned previously, we will measure from two different views. First, let's look at the bird's eye view.

Measuring the distance between cars in a bird's eye view

To be able to see cars from a bird's eye view, I fixed my camera to a window in my office, which is on the eighth floor, and let it face the ground. Here's one of the pictures I got from my camera:

You can see that the cars on the road are running from the left of the picture to the right. It is not an absolute bird's eye view, but we can approximate the distance between the cars using the method we talked about in the preceding section. Let's do this in our code.

In the `capture_thread.cpp` source file, we will add a new function named `distanceBirdEye`:

```
void distanceBirdEye(cv::Mat &frame, vector<cv::Rect> &cars)
{
    // ...
}
```

It takes two arguments:

- A frame of the `cv::Mat` type from the video
- A vector of the bounding boxes of the detected cars in the given frame

We will calculate the distances of the bounding boxes in the horizontal direction in pixels first. However, these boxes may be partially overlapping in the horizontal direction. For example, in the preceding photo, the two white cars on the left-hand side are nearly in the same position on the horizontal direction, and, obviously, the distance between them in the horizontal direction that we are interested in, is zero, and we have no necessity to measure it. So, before we calculate every distance of any two given boxes, we should merge the ones that are overlapping in the horizontal direction into one box.

Here's how we merge the boxes:

```
vector<int> length_of_cars;
vector<pair<int, int>> endpoints;
vector<pair<int, int>> cars_merged;
```

First, in the preceding code, we declare the variables:

- The `length_of_cars` variable, which is a vector of integers, will hold the length of the cars in pixels, that is, the widths of the bounding boxes.
- The `endpoints` variable will hold the position of both ends of the cars. This variable is a vector of pairs of integers. Each pair in it is an end (either the front end or back end) of a car. If it is a back end, the pair will be `(X, 1)`, otherwise, it will be `(X, -1)`, where `X` is the *x* coordinate of the endpoint.
- The `cars_merged` variable is for the position information of cars after they are merged. We only care about their position in the horizontal direction, so we use pairs instead of rectangles to represent the position. The first element of the pair is the back end of the car, which is on the left, and the second one is the front end of the car, which is on the right.

Then, we iterate over the bounding boxes of the detected cars to fill these three vectors:

```
for (auto car: cars) {
    length_of_cars.push_back(car.width);
    endpoints.push_back(make_pair(car.x, 1));
    endpoints.push_back(make_pair(car.x + car.width, -1));
}
```

After the vectors have been filled, we sort the vectors of the lengths and find the median as the int length variable. We will use this median value as one of the reference values later:

```
sort(length_of_cars.begin(), length_of_cars.end());
int length = length_of_cars[cars.size() / 2];
```

Now, we implement our final step:

```
sort(
    endpoints.begin(), endpoints.end(),
    [](pair<int, int> a, pair<int, int> b) {
        return a.first < b.first;
    }
);

int flag = 0, start = 0;
for (auto ep: endpoints) {
    flag += ep.second;
    if (flag == 1 && start == 0) { // a start
        start = ep.first;
    } else if (flag == 0) { // an end
        cars_merged.push_back(make_pair(start, ep.first));
        start = 0;
    }
}
```

In the preceding code, we sort the endpoints vector by the first element of each pair in it. After sorting, we iterate over the sorted endpoints to do the merging. In the iteration, we add the second integer in the pair to a flag whose initial value is zero and then check the value of the flag. If it's 1 and we haven't started a merged range yet, it is a start point. When the flag decreases to zero, we get an endpoint of the range. In other words, we go through all the endpoints of the cars, from left to right. When we encounter a back end point of a car, we add one to the flag, and when we encounter a front end point of a car, we take one away from the flag. When the flag changes from zero to one, it is a start point of the merged range, and when it changes from non-zero to zero, it is an endpoint of the merged range.

The following diagram describes this algorithm in more detail:

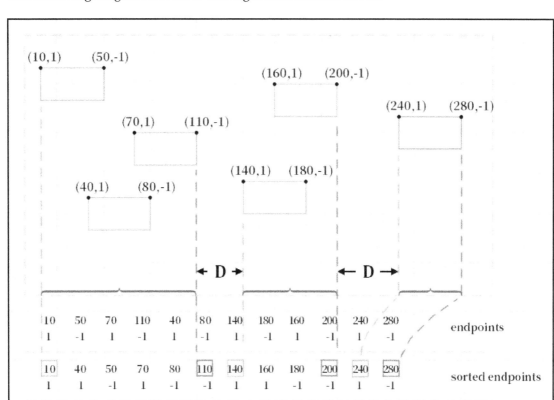

With pushing the start point and end point as a pair to the `cars_merged` vector, we will get all the merged boxes or the merged ranges, since we only care about the horizontal direction.

When we talked about measuring distances in the bird's eye view, we said that we must have a reference object with a fixed and known size, for instance, a coin. But in these circumstances, we don't have an object which meets this condition. To resolve this issue, we will pick the median of the lengths of the detected cars and assume that it has a length of 5 meters in the real world, and use it as the reference object. Let's see how we can calculate the distances between the merged ranges with this reference car:

```
for (size_t i = 1; i < cars_merged.size(); i++) {
    // head of car, start of spacing
    int x1 = cars_merged[i - 1].second;
```

```
    // end of another car, end of spacing
    int x2 = cars_merged[i].first;
    cv::line(frame, cv::Point(x1, 0), cv::Point(x1, frame.rows),
        cv::Scalar(0, 255, 0), 2);
    cv::line(frame, cv::Point(x2, 0), cv::Point(x2, frame.rows),
        cv::Scalar(0, 0, 255), 2);
    float distance = (x2 - x1) * (5.0 / length);

    // TODO: show the distance ...
}
```

In the preceding code, we iterate over the merged ranges, find the head of a range (car) and the back end of the next range (car), and then draw a green vertical line and a red vertical line at the two found points, respectively.

Then, we calculate the distance between the two vertical lines by using the `(x2 - x1) * (5.0 / length)` expression, where `5.0` is the approximate average length of the cars in common sense and `length` is the median of the lengths of the cars we detected in the video.

Now, let's display the calculated distances on the frame:

```
    // display the label at the top of the bounding box
    string label = cv::format("%.2f m", distance);
    int baseLine;
    cv::Size labelSize = cv::getTextSize(
        label, cv::FONT_HERSHEY_SIMPLEX, 0.5, 1, &baseLine);
    int label_x = (x1 + x2) / 2 - (labelSize.width / 2);
    cv::putText(
        frame, label, cv::Point(label_x, 20),
        cv::FONT_HERSHEY_SIMPLEX, 0.5, cv::Scalar(255, 255, 255));
```

The preceding code is also in the `for` loop. Here, we format the `distance` variable, which is a floating-point number to a string, and draw it on the top of the frame and in the middle of the two lines with the size of the text measured by the `cv::getTextSize` function.

At this point, the function of measuring the distance between cars in the bird's eye view is complete. Let's call it in the `CaptureThread::detectObjectsDNN` method:

```
    for(size_t i = 0; i < outBoxes.size(); i ++) {
        cv::rectangle(frame, outBoxes[i], cv::Scalar(0, 0, 255));
    }
    distanceBirdEye(frame, outBoxes);
```

As you can see, after drawing the bounding boxes of the detected cars in the
`CaptureThread::detectObjectsDNN` method, we call the newly added function with the
frame and the vector of the bounding boxes directly. Now, let's compile and start our
application and open the camera to see what it looks like:

As expected, we find many green and red line pairs in the video, which indicate the distances, and the approximate length of the distances are marked at the top of the video between the lines.

The key points of this approach are viewing the objects of interest in the bird's eye view and finding a fixed size reference object. Here, we use an empirical value as the reference value because we don't always get an appropriate reference object in the real world. We use the median of the lengths of the cars because there may be half cars that are entering or leaving the sight of the camera, which makes using an average value not very appropriate.

We have successfully measured the distance of cars in a bird's eye view, so let's move on to see how we cope with the eye-level view.

Measuring the distance between a car and the camera in the eye-level view

In the preceding subsection, we measured the distance between cars in the bird's eye view. In this subsection, we will measure the distance between a car and the camera.

When we talk about distance measurement in this circumstance, we understand that before measuring the distance, we must have our camera installed at a fixed position and then take a photo from it to get two reference values:

- The height or width of the object in the photo, measured in pixels. We called this value H0 or W0.
- The distance between the camera and the object when the photo is taken. We called this value D0.

The following photo has been taken from my camera—it's a photo of my car:

The two reference values of this photo are as follows:

- `W0 = 150 pixels`
- `D0 = 10 meters`

Now that we've got the reference values, let's start to do the distance measurement in the code. First, we will add a new function named `distanceEyeLevel`:

```
void distanceEyeLevel(cv::Mat &frame, vector<cv::Rect> &cars)
{
    const float d0 = 1000.0f; // cm
    const float w0 = 150.0f; // px

    // ...
}
```

Like the `distanceBirdEye` function, this function takes a frame of the video and the bounding boxes of the detected cars as its arguments as well. At the beginning of its body, we define the two reference values. Then, we try to find the car of interest:

```
// find the target car: the most middle and biggest one
vector<cv::Rect> cars_in_middle;
vector<int> cars_area;
```

```
            size_t target_idx = 0;

            for (auto car: cars) {
                if(car.x < frame.cols / 2 && (car.x + car.width) > frame.cols
    / 2) {
                    cars_in_middle.push_back(car);
                    int area = car.width * car.height;
                    cars_area.push_back(area);
                    if (area > cars_area[target_idx]) {
                        target_idx = cars_area.size() - 1;
                    }
                }
            }

            if(cars_in_middle.size() <= target_idx) return;
```

Considering that there may be more than one car detected in the video, we must figure out a way to choose one as the target. Here, we chose the biggest one in the middle of the view. To do this, we must declare three variables:

- `cars_in_middle` is a vector of rectangles which will hold the bounding boxes of cars, which are in the middle of the view.
- `cars_area` is a vector of integers, which is used to save the areas of the rectangles in the `cars_in_middle` vector.
- `target_idx` will be the index of the target car we find.

We iterate over the bounding boxes and check on each of them. If its top-left corner is on the left-hand side of the video and its top-right corner is on the right-hand side, we say it is in the middle of the video. Then, we push it and its area to the `cars_in_middle` vector and `cars_area` vector, respectively. After doing this, we check if the area we just pushed is bigger than the area of the current target. If it's true, we set the current index as the target index. When the iteration finishes, we will get the index of the target car in the `target_idx` variable. Then, we get the rectangle of the target car to measure the distance:

```
            cv::Rect car = cars_in_middle[target_idx];
            float distance = (w0 / car.width) * d0; // (w0 / w1) * d0
            // display the label at the top-left corner of the bounding box
            string label = cv::format("%.2f m", distance / 100);
            int baseLine;
            cv::Size labelSize = cv::getTextSize(
                label, cv::FONT_HERSHEY_SIMPLEX, 0.5, 1, &baseLine);
            cv::putText(frame, label, cv::Point(car.x, car.y +
    labelSize.height),
                cv::FONT_HERSHEY_SIMPLEX, 0.5, cv::Scalar(0, 255, 255));
```

In the preceding code, we find the rectangle and calculate the distance with the `(w0 / car.width) * d0` expression, according to equation **(7)**. Then, we format the `distance` variable into a string and draw it in the bounding box of the target car in the top-left corner.

Finally, we change the call to the `distanceBirdEye` function to a call to the newly added `distanceEyeLevel` function in the `CaptureThread::detectObjectsDNN` method, and then compile and run our application again. This is what it looks like:

As you can see, we detected more than one car in the video, but only the distance between the one in the middle and the camera is measured. The length of the distance is marked at the top-left corner of the bounding box of the target car in yellow text.

Switching between view modes

In the previous two subsections, we measured distance in two modes: the bird's eye view and the eye-level view. However, in our DiGauge application, the only way to switch between these modes is to change the code and recompile the application. Obviously, the end users cannot do this. In order to introduce this feature to the end users, we will add a new menu in the application to give the user a chance to switch between the modes. Let's start coding.

First, let's add some lines in the `capture_thread.h` file:

```
class CaptureThread : public QThread
{
    // ...
public:
    // ...
    enum ViewMode { BIRDEYE, EYELEVEL, };
    void setViewMode(ViewMode m) {viewMode = m; };

    // ...
private:
    // ...
    ViewMode viewMode;
};
```

In the preceding code, we define a public enumeration named `ViewMode`, which has two values to represent the two view modes, and a private member field of that type to indicate the current mode. There's also a public inline setter to update the current mode.

Then, in the constructor of the `CaptureThread` class, in the `capture_thread.cpp` file, we initialize the newly added field:

```
CaptureThread::CaptureThread(int camera, QMutex *lock):
    running(false), cameraID(camera), videoPath(""), data_lock(lock)
{
    frame_width = frame_height = 0;
    taking_photo = false;
    viewMode = BIRDEYE; // here
}

CaptureThread::CaptureThread(QString videoPath, QMutex *lock):
```

```
            running(false), cameraID(-1), videoPath(videoPath),
    data_lock(lock)
        {
            frame_width = frame_height = 0;
            taking_photo = false;
            viewMode = BIRDEYE; // and here
        }
```

In the `CaptureThread::detectObjectsDNN` method, we call `distanceBirdEye` or `distanceEyeLevel`, according to the value of the `viewMode` member field:

```
        if (viewMode == BIRDEYE) {
            distanceBirdEye(frame, outBoxes);
        } else {
            distanceEyeLevel(frame, outBoxes);
        }
```

Now, let's go to the `mainwindow.h` header file to add some methods and fields to the `MainWindow` class:

```
        class MainWindow : public QMainWindow
        {
            // ...
        private slots:
            // ...
            void changeViewMode();

        private:
            // ...
            QMenu *viewMenu;

            QAction *birdEyeAction;
            QAction *eyeLevelAction;
            // ...
        };
```

In this changeset, we add a `QMenu` and two `QAction` to the `MainWindow` class, as well as a slot named `changeViewMode` for the newly added actions. Now, let's instantiate the menu and the actions in the `mainwindow.cpp` source file.

In the `MainWindow::initUI()` method, we create the menu:

```
        // setup menubar
        fileMenu = menuBar()->addMenu("&File");
        viewMenu = menuBar()->addMenu("&View");
```

Then, in the `MainWindow::createActions` method, we instantiate the actions and add them to the view menu:

```
birdEyeAction = new QAction("Bird Eye View");
birdEyeAction->setCheckable(true);
viewMenu->addAction(birdEyeAction);
eyeLevelAction = new QAction("Eye Level View");
eyeLevelAction->setCheckable(true);
viewMenu->addAction(eyeLevelAction);

birdEyeAction->setChecked(true);
```

As you can see, this time, this was a little different from when we created actions before. We call the `setCheckable` method of the action instances with true after creating them. This makes the actions checkable, and a checkbox on the left of the text of the action will appear. The last line sets the state of the action, `birdEyeAction`, to checked. Then, we connect the `triggered` signal of the actions to the slot we just declared in the same method:

```
connect(birdEyeAction, SIGNAL(triggered(bool)), this,
SLOT(changeViewMode()));
connect(eyeLevelAction, SIGNAL(triggered(bool)), this,
SLOT(changeViewMode()));
```

Now, let's see how the slot is implemented:

```
void MainWindow::changeViewMode()
{
    CaptureThread::ViewMode mode = CaptureThread::BIRDEYE;
    QAction *active_action = qobject_cast<QAction*>(sender());
    if(active_action == birdEyeAction) {
        birdEyeAction->setChecked(true);
        eyeLevelAction->setChecked(false);
        mode = CaptureThread::BIRDEYE;
    } else if (active_action == eyeLevelAction) {
        eyeLevelAction->setChecked(true);
        birdEyeAction->setChecked(false);
        mode = CaptureThread::EYELEVEL;
    }
    if(capturer != nullptr) {
        capturer->setViewMode(mode);
    }
}
```

In this slot, we get the signal sender, which must be one of the two newly added actions, set the sender as checked and another one as unchecked, and then save the view mode according to the action which is checked. After that, we check if the capturing thread is null; if it's not, we set its view mode by calling its `setViewMode` method.

The last thing we need to do is reset the state of these actions when a new capturing thread is created and started. At the end of the body of the `MainWindow::openCamera` method, we need to add a few lines:

```
birdEyeAction->setChecked(true);
eyeLevelAction->setChecked(false);
```

Now, everything has been done. Let's compile and run the application to test the new feature:

As we can see in the preceding screenshot, we can switch the view mode through the **View** menu, and our DiGauge application is finally complete.

Summary

In this chapter, we planned to measure the distance between cars or between a car and a camera using OpenCV. First, we created a new application named **DiGauge** to detect cars from the camera by abridging the **Detective** application we developed in the previous chapter. Then, we talked about the principles of distance measuring in the computer vision domain in two view modes—the bird's eye view and the eye-level view. After that, we implemented the distance measurement features in these two view modes in our application and added a menu on the UI to switch between the two view modes.

In the next chapter, we will introduce a new technology called OpenGL and see how we can use it in Qt and how it can help us in the computer vision domain.

Questions

Try to answer the following question to test your knowledge of this chapter:

1. Is there a better reference object that we can use when we're measuring the distance between cars?

8
Using OpenGL for the High-Speed Filtering of Images

In the previous chapters, we learned a lot about how to use OpenCV to deal with images and videos. Most of these processes are done by the CPU. In this chapter, we will explore another way to process images, that is, by moving the image filtering from the CPU to the **graphics processing unit** (**GPU**) using OpenGL.

In many types of software, such as the Google Chrome browser, you may see an option for hardware acceleration, or similar, on the Settings page. Usually, these settings mean that the graphics card (or the GPU) is being used to do rendering or computing. This approach, which uses another processor rather than the CPU to do the computing or rendering, is called **heterogeneous computing**. There are many ways to do heterogeneous computing, including OpenCL, which we mentioned in Chapters 6, *Object Detection in Real Time* while we were running a deep learning model using OpenCV with its OpenCL backend. OpenGL, which we will introduce in this chapter, is also an approach to heterogeneous computing, though it is mostly used for 3D graphics rendering. Here, we will use it to filter images on our GPU rather than render 3D graphics.

The following topics will be covered in this chapter:

- A brief introduction to OpenGL
- Using OpenGL with Qt
- Filtering images on GPU with OpenGL
- Using OpenGL with OpenCV

Technical requirements

A basic knowledge of the C and C++ programming languages is a requirement to follow this chapter. Since OpenGL will be a predominant part of this chapter, a good understanding of OpenGL will also be a big advantage.

Considering that we will use Qt and OpenCV along with OpenGL, readers are required, at the very least, to have Qt version 5 and OpenCV 4.0.0 installed, in the same way as for previous chapters.

All the code for this chapter can be found in our code repository at `https://github.com/PacktPublishing/Qt-5-and-OpenCV-4-Computer-Vision-Projects/tree/master/Chapter-08`.

You can check out the following video to see the code in action: `http://bit.ly/2Fj4z3Y`

Hello OpenGL

OpenGL is not a typical programming library like OpenCV or Qt. Its maintainer, the Khronos group, only designs and defines the API of OpenGL as a specification; however, it is not responsible for the implementation. Instead, it is the graphics card manufacturer's responsibility to give the implementation. Most manufacturers, such as Intel, AMD, and Nvidia, give their implementation in the drivers of their graphics cards. On Linux, there's an OpenGL implementation called Mesa, which can do software rendering while hardware rendering is also supported if the graphics card is driven correctly.

Nowadays, OpenGL has a steep learning curve; this is because you need to understand the heterogeneous architecture and another programming language, called the OpenGL Shading Language, as well as C and C++. In this chapter, we will use the new style API, which was introduced in OpenGL V4.0 and backported to V3.3, in our code to render and filter images. We will start with a simple example to say "Hello" to OpenGL.

Before starting the example, we should ensure that OpenGL and some helper libraries are installed on our computer. On Windows, if you have the latest driver for your graphics card installed, the OpenGL library is also installed. On modern macOS, the OpenGL library implemented by Apple is preinstalled. On Linux, we can use the Mesa implementation or the proprietary hardware driver of the installed graphics card; using Mesa is easier because, once the runtime and development packages of Mesa are installed, we will get a working OpenGL installation.

Before doing anything with OpenGL, we must create an OpenGL context to operate on and a window that is associated with the context to show the rendered graphics. This work is usually platform-dependent. Fortunately, there are many libraries that hide these platform-dependent details and wrap up a universal API for that use. Here, we will use the GLFW (https://www.glfw.org/) and GLEW (http://glew.sourceforge.net/) libraries. The GLFW library will help us to create the OpenGL context and a window to show rendered graphics, while the GLEW library will take care of the OpenGL headers and extensions. On a UNIX-like system, we can build them from the source or easily install them using the system package manager. On Windows, we can download the binary packages that are provided on the official websites of the two helper libraries to install them.

Finally, after all the prerequisites are installed, we can start the `Hello OpenGL` example. Writing an OpenGL program usually involves the following steps, as follows:

1. Create the context and window.
2. Prepare the data of the objects that we want to draw (in 3D).
3. Pass the data to the GPU by calling some OpenGL APIs.
4. Call the drawing instructions to tell the GPU to draw the objects. During the drawing, the GPU will do many manipulations on the data, and these manipulations can be customized by writing shaders in the OpenGL Shading Language.
5. Write shaders that will run on the GPU to manipulate the data on the GPU.

Let's take a look at how we can perform these steps in our code. First, we create a source file named `main.c`, and then add in the essential `include` directives and the main function, as follows:

```c
#include <stdio.h>

#include <GL/glew.h>
#include <GLFW/glfw3.h>

int main() {
    return 0;
}
```

Then, as we mentioned, the first step is to create the OpenGL context and the window for showing the graphics:

```c
// init glfw and GL context
if (!glfwInit()) {
    fprintf(stderr, "ERROR: could not start GLFW3\n");
    return 1;
}
```

```
glfwWindowHint(GLFW_CONTEXT_VERSION_MAJOR, 3); // 3.3 or 4.x
glfwWindowHint(GLFW_CONTEXT_VERSION_MINOR, 3);
glfwWindowHint(GLFW_OPENGL_FORWARD_COMPAT, GL_TRUE);
glfwWindowHint(GLFW_OPENGL_PROFILE, GLFW_OPENGL_CORE_PROFILE);


GLFWwindow *window = NULL;
window = glfwCreateWindow(640, 480, "Hello OpenGL", NULL, NULL);
if (!window) {
    fprintf(stderr, "ERROR: could not open window with GLFW3\n");
    glfwTerminate();
    return 1;
}
glfwMakeContextCurrent(window);
```

In this piece of code, we first initialize the GLFW library by calling its `glfwInit` function. Then, we set some hints with the `glfwWindowHint` function, as follows:

- `GLFW_CONTEXT_VERSION_MAJOR` and `GLFW_CONTEXT_VERSION_MINOR` are used to specify the version of OpenGL; as we mentioned, we are using the new style API, which was introduced in V4.0 and backported to V3.3, so, here, at least V3.3 should be used.
- `GLFW_OPENGL_FORWARD_COMPAT` sets the OpenGL forward-compatibility to true.
- `GLFW_OPENGL_PROFILE` is used to set the profile we used to create the OpenGL context. Generally, there are two profiles we can choose: the core profile and the compatibility profile. With the core profile, only the new style API can be used, while with the compatibility profile, the manufacturers may provide support for both the old and the new API. However, when the compatibility profile is used, there may be some glitches when running the new version shaders on some implementation. So, here, we use the core profile.

After the hints are set, we declare and create the window. As you see from the arguments to the `glfwCreateWindow` function, the newly created window has a width of 640 pixels, a height of 480 pixels, and has the `Hello OpenGL` string as its title.

An OpenGL context associated with the window is also created along with the window. We call the `glfwMakeContextCurrent` function to set that context as the current context.

Following this, the `GLEW` library also needs to be initialized:

```
// start GLEW extension handler
GLenum ret = glewInit();
if ( ret != GLEW_OK) {
    fprintf(stderr, "Error: %s\n", glewGetErrorString(ret));
}
```

Next, let's go to the second step and prepare the data of the objects that we want to draw. We will draw a triangle here; a triangle is the most primitive shape in OpenGL since almost all things we draw in OpenGL are composed of triangles. The following is the data for our triangle:

```
GLfloat points[] = {+0.0f, +0.5f, +0.0f,
                    +0.5f, -0.5f, +0.0f,
                    -0.5f, -0.5f, +0.0f };
```

As you can see, the data is a nine-element array of floats. That is, we use three float numbers to describe each vertex of the triangle in the 3D space and there are three vertices of one triangle. In this book, we won't pay much attention to the 3D rendering, so we give the z coordinate of each vertex as 0.0 to draw the triangle as a 2D shape.

OpenGL uses a coordinate system called **normalized device coordinates** (**NDC**). In this coordinate system, all coordinates are confined within a range of -1.0 and 1.0. If the coordinates of objects are out of this range, they will not be shown in the OpenGL viewport. By omitting the z axis, the viewport of OpenGL and the points (which make the triangle) we give can be demonstrated by the following diagram:

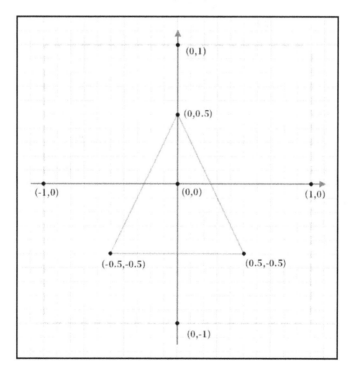

The data of vertices is ready, and we should now pass it onto the GPU. This is done by the **vertex buffer object** (**VBO**) and **vertex array object** (**VAO**); let's take a look at the following code:

```
// vbo
GLuint vbo;
glGenBuffers(1, &vbo);
glBindBuffer(GL_ARRAY_BUFFER, vbo);
glBufferData(GL_ARRAY_BUFFER, 9 * sizeof(GLfloat), points,
GL_STATIC_DRAW);
```

In the preceding code, the call to the `glGenBuffers` function generates one vertex buffer object (the first argument) and stores the name of the object to the `vbo` variable (the second argument). Then, we call the `glBindBuffer` function to bind the vertex buffer object to the current OpenGL context as a `GL_ARRAY_BUFFER` type, which means that the object is for the data of vertex attributes. Finally, we call the `glBufferData` function to create the data store and initialize it with our data of vertices for the currently bound buffer. The last argument to the function call tells OpenGL that our data will not be changed, and it is a hint for optimization.

Now, we have filled our data into a vertex buffer object, but the buffer is not visible on the GPU. In order to make it visible on the GPU, we should introduce a vertex array object and place a pointer that points to the buffer in it:

```
GLuint vao;
glGenVertexArrays(1, &vao);
glBindVertexArray(vao);
glEnableVertexAttribArray(0);
glVertexAttribPointer(0, 3, GL_FLOAT, GL_FALSE, 0, NULL);
```

Like the vertex buffer object, the vertex array object should be generated and bound before being used. After that, we call the `glEnableVertexAttribArray` function to enable a generic vertex attribute array pointer whose index is 0; in the vertex array object. You can think of this as reserving a seat for the vertex buffer object we created in the vertex array object and the number of the seat is 0. Then, we call the `glVertexAttribPointer` function to let the currently bound vertex buffer object sit on the reversed seat. The function accepts many arguments, and its signature is as follows:

```
void glVertexAttribPointer(
    GLuint index,
    GLint size,
    GLenum type,
    GLboolean normalized,
    GLsizei stride,
```

```
    const GLvoid * pointer
);
```

Let's explore each of them one by one, as follows:

- `index` specifies the index (or the seat number).
- `size` specifies the number of components per vertex attribute; we have three float numbers for each vertex (or point), so we use 3 here.
- `type` is the element type of the buffer or the data type of the components of the vertex attributes.
- `normalized` specifies whether our data should be normalized by OpenGL before it is accessed on the GPU. In our case, we used the normalized data (between -1.0 and 1.0), so it doesn't need to be normalized again.
- `stride` is the offset between consecutive generic vertex attributes. We use 0 here to tell OpenGL that our data is tightly packed and has no offset.
- `pointer` is the offset of the first component of the first generic vertex attribute in our buffer. We use NULL to indicate a zero offset.

At this point, we have successfully passed our vertex data onto the GPU by using the vertex buffer object and the vertex array object. The data will then be sent to the graphics pipeline of OpenGL. The OpenGL graphics pipeline has several stages: it accepts our 3D vertices, data and some other data, transforms them into colored pixels in 2D graphics, and displays them on the screen. The GPU has a large number of processors, and the transformation of the vertices can be done on these processors in parallel. That's why, by using a GPU, we can improve the performance while we are processing images or doing numerical computing that can be parallelized.

Before going on, let's take a look at the stages of the OpenGL graphics pipeline first. We can roughly divide it into six stages, as follows:

- **Vertex shader**: This stage takes the vertex attribute data (which, in our case, we had passed to the GPU) as its input, and gives the position of each vertex as its output. OpenGL doesn't provide a default shader program in this stage, so we should write one by ourselves.
- **Shape assembly**: This stage is used to assemble the shapes; for example, generating vertices and positioning them. This is an optional stage, and, in our case, we will ignore it.
- **Geometry shader**: This stage is for generating or deleting geometries and it is also an optional stage for which we don't have to write a shader program.

- **Rasterization**: This stage transforms 3D shapes (which are mainly triangles in OpenGL) to 2D pixels. This stage doesn't require any shader program.
- **Fragment shader**: This stage is used to colorize the fragments from the rasterization stage. Like the vertex shader stage, OpenGL doesn't provide a default shader program in this stage, so we should write one by ourselves.
- **Blending**: This stage renders the 2D graphics on the screen or a frame buffer.

Each of these six stages takes the output of its preceding stage as its input and gives output to its next stage. Additionally, in some stages, we can or need to write a shader program to participate in the work. A shader program is a piece of code that is written in the OpenGL Shading Language and runs on the GPU. It is compiled in the runtime of our application by the OpenGL implementation. As you can see in the preceding list of stages, there are at least two stages, that is, the vertex shader and the fragment shader, which require us to provide shader programs even in the most minimal OpenGL application. That's the steepest part of the learning curve for OpenGL. Let's examine what these shader programs look like:

```
// shader and shader program
GLuint vert_shader, frag_shader;
GLuint shader_prog;
const char *vertex_shader_code = "#version 330\n"
    "layout (location = 0) in vec3 vp;"
    "void main () {"
    " gl_Position = vec4(vp, 1.0);"
    "}";

const char *fragment_shader_code = "#version 330\n"
    "out vec4 frag_colour;"
    "void main () {"
    " frag_colour = vec4(0.5, 1.0, 0.5, 1.0);"
    "}";

vert_shader = glCreateShader(GL_VERTEX_SHADER);
glShaderSource(vert_shader, 1, &vertex_shader_code, NULL);
glCompileShader(vert_shader);

frag_shader = glCreateShader(GL_FRAGMENT_SHADER);
glShaderSource(frag_shader, 1, &fragment_shader_code, NULL);
glCompileShader(frag_shader);

shader_prog = glCreateProgram();
glAttachShader(shader_prog, frag_shader);
glAttachShader(shader_prog, vert_shader);
glLinkProgram(shader_prog);
```

In this piece of code, we start by defining three variables: vert_shader and frag_shader for the required shader programs of the corresponding stages, and shader_prog for the whole shader program, which will contain all the shader programs of all the stages. Then, we write the shader programs as strings in the code, which we will explain later. Following this, we create each shader program by calling the glCreateShader function and attaching the source string to them, and then compiling them.

After the shader programs for the stages are ready, we create the whole shader program object, attach the stage shader programs to it, and then link the program. At this point, the whole shader program is ready to use, and we can call glUseProgram with it to use it; we will do this later after explaining the code for shader programs.

Now, let's take a look at the vertex shader:

```
#version 330
layout (location = 0) in vec3 vp;
void main() {
    gl_Position = vec4(vp, 1.0);
}
```

The first line of the preceding code is a version hint, that is, it specifies the version of the OpenGL Shading Language. Here, we use version 330, which corresponds to the version of OpenGL that we use.

Then, in the second line, we declare the variable of the input data. The layout (location = 0) qualifier indicates that this input data is associated with index 0 (or, the seat whose number is 0) of the currently bound vertex array object. Additionally, the in keyword says that it is an input variable. The word vec3, which stands for a vector of 3 float numbers, is the data type and vp is the variable name. In our case, vp will be the coordinates of one of the vertices we stored in the points variable, and the three vertices will be dispatched to three different processors on the GPU, so this piece of code will run on these processors in parallel for each vertex. If we only have one input array, the layout qualifier can be omitted in this shader.

After the input data is correctly described, we define the main function, which is the entry point of the program, just as we do in the C programming language. In the main function, we construct a vector of four float numbers from the input and then assign it to the gl_Position variable. The gl_Position variable is a predefined variable that is the output for the next stage and represents the position of the vertex.

The type of this variable is `vec4` but not `vec3`; the fourth component is named `w`, while the first three are `x`, `y`, and `z`, which we can guess. The `w` component is a factor that is used to divide the other vector components to homogenize them; we use 1.0 in our case since our values are normalized values already.

In conclusion, our vertex shader gets the input from the vertex array object and returns it untouched.

Now, let's take a look at the fragment shader:

```
#version 330
out vec4 frag_colour;
void main () {
    frag_colour = vec4(0.5, 1.0, 0.5, 1.0);
}
```

In this shader, we define an output variable with the `out` keyword of the `vec4` type and it represents the color in RGBA format. Then, in the main function, we assign a constant color, that is, light green, to the output variable.

Now the shader programs are clear and ready, let's start the graphics pipeline:

```
while (!glfwWindowShouldClose(window)) {
    glClear(GL_COLOR_BUFFER_BIT | GL_DEPTH_BUFFER_BIT);
    glUseProgram(shader_prog);
    glBindVertexArray(vao);
    glDrawArrays(GL_TRIANGLES, 0, 3);
    // update other events like input handling
    glfwPollEvents();
    // put the stuff we've been drawing onto the display
    glfwSwapBuffers(window);
}

glfwTerminate();
```

In the preceding code, we will continuously run a code block unless the application window is closed. In the code block, we clear the bitplane area on the window, then use the shader program we created and bind the vertex array object. This operation connects the shader program and the array or buffer with the current OpenGL context. Following this, we call `glDrawArrays` to start the graphics pipeline to draw the objects. The first argument to the `glDrawArrays` function is the primitive type; here, we want to draw a triangle, so `GL_TRIANGLES` is used. The second argument is the buffer index that we enabled for the vertex buffer object, and the last one is the count of the vertices we want to use.

At this point, the work of drawing the triangle is done, but we still have something more to do: we call the `glfwPollEvents` function to grab the events that occurred on the window and call the `glfwSwapBuffers` function with the window object to show the graphics we draw. We need the latter function call because the GLFW library uses double-buffer optimization.

When the window is closed by the user, we will jump out of the code block and initiate the call to the `glfwTerminate` function to release all the resources allocated by the GLFW library; then the application exits.

Okay, so let's compile and run the application:

```
gcc -Wall -std=c99 -o main.exe main.c -lGLEW -lglfw -lGL -lm
./main.exe
```

You will see the following green triangle:

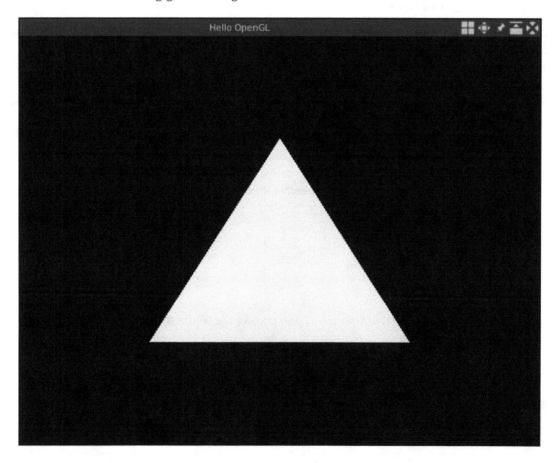

If you are using Windows, you can compile the application on MinGW with the `gcc -Wall -std=c99 -o main.exe main.c libglew32.dll.a glfw3dll.a -lOpenGL32 -lglew32 -lglfw3 -lm` command. Don't forget to specify the include paths and library paths of the GLFW and GLEW libraries with the `-I` and `-L` options.

Okay, so our first application with OpenGL is done. However, as you can see, GLFW is not a full-fledged GUI library, especially when we compare it to the Qt library, which we have used a lot in this book. The GLFW library can create windows and capture and respond to UI events, but it doesn't have many kinds of widget. So, what happens if we require OpenGL and some widgets at the same time in an application? Could we use OpenGL in Qt? The answer is yes, and we will demonstrate how to do this in the next section.

OpenGL in Qt

In the early days, Qt had a module named `OpenGL`, but in Qt 5.x, that module is deprecated. A new version of facilities for OpenGL supports is put into the `gui` module; if you search classes whose names start with `QOpenGL` in the Qt docs, you will find them. Besides the facilities that reside in the `gui` module, there's another important class named `QOpenGLWidget` in the `widgets` module. In this section, we will use some of these facilities to draw a triangle with OpenGL in Qt.

First, let's create the required Qt projects:

```
$ pwd
/home/kdr2/Work/Books/Qt5-And-OpenCV4-Computer-Vision-Projects/Chapter-08
$ mkdir QtGL
$ cd QtGL/
$ touch main.cpp
$ qmake -project
$ ls
QtGL.pro main.cpp
$
```

Then, we change the content of the `QtGL.pro` project file to the following:

```
TEMPLATE = app
TARGET = QtGL

QT += core gui widgets

INCLUDEPATH += .
```

```
DEFINES += QT_DEPRECATED_WARNINGS

# Input
HEADERS += glpanel.h
SOURCES += main.cpp glpanel.cpp

RESOURCES = shaders.qrc
```

This refers to many files that don't exist for now, but don't worry—we will create all of them before we compile the project.

First, we will create a widget class named GLPanel to show the graphics that will be drawn in the OpenGL context; the code we used to prepare the data as well as draw the graphics will also be in this class. Let's examine the declaration of this GLPanel class in the glpanel.h header file:

```
    class GLPanel : public QOpenGLWidget, protected
QOpenGLFunctions_4_2_Core
    {
        Q_OBJECT

    public:
        GLPanel(QWidget *parent = nullptr);
        ~GLPanel();

    protected:
        void initializeGL() override;
        void paintGL() override;
        void resizeGL(int w, int h) override;
    private:
        GLuint vbo;
        GLuint vao;
        GLuint shaderProg;
    };
```

The class is derived from two classes: the QOpenGLWidget class and the QOpenGLFunctions_4_2_Core class.

The QOpenGLWidget class provides three protected methods that we must implement in our class, as follows:

- The initializeGL method is for the initialization; for example, preparing the vertex data, the vertex buffer object, the array buffer object, and the shader programs.

- The `paintGL` method is for the drawing work; for example, in it we will call the `glDrawArrays` functions.
- The `resizeGL` method is the function that will be called when the widget is resized.

The `QOpenGLFunctions_4_2_Core` class contains many functions that have similar names to the OpenGL V4.2 API from Khronos. The `4_2` string in the class name indicates the version of OpenGL we are using and the `Core` string tells us that the core profile of OpenGL is used. We derive our class from this class so that we can use all of the OpenGL functions with the same names without any prefix in our class, though these functions are actually wrappers provided by Qt.

Let's go to the `glpanel.cpp` source file to see the implementation. The constructor and destructor are very simple so I won't explain them here. First, let's see the initialization method, `void GLPanel::initializeGL()`:

```
void GLPanel::initializeGL()
{
    initializeOpenGLFunctions();
    // ... omit many lines
    std::string vertex_shader_str =
textContent(":/shaders/vertex.shader");
    const char *vertex_shader_code = vertex_shader_str.data();

    std::string fragment_shader_str =
textContent(":/shaders/fragment.shader");
    const char *fragment_shader_code = fragment_shader_str.data();
    // ... omit many lines
}
```

Most of the code in this method is copied from the main function in the preceding section; so, I have omitted many lines here, and will only explain the similarities and differences. In this method, we prepare the vertex data, vertex buffer object, and vertex array object; pass the data to the GPU; and write, compile, and link the shader program. This is the same process as the preceding application except that, here, `vao`, `vbo`, and `shaderProg` are class members but not local variables.

Besides that, we call the `initializeOpenGLFunctions` method at the beginning to initialize the OpenGL function wrappers. Another difference is that we move the shader code into separate files to improve the maintainability of the shader programs. We place the files under a subdirectory named `shaders` and reference them in a `shaders.qrc` Qt resource file:

```
<!DOCTYPE RCC>
```

```
<RCC version="1.0">
  <qresource>
    <file>shaders/vertex.shader</file>
    <file>shaders/fragment.shader</file>
  </qresource>
</RCC>
```

Then, we use the `textContent` function to load the content of these files. This function is also defined in the `glpanel.cpp` file:

```
std::string textContent(QString path) {
    QFile file(path);
    file.open(QFile::ReadOnly | QFile::Text);
    QTextStream in(&file);
    return in.readAll().toStdString();
}
```

Now that the initialization is done, let's move on to the `paintGL` method:

```
void GLPanel::paintGL()
{
    glClear(GL_COLOR_BUFFER_BIT | GL_DEPTH_BUFFER_BIT |
GL_STENCIL_BUFFER_BIT);
    glUseProgram(shaderProg);
    glBindVertexArray(vao);
    glDrawArrays(GL_TRIANGLES, 0, 3);
    glFlush();
}
```

As you can see, all the things we do to draw the triangle in this method are exactly the same as the last code block in the preceding application.

Finally, we resize the OpenGL viewport when the widget is resized:

```
void GLPanel::resizeGL(int w, int h)
{
    glViewport(0, 0, (GLsizei)w, (GLsizei)h);
}
```

At this point, we have finished our `GLPanel` OpenGL widget, so let's use it in the `main.cpp` file:

```
int main(int argc, char *argv[])
{
    QApplication app(argc, argv);

    QSurfaceFormat format = QSurfaceFormat::defaultFormat();
    format.setProfile(QSurfaceFormat::CoreProfile);
```

```
        format.setVersion(4, 2);
        QSurfaceFormat::setDefaultFormat(format);

        QMainWindow window;
        window.setWindowTitle("QtGL");
        window.resize(800, 600);
        GLPanel *panel = new GLPanel(&window);
        window.setCentralWidget(panel);
        window.show();
        return app.exec();
    }
```

In the main function, we get the default `QSurefaceFormat` type and update some key settings that are relevant to OpenGL, as follows:

- Set the profile to the core profile.
- Set the version to V4.2, since we are using the `QOpenGLFunctions_4_2_Core` class.

Then, we create the main window and an instance of the `GLPanel` class, set the `GLPanel` instance as the central widget of the main window, show the window, and execute the application. Our first Qt application in OpenGL is finished, so you can compile and run it now. However, you may find that there is no difference from the window in our preceding example. Yes, we showed you how to use OpenGL in a Qt project, but not how to make a complex application with many widgets. Since we have already learned a lot about how to build a complex GUI application with Qt in the previous chapters and we now have an OpenGL widget, you can try to develop complex Qt applications that feature OpenGL by yourself. In the next section, we will dive a little deeper into OpenGL to explore how to filter images with OpenGL.

 Apart from the OpenGL API functions in the `QOpenGLFunctions_*` classes, Qt also wraps many other classes for the concepts in OpenGL; for example, the `QOpenGLBuffer` class is for the vertex buffer object, the `QOpenGLShaderProgram` type is for the shader program, and more. These classes are also very convenient to use, but may (or will) be a little behind compared to the latest version of OpenGL.

Filtering images with OpenGL

So far, we have learned how to draw a simple triangle in OpenGL. In this section, we will learn how to draw images and filter them with OpenGL.

We will do this work in a copy of the QtGL project, that is, a new project named `GLFilter`. The creation of the project simply involves straightforward copying and a little bit of renaming, just as we did in the previous chapters. I won't repeat it again here, so please copy it by yourself.

Drawing images with OpenGL

In order to draw an image on the OpenGL viewport, we should introduce another concept of OpenGL—the texture. A texture in OpenGL is usually a 2D image, and it is generally used to add visual detail to an object, which is mainly a triangle.

Since any kind of digital image is usually a rectangle, we should draw two triangles to compose a rectangle for the image, and then load the image as a texture and map it to the rectangles.

The texture uses a coordinate system that differs from the NDC that is used when we draw the triangles. Both of the x and y (axes) of the texture coordinate system are between **0** and **1**, that is, the bottom-left corner is (0, 0), while the top-right corner is (1, 1). So, our vertices and coordinate mapping will look like the following:

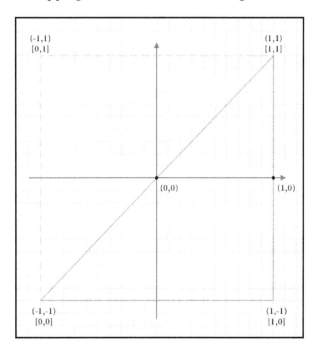

The preceding diagram shows one of the two triangles we will draw, that is, the bottom-right one. The coordinates in the parentheses are those of the triangle vertices, and the ones in the brackets are of the texture.

As the diagram shows, we define our vertex attribute data as follows:

```
GLfloat points[] = {
        // first triangle
        +1.0f, +1.0f, +0.0f, +1.0f, +1.0f, // top-right
        +1.0f, -1.0f, +0.0f, +1.0f, +0.0f, // bottom-right
        -1.0f, -1.0f, +0.0f, +0.0f, +0.0f, // bottom-left
        // second triangle
        -1.0f, -1.0f, +0.0f, +0.0f, +0.0f, // bottom-left
        -1.0f, +1.0f, +0.0f, +0.0f, +1.0f, // top-left
        +1.0f, +1.0f, +0.0f, +1.0f, +1.0f // top-right
    };
```

As you can see, we define six vertices for the two triangles. Additionally, there are five float numbers for each vertex—the first three are the coordinates for the triangle vertex, while the last two are the coordinates of the texture corresponding to the vertex.

Now, let's pass the data on to the GPU:

```
        // VBA & VAO
        glGenBuffers(1, &vbo);
        glBindBuffer(GL_ARRAY_BUFFER, vbo);
        glBufferData(GL_ARRAY_BUFFER, sizeof(points), points,
    GL_STATIC_DRAW);

        glGenVertexArrays(1, &vao);
        glBindVertexArray(vao);
        glEnableVertexAttribArray(0);
        glVertexAttribPointer(0, 3, GL_FLOAT, GL_FALSE, 5 * sizeof(float),
    NULL);
        glEnableVertexAttribArray(1);
        glVertexAttribPointer(1, 2, GL_FLOAT, GL_FALSE, 5 * sizeof(float),
    (void*)(3 * sizeof(float)));
```

In the preceding code, we create the vertex buffer object, fill the float numbers into it, and then create the vertex array object. Here, in comparison to the last time we bound vertex buffer objects to a vertex array object when we draw the single triangle in the Hello OpenGL example, we enable two pointers in the vertex array object but not one; that is, we reserve two seats there. The first one, whose index is 0, is for the coordinates of the triangle vertices; the second one, whose index is 1, is for the texture coordinates mapping to the vertices.

The following diagram shows the data layout for three vertices in the buffer and how we use it in the vertex array object:

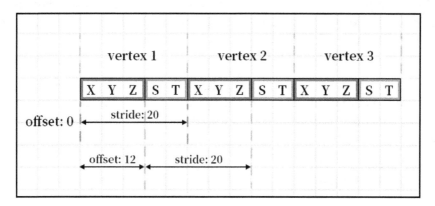

We use the vertices' coordinates as the pointer whose index is 0, as the diagram shows, its element count for each vertex is 3, its stride is 20 (5 * `sizeof(float)`), and its offset is 0. These are the arguments we pass to the first call to the `glVertexAttribPointer` function. For the coordinates of the texture, the element count is 2, the stride is 20, and the offset is 12. With these numbers, we call the `glVertexAttribPointer` function again to set the array pointer.

Okay, so the data of the vertices attributes is passed to the GPU; let's now demonstrate how to load the image (or the texture) onto the GPU:

```
// texture
glEnable(GL_TEXTURE_2D);
// 1. read the image data
QImage img(":/images/lizard.jpg");
img = img.convertToFormat(QImage::Format_RGB888).mirrored(false,
true);
// 2. generate texture
glGenTextures(1, &texture);
glBindTexture(GL_TEXTURE_2D, texture);
glTexImage2D(
    GL_TEXTURE_2D, 0, GL_RGB,
    img.width(), img.height(), 0, GL_RGB, GL_UNSIGNED_BYTE,
img.bits());
glGenerateMipmap(GL_TEXTURE_2D);
```

In this piece of code, we enable the 2D texture feature of OpenGL, load an image from the Qt resource system, and then convert the image to RGB format. You may notice that we flip the image in the vertical direction by calling its `mirrored` method. That's because the image in Qt and the texture in OpenGL use different coordinate systems: (0, 0) is the top-left point in the Qt image, while it is the bottom-left point in the OpenGL texture. In other words, they have the y axis in opposite directions.

After the image is loaded, we generate one texture object and save its name to the `texture` class member, and bind it to the current OpenGL context. Then, we call the `glTexImage2D` function to copy the data of the image to the texture memory of the GPU. Here is the signature of this function:

```
void glTexImage2D(
    GLenum target,
    GLint level,
    GLint internalformat,
    GLsizei width,
    GLsizei height,
    GLint border,
    GLenum format,
    GLenum type,
    const GLvoid * data
);
```

Let's examine the arguments of this function call one by one, as follows:

- `target`, with `GL_TEXTURE_2D` as its value, specifies the texture target. OpenGL also supports 1D and 3D textures, so we use this value to ensure that it's the currently bound 2D texture that we are operating on.
- `level` is the mipmap level. In OpenGL, a mipmap is a series of images of different sizes generated by resizing the original image; in the series, each subsequent image is twice as small as the previous one. The images in the mipmap are automatically selected for use with different object sizes, or a certain object when it is in different positions. For instance, if the object is far away in our view, a small image will be used. Compared to resizing the texture to a proper size on-the-fly, using a pre-calculated one from the mipmap can reduce computing and improve the image quality. If you want to manipulate the mipmap manually, you should use a nonzero value. Here, we will use an OpenGL-provided function to generate the mipmap, so we simply use 0.
- `internalformat` tells OpenGL what type of format we want to store the texture in. Our image only has RGB values, so we'll store the texture with RGB values as well.

- `width` and `height` are the width and height of the target texture. We use the dimension of the image here.
- `border` is a legacy argument that has no meaning and should always be 0.
- `format` and `type` are the format and data type of the source image.
- `data` is the pointer to the actual image data.

After the call returns, the texture data is ready on the GPU, and then we call `glGenerateMipmap(GL_TEXTURE_2D)` to generate the mipmap for the currently bound 2D texture.

At this point, the texture is ready, so let's take a look at our shader programs. First is the vertex shader, as follows:

```
#version 420

layout (location = 0) in vec3 vertex;
layout (location = 1) in vec2 inTexCoord;

out vec2 texCoord;

void main()
{
    gl_Position = vec4(vertex, 1.0);
    texCoord = inTexCoord;
}
```

In this shader, the two input variables (whose locations are 0 and 1) correspond to the two pointers we enabled in the vertex array object, which represent the triangle vertices' coordinates and the texture mapping coordinates. In the main function, we set the position of the vertex by assigning it to the predefined variable, `gl_Position`. Then, we pass the texture coordinates to an output variable that is declared with the `out` keyword. This output variable will be passed to the next shader, which is the fragment shader; the following is our fragment shader:

```
#version 420

in vec2 texCoord;
out vec4 frag_color;
uniform sampler2D theTexture;

void main()
{
    frag_color = texture(theTexture, texCoord);
}
```

There are three variables in this fragment shader, as follows:

- in vec2 texCoord is the texture coordinate from the vertex shader.
- out vec4 frag_color is the output variable that we will update to pass out the color of the fragment.
- uniform sampler2D theTexture, is the texture. It is a uniform variable; unlike the in and out variables, a uniform variable can be seen in any shader at any stage in the OpenGL graphics pipeline.

In the main function, we use the built-in texture function to get the color corresponding to the given texture coordinate texCoord, and assign it to the output variable. This process, picking colors from texture, is called a texture sampling in OpenGL terms.

Now the shaders are ready; the final thing we need to do in the initialization function is to resize the main window to fit the image size:

```
((QMainWindow*)this->parent())->resize(img.width(), img.height());
```

Okay, so let's now draw the objects in the GLPanel::paintGL method:

```
glClear(GL_COLOR_BUFFER_BIT | GL_DEPTH_BUFFER_BIT |
GL_STENCIL_BUFFER_BIT);

glUseProgram(shaderProg);
glBindVertexArray(vao);
glBindTexture(GL_TEXTURE_2D, texture);
glDrawArrays(GL_TRIANGLES, 0, 6);
glFlush();
```

In comparison to the last time we drew a triangle, here we add a new function call to glBindTexture to bind the newly created texture to the current OpenGL context, and use 6 as the third argument to the glDrawArrays function, since we want to draw two triangles.

Now, it's time to compile and run our application. If all goes well, you will see the image rendered by OpenGL:

TIP

Although in our code, we load the image from the Qt resource system, we can load any image on our local disk—just change the path to do that.

Filtering images in the fragment shader

In the preceding subsection, we drew an image with OpenGL. While drawing the image, we picked colors from the texture (which has the same data as the original image) in the fragment shader. So, if we, in the fragment shader, change the color according to a particular rule before passing it out, will we get a modified image?

Following this thought, let's try a simple linear blur filter within the fragment shader program. The principle of the linear blur filter can be displayed in the following diagram:

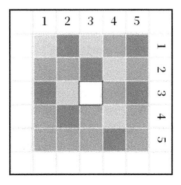

For a given pixel, we determine its color according to the color of the pixels around it. In the preceding diagram, for the given pixel, we draw a 5 x 5 square around it and ensure that it is the center pixel of the square. Then, we sum up the color of all the pixels in the square except the center pixel itself, work out the average value (by dividing the sum by 5 x 5 − 1), and then use the average as the color of the given pixel. Here, we call the square the filter kernel and its side length, which is **5**, the kernel size.

However, we have a problem here. The coordinates that are stored in the texCoord variable are the float numbers between 0 and 1, not the number of pixels. Within such a range, we can't directly determine the kernel size, so we need to know how long one pixel stands for in the texture coordinate system. This can be worked out by dividing 1.0 by the image width and height. By doing so, we will get two float numbers that stand for one-pixel width and one-pixel height, respectively, in the texture coordinate system. We will store the two numbers in a uniform two-element vector later. Let's update our fragment shader, as follows:

```
#version 420

in vec2 texCoord;
out vec4 frag_color;
uniform sampler2D theTexture;
uniform vec2 pixelScale;

void main()
{
    int kernel_size = 5;
    vec4 color = vec4(0.0, 0.0, 0.0, 0.0);
    for(int i = -(kernel_size / 2); i <= kernel_size / 2; i++) {
        for(int j = -(kernel_size / 2); j <= kernel_size / 2; j++) {
            if(i == 0 && j == 0) continue;
            vec2 coord = vec2(texCoord.x + i * pixelScale.x,
texCoord.y + i * pixelScale.y);
            color = color + texture(theTexture, coord);
        }
    }
    frag_color = color / (kernel_size * kernel_size - 1);
}
```

The uniform vec2 pixelScale variable in the preceding code is the ratio numbers we just discussed. In the main function, we use 5 as the kernel size, work out the texture coordinates of the pixels in the kernel square, pick up the color, and sum them up in a two-level nested for loop. After the loop, we calculate the average and assign it to the output variable.

The next step is setting the value to the `uniform vec2 pixelScale` variable. This is done in the `GLPanel::initializeGL` method after the shader program is linked:

```
// ...
glLinkProgram(shaderProg);
// scale ration
glUseProgram(shaderProg);
int pixel_scale_loc = glGetUniformLocation(shaderProg,
"pixelScale");
glUniform2f(pixel_scale_loc, 1.0f / img.width(), 1.0f /
img.height());
```

After the shader program is linked, we activate (that is, use) the shader program in the current OpenGL context, and then call `glGetUniformLocation` with the shader program and the uniform variable name as its arguments. The call will return the location of the uniform variable. With this location, we can call `glUniform2f` to set its value. The `2f` suffix in the function name means two floats, hence, we pass the two scale ratios to it.

At this point, our filter is almost done, except for one situation. Consider what would happen if the given pixel whose color we are calculating, is on the edge of the image. In other words, how do we handle the edge of the image? The following is the solution:

```
glTexParameteri(GL_TEXTURE_2D, GL_TEXTURE_WRAP_S,
GL_MIRRORED_REPEAT);
glTexParameteri(GL_TEXTURE_2D, GL_TEXTURE_WRAP_T,
GL_MIRRORED_REPEAT);
```

Add these two lines in the `GLPanel::initializeGL` method next to the lines where we generate and bind the texture. These lines set the behavior of texture wrapping: `GL_TEXTURE_WRAP_S` is for the horizontal direction and `GL_TEXTURE_WRAP_T` is for the vertical direction. We set both of them to `GL_MIRRORED_REPEAT` so that if we use a coordinate less than 0 or greater than 1, a mirrored repeat of the texture image will be there for sampling. In other words, it has the same effect as `BORDER_REFLECT` in the OpenCV library, which is interpolated as `fedcba|abcdefgh|hgfedcb` when we call the `cv::warpAffine` function. For example, when we access a point with the coordinate (`1`, `1 + y`) coordinate, it returns the color of the point (`x`, `1 - y`).

For now, our linear blur filter is done, so let's recompile and run our application to see the effect:

Well, it works as expected. In order to see its effect in a clearer way, we can even blur part of the image only. Here's the main function of the updated fragment shader:

```
void main()
{
    int kernel_size = 7;
    vec4 color = vec4(0.0, 0.0, 0.0, 0.0);
    if(texCoord.x > 0.5) {
        for(int i = -(kernel_size / 2); i <= kernel_size / 2; i++) {
            for(int j = -(kernel_size / 2); j <= kernel_size / 2; j++)
{
                if(i == 0 && j == 0) continue;
                vec2 coord = vec2(texCoord.x + i * pixelScale.x,
texCoord.y + i * pixelScale.y);
                color = color + texture(theTexture, coord);
            }
        }
        frag_color = color / (kernel_size * kernel_size - 1);
    } else {
        frag_color = texture(theTexture, texCoord);
    }
}
```

In this version, we only blur the right-side of the image (the part that is `texCoord.x > 0.5`); the following is the effect:

Since we compile all the resources into the executable, we need to recompile the application after an update of the resource file to take effect, including the shaders.

In this section, we implement a simple linear blur filter in the fragment shader that runs on the GPU. If you have a decent GPU and apply this on a large image, you will gain a big performance improvement, compared to running a similar filter on the CPU.

Since we can access all the pixels of the texture (or the image) and determine the color of all the pixels of the rendered image in the fragment shader, we can implement any filter in the shader program. You can try the Gaussian blur filter by yourself.

Saving the filtered images

In the preceding subsection, we implemented a blur filter and successfully blurred an image with it—the blurred image was rendered on the OpenGL viewport. So, can we save that resulting image as a file on our local disk? Sure; let's do it as follows:

```
void GLPanel::saveOutputImage(QString path)
{
    QImage output(img.width(), img.height(), QImage::Format_RGB888);
    glReadPixels(
        0, 0, img.width(), img.height(), GL_RGB, GL_UNSIGNED_BYTE,
output.bits());
    output = output.mirrored(false, true);
    output.save(path);
}
```

We add a new `GLPanel::saveOutputImage` method that accepts a file path as its argument to save the image. Another thing worth noting is that we change the original image, `QImage img`, from a local variable in the `initializeGL` method to a class member, since we will use it in the class scope.

In this newly added method, we define a new `QImage` object that has the same dimension as the original image, and then call the `glReadPixels` function to read the data in the rectangle described by the first four arguments to the image object. Then, we flip the image in the vertical direction because of the different coordinate systems, which we mentioned previously. Finally, we save the image to the disk.

If you call this method at the end of the `paintGL` method, you will find the saved image after you see the image on the screen.

Using OpenGL with OpenCV

In the preceding section, when we load the source image and flip it, we use Qt to do the work. This work can also be done by using the OpenCV library:

```
img = cv::imread("./images/lizard.jpg");
cv::Mat tmp;
cv::flip(img, tmp, 0);
cvtColor(tmp, img, cv::COLOR_BGR2RGB);
// ...
glTexImage2D(
    GL_TEXTURE_2D, 0, GL_RGB,
    img.cols, img.rows, 0, GL_RGB, GL_UNSIGNED_BYTE, img.data);
// ...
```

Similarly, when saving the resulting image, we can do it like this:

```
cv::Mat output(img.rows, img.cols, CV_8UC3);
glReadPixels(
    0, 0, img.cols, img.rows, GL_RGB, GL_UNSIGNED_BYTE,
output.data);
cv::Mat tmp;
cv::flip(output, tmp, 0);
cvtColor(tmp, output, cv::COLOR_RGB2BGR);
cv::imwrite(path.toStdString(), output);
```

Both `QImage` and `cv::Mat` represent images, so it is easy to exchange them forth and back.

Apart from simply using the `cv::Mat` class to exchange data with the texture, OpenCV also has the ability to create the OpenGL context. It requires the library to be configured with the `-D WITH_OPENGL=on` option when building it from the source. Once OpenGL support is enabled, we can create a window (using the `highgui` module) with an OpenGL context associated with it:

```
cv::namedWindow("OpenGL", cv::WINDOW_OPENGL);
cv::resizeWindow("OpenGL", 640, 480);
```

The key point here is the `cv::WINDOW_OPENGL` flag; with this flag set, an OpenGL context will be created and set as the current one. But OpenCV doesn't provide a way to select the OpenGL version we want to use and it doesn't always use the latest version available on a machine.

I provide a sample of drawing a triangle with an OpenGL context and the OpenCV `highgui` module in our code repository, in the `Chapter-08/CVGLContext` directory—you can refer to it to learn more. The core module of the OpenCV library provides a namespace, `cv::ogl`, which includes many facilities used to interoperate with OpenGL as well.

However, these facilities have the same issue as the Qt-provided OpenGL-relevant classes, that is, they may be far behind the latest OpenGL. So, here, I recommend that, if you want to use OpenGL, you just use the raw OpenGL API and not any wrapper for it. Most OpenGL implementations are flexible enough and can be easily integrated with common libraries, and you can always use the latest API in this way.

Summary

OpenGL is a specification for developing 2D and 3D graphics applications, and it has many implementations. In this chapter, we learned a lot about it, including drawing primitives such as triangles, integrating it with the Qt library, using a texture to render images, and filtering images in the fragment shaders. Additionally, we used OpenGL in a non-typical way, that is, we didn't use it for graphics rendering, but for heterogeneous computing and processing images on the GPU in parallel.

Finally, we learned how to integrate OpenCV and OpenGL, and, in my opinion, by comparing this approach to using the raw OpenGL API, this is not a recommended way for a production application, but feel free to use it in your attempts.

With the end of this chapter, we have finished the book. I hope that all the projects we developed with Qt, OpenCV, Tesseract, the many DNN models, and OpenGL will bring you closer to the world of computer vision.

Further reading

There is a lot more to OpenGL than what we have covered in this chapter. Since we mainly focused on image processing in this book, we only showed how to use it to filter images. If you are interested in OpenGL, you can find more resources on its official website at `https://www.opengl.org`. There are also a number of awesome tutorials on the internet, for example, `https://learnopengl.com` and `https://open.gl/`.

If you are not so interested in OpenGL, which is mainly for 2D and 3D graphics development, but are interested in heterogeneous computing, then you can refer to OpenCL or CUDA. OpenCL is very similar to OpenGL; it is a specification maintained by the Khronos group. Additionally, the next generations of OpenGL and OpenCL are now consolidated into one specification named Vulkan, so Vulkan is also a good option to choose. CUDA is a proprietary solution for heterogeneous computing from Nvidia, and it is the most mature solution in this domain, so using it to do heterogeneous computing is the best choice if you have an Nvidia graphics card.

Assessments

Chapter 1, Building an Image Viewer

1. We use a message box to tell users that they are already viewing the first or last image as they attempt to view the image prior to the first image, or the image following the last image. However, there is another way to handle this: disable prevAction when users are viewing the first image, and disable nextAction when users are viewing the last image. How do we go about this?

   The QAction class has a bool enabled property and, hence, a setEnabled(bool) method, and we call it to enable or disable the corresponding action in the prevImage and nextImage methods.

2. There is only text on our menu items or tool buttons. How can we add an icon image to them?

   The QAction class has a QIcon icon property and, hence, a setIcon method, and you can create and set an icon for the action. To create a QIcon object, please refer to its corresponding documentation at https://doc.qt.io/qt-5/qicon.html.

3. We use QGraphicsView.scale to zoom in or out of an image view. How can an image view be rotated?

   Use the QGraphicsView.rotate method.

4. What does moc do? What do the SIGNAL and SLOT macros do?

   The moc command is the Qt meta-object system compiler. It mainly extracts all the meta object system-relevant information from a user-defined class that contains the QOBJECT macro, including signals and slots. Then, it creates a C++ source file whose name starts with moc_ to manage this meta information (primarily, the signals and slots). It also gives the implementations of the signals in that file. The SIGNAL and SLOT macros convert their arguments to a string that can be used to find the corresponding signal or slot in the meta information managed by the moc command.

Chapter 2, Editing Images Like a Pro

1. How would we know whether an OpenCV function supports in-place operations?

   As we mentioned in the chapter, we can refer to the official document pertaining to the function. If the document stipulates that it supports in-place operations, then it does, otherwise, it doesn't.

2. How can a hotkey be added to each action we added as a plugin?

   We can add a new method to the plugin interface class that returns a `QList<QKeySequence>` instance and implement it in the concrete plugin class. When we load the plugin, we call that method to get the shortcut key sequence and set it as the hotkey of the action for that plugin.

3. How can a new action be added to discard all the changes in the current image in our application?

   First of all, add a class field of the `QPixmap` type to the `MainWindow` class. Before editing the current image, we save a copy of the image to that field. Then, we add a new action and a new slot connected to the action. In the slot, we set the saved image to the graphics scene.

4. How can images be resized using OpenCV?

   There is a function for this, which can be found at the following link: `https://docs.opencv.org/4.0.0/da/d54/group__imgproc__transform.html#ga47a974309e9102f5f08231edc7e7529d`

Chapter 3, Home Security Applications

1. Can we detect motion from a video file instead of from a camera? How is this achieved?

   Yes, we can. Just use the video file path to construct the `VideoCapture` instance. More details can be found at `https://docs.opencv.org/4.0.0/d8/dfe/classcv_1_1VideoCapture.html`.

2. Can we perform the motion detection work in a thread that differs from the video capturing thread? If so, how is this possible?

   Yes. But we should use a number of synchronization mechanisms to ensure data safety. Also, if we dispatch the frames to different threads, we must ensure that the order of the resulting frames is also correct when they are sent back and are about to be shown.

3. IFTTT allows you to include images in the notifications it sends—How could we send an image with the motion we detected while sending notifications to your mobile phone via this feature of IFTTT?

   First, select **Send a rich notification from the IFTTT app** as **that** service while creating the applet on IFTTT. Then, when motion is detected, we upload the frame as an image to a location such as `https://imgur.com` and get a URL for it. Then, post the image URL to the IFTTT webhook as a parameter and use the URL as the image URL in the rich format notification, which can have an image URL in its body.

Chapter 4, Fun with Faces

1. Can the LBP cascade classifier be used to detect faces by yourself?

   Yes. Just use the OpenCV built-in `lbpcascades/lbpcascade_frontalface_improved.xml` classifier data file.

2. There are a number of other algorithms that can be used to detect facial landmarks in the OpenCV library. The majority of these can be found at `https://docs.opencv.org/4.0.0/db/dd8/classcv_1_1face_1_1Facemark.html`. Try them for yourself.

   Different functions can be used from the following link—`https://docs.opencv.org/4.0.0/d4/d48/namespacecv_1_1face.html`—to create different algorithm instances. All these algorithms have the same API as the one we used in the chapter, so you can try these algorithms easily by just changing their creation statement.

3. How can a colored ornament be applied to faces?

In our project, both the video frame and the ornament are of the BGR format and have no alpha channel. In view of the fact that the ornament has a white background, we can use the cv::threshold function to generate a mask first. The mask is a binary image whose background is white and whose foreground (the part of the ornament) is black. Then, we can use the following code to apply the ornament:

```
frame(rec) &= mask;
ornament &= ^mask;
frame(rec) |= ornament;
```

Chapter 5, Optical Character Recognition

1. How is it possible to recognize characters in non-English languages with Tesseract?

Specify the corresponding language name when initializing the TessBaseAPI instance.

2. When we used the EAST model to detect text areas, the detected areas are actually rotated rectangles, and we simply use their bounding rectangles instead. Is this always correct? If not, how can this approach be rectified?

It is correct, but this is not the best approach. We can copy the region in the bounding boxes of the rotated rectangles to new images, and then rotate and crop them to transform the rotated rectangles into regular rectangles. After that, we will generally get better outputs by sending the resulting regular rectangles to Tesseract in order to extract the text.

3. Try to figure out a way to allow users to adjust the selected region after dragging the mouse while capturing images from the screen.

The general approach is to insert eight handles on the vertices and sides of the bounding rectangle of the selected region and users can then drag these handles to adjust the selected region. This can be done by extending the paintEvent and mouse*Event methods of our ScreenCapturer class. In the paintEvent method, we paint the selection rectangle and its handles. In the mouse*Event method, we check whether the mouse is pressed down on a handle, and then repaint the selection rectangle by dragging the mouse.

Chapter 6, Object Detection in Real Time

1. When we trained the cascade classifier for the faces of Boston bulls, we annotated the dog faces on each image by ourselves. The annotation process was very time-consuming. There is a tarball of annotation data for that dataset on its website: `http://vision.stanford.edu/aditya86/ImageNetDogs/annotation.tar`. Is it possible to generate the `info.txt` file from this annotation data by using a piece of code? How can this be done?

   The annotation data in that tarball relates to the dogs' bodies, and not to the dogs' faces. So, we can't use it to train a classifier for the dogs' faces. However, if you want to train a classifier for the full bodies of the dogs, this can help. The data in that tarball is stored in XML format, and the annotation rectangles are the nodes with the `//annotation/object/bndbox` path, which we can extract easily.

2. Try to find a pretrained (Fast/Faster) R-CNN model and a pretrained SSD model, run them, and then compare their performance with that of YOLOv3.

   The following list provides some Faster R-CNN and SSD models. Please test them by yourself if you are interested in any one of them:

   - `https://github.com/smallcorgi/Faster-RCNN_TF`
   - `https://github.com/endernewton/tf-faster-rcnn`
   - `https://github.com/balancap/SSD-Tensorflow`

3. Could we use YOLOv3 to detect a certain kind of object, but not all 80 classes of objects?

   Yes, you can filter the result according to the particular class ID. We employed this approach to detect cars in `Chapter 7`, *Real-Time Car Detection and Distance Measurement*. Just refer to that chapter.

Chapter 7, Real-Time Car Detection and Distance Measurement

1. Is there a better reference object when measuring the distance between cars?

    There are many classes in the coco dataset in which the objects generally have fixed positions; for instance, traffic lights, fire hydrants, and stop signs. We can find some of them in the view of our camera, choose any two of them, measure the distance between them, and then use the chosen objects and their distance as the references.

Other Books You May Enjoy

If you enjoyed this book, you may be interested in these other books by Packt:

Computer Vision with OpenCV 3 and Qt5
Amin Ahmadi Tazehkandi

ISBN: 9781788472395

- Get an introduction to Qt IDE and SDK
- Be introduced to OpenCV and see how to communicate between OpenCV and Qt
- Understand how to create UI using Qt Widgets
- Know to develop cross-platform applications using OpenCV 3 and Qt 5
- Explore the multithreaded application development features of Qt5
- Improve OpenCV 3 application development using Qt5
- Build, test, and deploy Qt and OpenCV apps, either dynamically or statically
- See Computer Vision technologies such as filtering and transformation of images, detecting and matching objects, template matching, object tracking, video and motion analysis, and much more
- Be introduced to QML and Qt Quick for iOS and Android application development

Mastering OpenCV 4 - Third Edition
Roy Shilkrot, David Millán Escrivá

ISBN: 9781789533576

- Build real-world computer vision problems with working OpenCV code samples
- Uncover best practices in engineering and maintaining OpenCV projects
- Explore algorithmic design approaches for complex computer vision tasks
- Work with OpenCV's most updated API (v4.0.0) through projects
- Understand 3D scene reconstruction and Structure from Motion (SfM)
- Study camera calibration and overlay AR using the ArUco Module

Leave a review - let other readers know what you think

Please share your thoughts on this book with others by leaving a review on the site that you bought it from. If you purchased the book from Amazon, please leave us an honest review on this book's Amazon page. This is vital so that other potential readers can see and use your unbiased opinion to make purchasing decisions, we can understand what our customers think about our products, and our authors can see your feedback on the title that they have worked with Packt to create. It will only take a few minutes of your time, but is valuable to other potential customers, our authors, and Packt. Thank you!

Index

F

faces
  detecting, with cascade classifiers 155, 156, 157, 158, 159, 160, 161
  masks, applying to 168
  masks, drawing on 171, 172, 173, 175
Facetious application
  about 146, 183
  photo taking feature 151, 153, 154, 155
  using 146, 147, 148, 151
facial landmarks
  detecting 161, 162, 163, 165, 166, 167
filtered images
  saving 320
fragment shader
  images, filtering in 315, 316, 317, 318, 319
frame frequency 112
frames per second (FPS)
  about 87, 148
  calculating 112, 113, 115, 116, 117
functions, implementing for actions
  about 18
  copy, saving 23, 24
  exit action 19
  image, opening 19, 20, 21
  navigating, in folder 25, 26
  opening 22
  responding, to hotkeys 26, 27
  zooming in 22, 23
  zooming out 22, 23

G

GaussianBlur function
  reference 65
Gazer application
  about 88, 89, 145, 183
  project, starting 89, 90, 91, 92, 93, 94, 95, 96
  user interface, setting up 89, 90, 91, 92, 93, 94, 95, 96
GLEW
  reference 295
GLFW
  reference 295
graphics processing unit (GPU) 293

H

Haar classifier 156
heterogeneous computing 293

I

ImageEditor application 30, 31
images, editing like pro
  about 62
  Affine transformation 81, 83, 84, 85
  Affine, transformation 80
  cartoon effect 67, 68, 69, 70, 71, 72, 73, 74, 75
  images, rotating 75, 77, 78, 79
  images, sharpening 62, 63, 64, 65, 66, 67
images
  blurring 38, 39, 40, 41, 42
  blurring, OpenCV used 31
  drawing, with OpenGL 309, 310, 311, 312, 313, 314
  eroding, ErodePlugin used 49, 50, 52, 53
  filtering, in fragment shader 315, 316, 317, 318, 319
  filtering, with OpenGL 308, 309
  rotating 75, 77, 78, 79
  sharpening 62, 63, 64, 65, 66, 67
integrated development environment (IDE) 10

K

Keras
  reference 261

L

Literacy
  creating 184
  user interface, designing 184
  user interface, setting up 185, 186, 187, 189, 190, 191, 192, 193
local binary pattern (LBP) cascade classifier 161
Long Short-Term Memory (LSTM) 195

M

masks, applying to faces
  about 168
  images, loading with Qt resource system 168, 169, 170, 171

www.ingramcontent.com/pod-product-compliance
Lightning Source LLC
Chambersburg PA
CBHW080619060326
40690CB00021B/4747